O9-CFU-200

Poetic Knowledge in the Early Yeats

A Study of *The Wind among the Reeds*

WILLIAM BLAKE: "THE REUNION OF SOUL AND BODY."

Poetic Knowledge in the Early Yeats

A Study of
The Wind among the Reeds

ALLEN R. GROSSMAN
DEPARTMENT OF ENGLISH
BRANDEIS UNIVERSITY

THE UNIVERSITY PRESS
OF VIRGINIA
CHARLOTTESVILLE

COLLEGE OF THE SEQUOIAS
LIBRARY

THE UNIVERSITY PRESS OF VIRGINIA
COPYRIGHT © 1969 BY THE RECTOR AND VISITORS
OF THE UNIVERSITY OF VIRGINIA

FIRST PUBLISHED 1969

Yeats' poems and passages therefrom are reprinted with permission of The Macmillan Company from *Collected Poems*
by William Butler Yeats. Copyright 1903, 1906, 1907, 1912,
1916, 1918, 1919, 1924, 1928, 1931, 1933, 1934, 1935, 1940,
1944, 1945, 1946, 1950, 1956, by The Macmillan Company.
Copyright 1940 by Georgie Yeats.

Citations here are to the first edition of *The Wind among
the Reeds* (1899) and to *The Variorum Edition of the
Poems of W. B. Yeats* (1965).

STANDARD BOOK NUMBER: 8139-0253-3
LIBRARY OF CONGRESS CATALOG CARD NUMBER: 68-8540
PRINTED IN THE UNITED STATES OF AMERICA

Preface

LIKE Parzifal, William Butler Yeats was a strong man slowly wise. His growth as a poet, although both extended and complex, was guided by an instinct for the conservation and reinterpretation of states of the self very early achieved. This style of development, by retrenchment and amplification, requires that the critic lay emphasis retrogressively on early states of the poet's mind, on the principle that what the poet always remembered his interpreters are not at liberty to forget. This book inquires into the most important of Yeats' early stages of development, the period between 1893 and 1899, of which the chief result was *The Wind among the Reeds*.

From the point of view of 1899 it is possible to pass in review virtually the whole range of Yeats' mind, and to participate with some intimacy in the founding events of the long series of major poems which followed. The premise of this study is that *The Wind among the Reeds* represents a poetic moment in which the determining conditions both of Yeats' later writing and of the modern movement in poetry can be seen with singular clarity. The procedure which I have followed, especially in the first few chapters, has been to examine closely and with as much fidelity as possible the crucial assertions of the young poet, even to the point of risking a presentation of Yeats' early positions so severe as to seem ingenuous. The reader who finds this procedure trying should note, at least, that inquiry of this sort calls attention to the extreme states of mind which underlie great poetic achievement. States of mind in Yeats which his readers find hardest to reconcile with their preferred interpretations of experience are likely to be just those without which his poetry is inconceivable. For this reason, more general considerations arising in the course of this study have to some extent been withheld in favor of exegesis and an attempt to get a just report of early attitudes.

For the same reason the text of *The Wind among the Reeds* used is that of 1899, and a table of early and later titles has been provided at the end of the book. The reader who wishes to use this study as a guide to the early poems of Yeats may do so by consulting the index.

It should be added that A. Norman Jeffares, *A Commentary on the Collected Poems of W. B. Yeats,* which appeared when this book was in the last stages of production, provides a useful compendium of materials and, in addition, offers some assurance that the large body of Yeats' unpublished manuscripts to which Professor Jeffares has had access does not raise further questions of substance about these poems.

The publication of this book has been made possible in part through the financial assistance of the President and Trustees of Brandeis University.

A. R. G.

Brandeis University
June 1968

Acknowledgments

GRATEFUL acknowledgment is due to the following for permission to quote copyrighted material:

To A. P. Watt and Son and Messrs. Macmillan and Company for permission to quote from the works of W. B. Yeats.

To the Chilmark Press for permission to quote from Frank Kermode, *The Romantic Image* (New York: Chilmark Press, 1964).

To E. P. Dutton and Co., Inc., for permission to quote from Evelyn Underhill's *Mysticism* (New York: Meridian Books, 1955).

To the Clarendon Press, Oxford, for permission to quote from E. R. Dodds, *Proclus: The Elements of Theology* (2d ed., Oxford: Oxford University Press, 1963).

To Harvard University Press for permission to quote from Horace Reynolds, ed., *Letters to the New Island by W. B. Yeats* (Cambridge: Harvard University Press, 1934).

To Columbia University Press for permission to quote from Robert Grant, ed., *A Source Book of Heretical Writings from the Early Christian Period* (New York: Columbia University Press, 1959).

To William Heinemann Ltd. for permission to quote from Arthur Symons, *Images of Good and Evil* (London: William Heinemann, 1899).

In addition, the author wishes to thank The Bodley Head Press for the use of the cover of Nora Hopper Chesson, *Ballads in Prose* (London:

John Lane, Bodley Head, 1887) and George Allen & Unwin Ltd. for
the use of the cover of W. B. Yeats, *The Wind among the Reeds* (London: Elkin Mathews, 1899), a copy of which was kindly made available
by the Harvard College Library.

The Blake engraving used as the frontispiece is from S. Foster
Damon, *William Blake's Illustrations for Robert Blair's* The Grave
(Providence: Brown University Press, 1963).

Contents

Illustrations

Introduction

Mallarmé's phrases will never grow old for they tell us nothing, the secret meaning is so deeply imbedded that generations will try to puzzle through them, and in the volume entitled *The Wind among the Reeds* Yeats has written poems so difficult . . . that even the adepts could not disentangle the sense; and since *The Wind among the Reeds* he has written a sonnet that clearly referred to a house. But to what house? —George Moore, *Hail and Farewell*

Once on Plato's feast, I read a poem, "The Sacred Marriage": my piece abounded in mystic doctrine conveyed in veiled words and was couched in terms of enthusiasm; someone exclaimed: "Porphyry has gone mad"; Plotinus said to me so that all might hear: "You have shown yourself at once poet, philosopher and hierophant." —Porphyry, *On Plotinus*

Introduction

POETIC KNOWLEDGE

WHEN W. B. Yeats began to write, no Irishman had written a major poem in English. The publication of *The Wind among the Reeds* in 1899 constituted Yeats' first effort to produce an integrated work in the lyric genre and the end of a major episode in his struggle with the problems of poetic knowledge. During the same period of apprenticeship Yeats laid the groundwork of his most characteristic contribution to the English poetic tradition, namely, the adaptation to the uses of poetry of the Wisdom tradition. At no time after *The Wind among the Reeds* did Yeats conceive the problem of style and the problem of Wisdom in such absolute terms. Yeats possessed a genius for culture in the constructive sense; with some right he boasted of his ambition as a young man "and I, that my native scenery might find imaginary inhabitants, half-planned a new method, a new culture."[1] The new culture which Yeats "half-planned" in his early years was in a sense the modern poetic culture of the English-speaking world.

The "pure" style and the vision of Wisdom were Yeats' answers in the last years of the nineteenth century to the question of unity. As the child of many cultures each in itself complex, Yeats required an account of himself which would unify the heterogeneity of his inheritance without nullifying its richness. His response was the construction out of perennial elements of a new and in large part imaginary civilization which permitted him to give an account of himself without commitment to the constraints of the several historical cultures which were

competing for his identity. *The Wind among the Reeds* is the poetry of
the heterocosm so constructed, and this study is in effect an anthropology of that culture based on the whole range of Yeats' early writing,
but in particular on its most unified product, *The Wind among the
Reeds*.

The content of Yeats' major poetry in the nineties is a mythology of
the processes of creation conceived in terms of a sacrificial relationship
to an overwhelming and almost inaccessible power in the self. The chief
business of Yeats' poetry in the period between 1893 and 1899 is to
master (primarily by ritual means) that relationship which seems to
demand nothing less than the exchange of life for art. *The Wind among
the Reeds* is a mythological poem in what Yeats called the "epic-lyric"
genre which takes as its subject the search for poetic knowledge; and
poetic knowledge in *The Wind among the Reeds* defines itself as an
account of personal origins. The achieved capacity for such an account
leads to self-identification in terms of unity, creativity, and the intelligibility of experience; but its personal cost (what Frank Kermode calls
"the cost of the image") is so great that the completed achievement is
prohibited by the necessity of life itself. In other words, *The Wind
among the Reeds* is a history of the poet's archetypal self-finding the
achievement of which, though necessarily incomplete, enables him to
emerge after 1900 as if reborn into a new phase of life characterized by
portraiture of a self which had not previously existed as a creative
possibility.

The study of Yeats' poetry in the nineteenth century is the study of
a tradition of poetry which has failed to sustain itself. But the importance of that tradition for the development of Yeats' art and the art of
the twentieth century as a whole is very great. *The Wind among the
Reeds* is the record of a daemonic episode which lies, like childhood, in
the background not only of Yeats' later work but also of much of the
poetry of Eliot, Pound, Stevens, and others who were to form the
modern poetic community. The period of Yeats' development which is
our concern is the moment prior to irony which the ironic medium of
twentieth-century poetry was to take as its subject matter. Above all,
however, it is evidence of a great mind struggling in a complex proto-

modern culture toward that archetypal self-identification which is the
substance of all poetic knowledge.

THE SOUL OF THE MAN
AND THE SOUL OF THE WORLD

Yeats came in the end to know the poet's trade with almost unexam-
pled thoroughness. The passage of life during which he learned that
trade was the years 1892 to 1899, the chief record of which is the poems
of *The Wind among the Reeds*. What Yeats learned in the process of
becoming a poet can be formulated as the answer to the following
question: "What relationship exists between *my* dreams, and visions,
the places and people given *me* by birth, that is to say *my* images, and
those images *not mine* which come to me from the great pool of
collective representations that constitutes the high traditional culture
of Europe?" This question the poet answered by devising an account of
personal origins in terms of an imaginary culture dominated by the
Wisdom figure which is both the source and the identifying soul of
personal existence. Yeats' prose is a complex history of lifelong experimentation in the relation between his experience of himself and his
experience of the human record. The discovery formulated in a dozen
different ways that the soul of man and the soul of the world have
mutual significance combined with the discovery of an account of
personal origins which gave him by virtue of birth the right of access to
the resource of universal human fantasy constituted for Yeats "poetic
knowledge."

But in order to be confident in this discovery a truly stable account
of his own identity in terms of the preferred tradition was required,
and this he was never able to give, largely because of the intensity of
awe and dread with which his mind invested the tradition. In *The
Wind among the Reeds* he attempts such an account, and the style of
procedure which he develops is determining for his later career and to
some extent for the poetry of the modern period as a whole. To state
the matter briefly once again, Yeats attempts to give an account of his

identity from the point of view of personal origins in terms of the Wisdom tradition, and by doing so strikes beneath the competing historical claims upon him, beneath the competition of Ireland (the mother) and Europe (the father) for the naming of their child. In the process of this effort he produces a counterhistorical civilization in which he enacts the dramas of creative self-finding.

On the validity of the discovery of the self in terms of a "third" culture rests the case both for and against Yeats as a poet. Yeats reproduced this effort at the ordering of history in relation to the self more than once in the course of his career; but the period between 1892 and 1899 is the crucial moment, the moment in which commitment or, if you like, alienation to the deep structures of mind was so great that mere survival made it possible to live on in another sense. It is obvious that Yeats' capacity to outlive this moment in his history gave him a sufficiently strong hold on life so that as time went on he attained the psychic leisure to be human.

THE MYTH

The drama of poetic knowledge in this period constitutes Yeats' first major myth. The principal actors are two: on the one hand, the child or creative fire-self whom we have called the figure at the center (Chapters VI and VII) and who appears in many shadowy forms as the hawk-headed youth, Mongan, and the triplicities of fire (Aedh, Hanrahan, Robartes); on the other hand, the Beloved who is the maternal symbol both of origins and selfhood, Ireland, the Muse, the white woman (Chapters II and IX). The drama of the relationship between these two orders of the self is rotated through a dozen different cultural systems in each of which a third figure emerges, the guardian of the mother, who also takes many forms as the cherubic Warder of Eden, the cabalistic Jehovah, the father in his many transformations (Chapter V). The prize of the contest of the creative self with the father for possession of the white woman is poetic identity or poetic knowledge which liberates the relationship of the self and the emotions, of which the predominant symbol in this period is the Moods, the perennial and reciprocal meanings of the collective and the individual mind conceived as one being (Chapter IV). The hard terms of this drama as they unfold in *The Wind among the Reeds* become the "cost of the image." Kermode describes Keats' encounter with the white woman:

Moneta is full of terrible knowledge, and this knowledge is about to be revealed to the poet. . . . She is immortal; her face is the emblem of the cost as well as of the benefits of knowledge and immortality. Moneta's face haunts many later poets as well as Keats. It has the pallor and equivocal life-in-death of Coleridge's spectre—whiter in disease than the hands of Venus and Adonis, which after the *Biographia Literaria,* were strongly associated with the act of imagination. The knowledge it represents is not malign, but is unrelated to "external things"; the eyes express nothing, looking inward to the "high tragedy in the dark chambers of the skull." To prostrate himself before this figure is the artist's joy and the reward of his suffering.[2]

It is the seed of modernity in Yeats that no relation to the white woman could compensate him for the sacrifice of that enforced oblation. No union with the immense and simplifying symbol of origin was possible to his imagination without that death which threatened to put an end to mind altogether. Kermode is correct in his observation that "Moneta's face haunts many later poets as well as Keats." Not only in the nineteenth century but also in the twentieth, encounter with this great figure determines the style of self-identification of man as poet. We find her in many forms in the work of Robinson, Stevens, and Hart Crane. She is present wherever the poetic act is authentically involved with the desire to know the self in terms of origins.

LITERATURE AND CULT

The world picture of modern literature is, in effect, first announced in *The Wind among the Reeds*. That world picture is basically a map of the Yeatsian experiment: the comparison of the experience of the individual mind with the world's perennial experience of collective representations. The universal syncretism which allows iconological and cultural configurations of diverse origin to enter a single system and thus become the structure of major works of art is in effect the modern world picture. This world picture is administered by Yeats, Eliot, Joyce, and Pound in different ways, but its premises are common to *A Vision, The Waste Land, Finnegans Wake,* and the *Cantos.* The concept of novelty in this version of poetic knowledge is bound up with a characteristic modern style of the incorporation of traditional elements, the model of which is to be found, of course, in cultural anthropology as exemplified in monumental fashion by James Frazer. Novelty for Yeats, as he makes clear in his notes to *The Wind among the Reeds,* is the rediscovery of the perennial nature of human identity. Yeats is seeking in the rapidly changing culture of late nineteenth-century Europe a version of the old sealed cultic society in which all images are conserved by processes of syncretism and metamorphosis, and in which any act of creation is a reaffirmation of the known and pre-existent whole. In such a conception the confrontation with personal origin will inevitably be crossed by the terrors of incest; and the dramas of self-finding will take on an archetypal character. All modern poetry seems retrospective of a lost wholeness which it locates in the historical past (Eliot's unity of sensibility) or in some unreachable aspect of the present (Crane's Helen) or which it ironically transvalues (Stevens' "One of Fictive Music"). Modern poetry begins with a rejected vision that Yeats recapitulated in his own person, an unconquerable delusion the reaction from which forms the motive of modern style. Yeats' career was more or less coterminous with the development of modern poetry itself, and his later art becomes in effect a medium for the incorporation of earlier absolute attitudes, as the art of the poets who followed him developed by the invention of ironic vehicles for lost states of being.

The Romantic period incorporated traditional elements in part by reducing historical *mystères cultuels* to ahistorical *mystères littéraires.* The obvious examples are Wordsworth's "priest of nature" and Whitman's "divine literatus." The modern or protomodern period of which *The Wind among the Reeds* is a part moved very powerfully in the opposite direction. Yeats seemed bent on affiliating literature with cult by transforming the processes of art back into acts of religion. We shall see very complete examples of this. Yeats takes the Romantic *mystères littéraires* and creates of them *mystères cultuels.* These cultic mysteries constitute the binding acts of Yeats' imaginative civilization. Yeats responds to his own time much as Arnold did retrospectively to the Romantic community: "The creative power of poetry wanted for success in the highest sense, materials and a basis; a thorough interpretation of the world was necessarily denied." Yeats' poetry in the nineties, slight as it is, constitutes, though not in the sense anticipated by Arnold, "a thorough interpretation of the world." Yeats' occult thought provides just that true community which Arnold desiderates retrospectively of the Romantics.

POET AS DAEMONIC MAN

In the early period Yeats was very busy reconciling divergent accounts of the origins of his mind. For a nation such as Ireland the dilemma of the alliance of the mind of its children was virtually insoluble. If the child married outside the *natio* (exogamically), the tribe was betrayed; if the child married inside the tribe (endogamically), he was destroyed by the complexities of guilt. The mysterious dramas of Yeats' early poems, like the plays of John Synge, turn round and round on problems of this kind. It should be borne in mind that Yeats wrote poetry with great difficulty, as the publication of his manuscripts makes increasingly clear. In the period with which we are dealing the impulse to silence and the impulse to speech were almost equally strong. The god Harpocrates who presides over the secrecy which gives power to mysteries is the ruling deity of this poetry. The reasons for its silence are intimately related to what is being said. We shall find clearly defined the origins of the impulse to hiddenness of meaning in Yeats and to some extent in modern poetry as a whole as we examine the dramas of Wisdom and her lover in the early poems.

In the second edition of his *A Vision* Yeats places himself among the daemonic men of his own system. The sense in which he is a "daemonic man" is undoubtedly that of Plato's *Symposium*:

Everything that is daemonic is intermediate between god and mortal. Interpreting and conveying the wishes of man to gods and the will of gods to men, it stands between the two and fills the gap. . . . God has no contact with man; only through the daemonic is there intercourse and conversation between man and gods whether in the waking state or during sleep. And the man who is expert in such intercourse is the daemonic man.

This is the daemonic concept of the artist. *The Wind among the Reeds* is a study of the cultural process in terms of daemonism. The Yeats of 1892–1899 had not yet discovered irony, the characteristic modern medium for the incorporation of lost contexts. Irony as a style enters Yeats only as Yeats enters the twentieth century. In this sense the nineties are very remote from us and require an act of historical imagination to enable understanding. In view of this there is some reason for inquiring briefly how *The Wind among the Reeds* was received in its period.

THE WIND AMONG THE REEDS IN ITS TIME

When *The Wind among the Reeds* appeared in 1899, it had been long awaited and was much reviewed. The so-called Celtic Revival had seemed, up to that time, to have issued in far more talk about writing than actual literary production. George Moore quotes Lady Gregory as having said in 1899:

For seven years we have been waiting for a new book from him [Yeats]; ever since *The Countess Kathleen* (1892) we have been reading the publisher's autumn announcement of *The Wind among the Reeds*. This volume was finished here last year; it would never have been finished if I had not asked him to Coole; and though we live in an ungrateful world, I think somebody will throw a kind word after me some day, if for nothing else, for *The Wind among the Reeds*.[3]

Moore, with the Irish genius for constructing history by analogy, had recently felt his commitment to his motherland heightened by the predicament of Kruger and the Boers and was known in 1899 to have complicated Yeats' reputation by publicly comparing him to Shakespeare.[4] Consequently, *The Wind among the Reeds* was received by reviewers outside the movement with skepticism, qualified by an admiration enforced by the obvious stylistic qualities of the book.

Reviewing *The Wind among the Reeds* for the *Speaker* in April of

1899, John Davidson comments, "It is difficult to believe that Mr. Yeats has not been dead for many years, and now revisits the glimpses of the moon, the first traveller to return from the undiscovered country."[5] With whatever literalness Davidson intends his remark to be taken, the notion of *The Wind among the Reeds* as utterance brought back from the world of the dead is not without relevance. The *Academy,* which a few months later awarded the book its prize of twenty-five guineas as the best of the year, emphasized that Yeats' work had been "slender" in quantity, adding with a significant absence of specification, "But it has quality."[6] No reviewer failed to locate Yeats within the Celtic movement, and most, while echoing the Arnoldian cliché about Celtic "magic," complained that "Irish mythology is unknown to English readers."[7] For the uninitiated reviewers of the *Academy,* the *Spectator,* the *Daily Mail,* the *Athenaeum,* and the *Nation* Yeats was amply described when he was located within the movement which also included Jane Barlow and Katharine Tynan. Indeed, the best evidence of the prepossessing character of the parochial auspices under which Yeats was presented to the English public was the persistence of that public in finding his symbols Irish.

By contrast to the reviewers whose sensibility lay outside the movement, the notice by "Fiona Macleod" in the *Fortnightly Review* and especially that by Arthur Symons in the *Saturday Review* provide us with a fairly distinct notion of how the book was understood within the circle of the Celtic adepts. Of all the members of the Celtic movement, William Sharp sustained the broadest view of its scope, including not only Irish and Scottish, but also Welsh, Cornish, and Breton writers. Echoing Renan and Arnold, Sharp defines Celticism in very general terms. "The Celtic writer is the writer the temper of whose mind is more ancient, more primitive, and in a sense more natural than his compatriot in whom the Teutonic strain prevails."[8] Consequently Sharp does not find *The Wind among the Reeds* wholly satisfactory. It possesses not only the virtues which Arnold attributes to the Celt, but also the faults. "It is not great poetry, but poetry with an air of greatness investing it." In particular, Sharp quarrels with Yeats' form of mysticism, finding it "sometimes mere vagueness" and his symbolism "arbitrary." Sharp accurately senses Yeats' alienation from literary parochialism, and finds it abhorrent. He regards Yeats' style of 1899

as transitional and, as many members of the movement must have
done, looks fondly back to the Yeats of *The Celtic Twilight*. The
objection of Sharp, George Russell, and others to Yeats' symbolism
in *The Wind among the Reeds* was that it seemed to them discursive or constructed, rather than ethnically limited and "natural," as
Celtic dogma demanded. We see Yeats in the position of being Irish in
the eyes of the English, but cosmopolitan and uncommitted in the eyes
of the "Celticist" and Irishman. Sharp is, however, deeply sympathetic
with Yeats' ambition to speak with the authority of the seer or magician, and the quotation with which he closes his review, Taliesin's
words to Merlin, might stand as an epigraph to a discussion of Yeats'
self-conception in the period. "Because thou art a seer men and demons
will continually assail thee. Great joys shall be thine and the Divine
Ray, but also thou mayst know madness, the scorn of men, solitude and
the bitter savor of death." [9]

The notice of Yeats' book by Symons in the *Saturday Review* comes
nearest of all the contemporary reviews to being an authoritative
statement.[10] It is less a critical notice than an exposition and requires
careful attention. He begins by pointing out that symbolism in *The
Wind among the Reeds* "extends to the cover, where reeds are woven
into a net to catch the wandering sounds." Like Sharp, Symons recog-
nizes the difference between the poetry of *The Wind among the Reeds*
and Yeats' earlier work, but with an opposite preference.

Technically the verse is far in advance of anything he has ever done. . . .
It is only gradually that Mr. Yeats has learnt to become quite human. Life
is the last thing he has learnt, and it is life, an extraordinary inner life,
that I find in this book of lyrics, which may also seem to be one long hymn
to intellectual beauty.[11]

We may agree that life was always the last thing which Yeats proved
capable of learning. Symons is accurately sensitive to Yeats' conquest
of the Victorian stylistic convention, but he is also aware that the life
represented in *The Wind among the Reeds* is the kind of Platonic inner
life which is convertible with the perception of "intellectual beauty."
In a comment which might have been written by Yeats himself, Symons makes quite clear the kind of humanity with which he conceives
his author to be concerned.

Never in these love songs . . . does an earthly circumstance divorce ecstasy from the impersonality of vision. This poet cannot see love under the form of time, cannot see beauty except as absolute beauty, cannot distinguish between the mortal person and the eternal idea.[12]

Finally Symons offers us a definition of "the conception of lyric poetry which Mr. Yeats has perfected in this volume":

A lyric is an unembodied ecstasy, and an ecstasy so profoundly personal that it loses the accidental qualities of personality, and becomes part of the universal consciousness. Itself, in its first merely personal stage a symbol, it can be expressed only by a symbol.[13]

The "life" that Symons discerns in the poetry of *The Wind among the Reeds* is the vitality of the essence. Symons' comment is the most discerning contemporary utterance about Yeats' book. It makes no mention of the Celtic convention at all and boldly sets forth Yeats' ambition for personality at the end of the nineteenth century. With respect to the problem of general structure Symons has this to say:

The poems which make up a volume apparently disconnected are subdivided dramatically among certain symbolic persons familiar to the readers of *The Secret Rose,* Aedh, Hanrahan, and Michael Robartes, each of whom . . . is but a pseudonym of a particular outlook of consciousness in its passionate, dreaming, or intellectual moments. It is by means of these dramatic symbols, refining still further upon the large mythological symbolism which he has built up into almost a system, that Mr. Yeats weaves about the simplicity of moods that elaborate web of atmosphere in which the illusion of love and cruelty of pain and the gross ecstasy of hope become changed into beauty.[14]

These statements, no doubt tutored by Yeats himself, provide a groundwork or conceptual prolegomenon for the study of *The Wind among the Reeds.*

Poetic Knowledge in the Early Yeats

A Study of *The Wind among the Reeds*

Ah! Druid, Druid, how great webs of sorrow
Lay hidden in the small slate-coloured thing!
— "Fergus and the Druid"

Chapter I

Those masterful images because complete
Grew in pure mind but out of what began?
    —"The Circus Animals' Desertion"

Unity and Diversity

A Problem of Style

THE earliest mention of a book of poems called *The Wind among the Reeds* occurs in an interview which Yeats gave to D. N. Dunlop, later editor of the *Irish Theosophist,* and which was published in that periodical on November 15, 1893.[1] In the same month another interview of much the same purport appeared over the name of Katharine Tynan in the *Sketch.*[2] Both interviews took place in Yeats' room in his father's house at 3 Blenheim Road, Bedford Park. Dunlop had come to Ireland on a theosophical errand to interpret Yeats' mysticism to the Irish; Katharine Tynan had come on a literary errand to interpret Yeats' Celticism to the English. It was in the nature of Yeats' position that both found what they were looking for.

Both interviewers came upon the poet in his disordered study environed by the symbols of his imaginary civilization. On the ceiling, as Katharine Tynan noted with the zeal of the Celticist, he had painted a map of Sligo with a ship at each corner. Dunlop found him with a Homer on his knees, surrounded by books on occult subjects. To the tradition of "aesthetic cheer" which built Bedford Park, Yeats had added the symbols of Ireland, with the concomitant heroic fantasy, and of Wisdom. "Prominent in the disorder," Katharine Tynan observes, "is a book bound like a medieval missal in cherry-coloured brocade and tarnished gold. 'What may that fine thing be?' I ask. He answers with a slight blush. 'That is my MS. book. A friend brought the cover from Paris and I had the book made to fit.'"[3] This book, redolent of the pseudo-sacramentalism of Huysmans' Des Esseintes and the medievalism of William Morris and a palpable symbol of the "jeweled paragraphs" of Walter Pater, contained in an early state several of the poems of *The Wind among the Reeds.*

In the course of an interview which was intended to elicit from Yeats anecdotes about Madame Blavatsky, who had died in 1891, Dunlop inquires, "Do you intend at any time publishing a book on 'Mysticism'?" Yeats replies, "Yes; at no very distant date I hope to publish a work dealing with mystics I have seen and stories I have heard but it will be as an artist, not as a controversialist." "And what about your present work?" " 'Celtic Twilight,' a work dealing with ghosts, goblins, and fairies, will be out shortly; also a small selection of 'Blake's poems.' . . . Then I am getting ready for publication next Spring, a book of poems I intend to call *The Wind among the Reeds;* and, as soon afterwards as possible, a collection of essays, and lectures dealing with Irish nationality and literature which will probably appear under the title of 'Watch Fire.' " [4]

Yeats' reply to Dunlop's question is adjusted to his interviewer's concern as a representative of the Irish Theosophical Society. In his answer to a similar question by Katharine Tynan, Yeats omits all reference to the "Blake," the "book on Mysticism" (which may have become "The Speckled Bird"), and "Watch Fire," a title deriving from A.E.'s apocalyptic Celticism, and replies in a way more acceptable to the Irish Catholic literary community. "I have two books coming out with Lawrence and Bullen. . . . One is a volume of Irish sketches . . . to be called the *Celtic Twilight.* . . . The other is to be called *The Secret Rose* and is to be a collection of weird stories about the middle ages in Ireland. . . . Also I am in treaty about a new volume of poems." Thus in 1893 Yeats' two major works of the nineties had already been planned, and publication of *The Wind among the Reeds* was intended to occur in the spring of 1894. In fact, *The Secret Rose* did not appear until 1897 and *The Wind among the Reeds* until 1899.

In 1899 *The Wind among the Reeds* was received into the literary world as an integral part of a brief but substantial tradition of Celtic style. Writing in *The Servant of the Queen,* Maude Gonne remarks, "Neither fairies nor ancient Gods had ever cause to complain of the new clothes Willie Yeats put on them and in which, round 1900, they became the fashion." William Sharp's *A Dominion of Dream*, Arthur Symons' *Images of Good and Evil*, and Yeats' *The Wind among the Reeds*, all published in the same year, are so closely related stylistically and iconologically that they seem products of the same mind. But in 1893 that style did not exist. Instead of publishing the volume of verse which he had projected for 1894, Yeats set about to revise all his earlier work and to issue that revision as the collected *Poems* of 1895. The style which he brought into existence in the process of that revision is in effect the style of *The Wind among the Reeds*.

Yeats defined his sense of the distinction between the poems in *The Wind among the Reeds* and the work which had preceded it in a note written for the *Collected Poems* of 1908:

When I wrote these poems [*The Wind among the Reeds*] I had so meditated over the images that came to me in writing "Ballads and Lyrics" [that is, *The Countess Kathleen* volume of 1892], "The Rose" and "The Wanderings of Oisin," and other images from Irish folk-lore, that they had become true symbols. I had sometimes when awake, but more often in sleep, moments of vision, a state very unlike dreaming, when these images took upon themselves what seemed an independent life and became a part of a mystic language, which seemed always as if it would bring some strange revelation. Being troubled at what was thought a reckless obscurity, I tried to explain myself in lengthy notes, into which I put what little learning I had, and more wilful phantasy than I now think admirable, though what is mystical still seems to me the most true.[5]

Yeats had conceived *The Wind among the Reeds* as the work which was to follow at no great distance in time his volume of 1892. But in 1893 he suffered (as the quotation above indicates) an estrangement from his earlier style which resulted in the transformation of his entire *oeuvre*. The deepening of "images" into "true symbols" and the association of his early repertory of myth and style with a "mystic language" record the alliance in Yeats' mind of Celticism and the rising symbolist movement in England—in short, his discovery of what in terms of the nineties was to become the muse of Ireland.

Within the general field of Irish national literature in the nineteenth century at least two basic styles must be distinguished. The first is the

purely national style allied to the rhetoric of '48, to the poetry of
Samuel Ferguson, who is the literary representative of the later Fenian
movement, and to Irish colloquial poetry. It continued to be written in
both Ireland and England throughout the nineties and is associated
with Catholicism and the less exacting, parochial audience of Catholic
nationalism.[6] The second is the literature of Celticism, which was
almost entirely a product of Yeats' mind and was intimately associated
with the development of post-Romantic literature in England and on
the continent.

No writer in the Celtic movement began either by writing about
Irish subjects or by writing in a way which might be called specifically
Irish. When Yeats sent John Synge from his middle-class Paris hotel to
Aran, he was merely drawing a fellow countryman into an imaginary
world which he himself, with his genius for culture, had in large part
invented. All the members of the Celtic movement had at one time or
another "gone Irish." Looked at from the point of view of any given
writer in 1885, there seems to have been little personal inevitability in
the turn to the Irish subject matter. Katharine Tynan's *Shamrocks* of
1889 was preceded by her *Louise de la Vallière,* which shows almost no
trace of any specifically Irish orientation. John Todhunter had had a
long ethnically anonymous poetic career before he produced his *Ban-
shee* in 1891. The same had been true of Sharp, whose first contribution
to Celticism, *Pharais,* was published in 1894 with a dedication to the
author of *The Celtic Twilight.* Lionel Johnson did not publish his
Ireland until 1897, although he had handled Welsh subjects much
earlier. Similarly, George Russell's *Homeward* of 1894 is much more
obviously an expression of the universalist characteristic of Indian
theology than the founding work of a local cult. Symons' Irish poems
do not make their appearance until the end of the decade. Yeats
himself began by writing Oriental and Arcadian drama, and he was far
more impressed before 1885 by the Sufistic religion of beauty as he
found it in Palmer's *Oriental Mysticism* (1867) or in Edward Fitzgerald, and by Hafiz and the Sakuntala of Kalidasa, from which he drew
his earliest lyric surrogate, than by Standish O'Grady's *History of
Ireland* (1878–80). Further, the chief members of the Celtic movement
were drawn from the children of a disaffected gentility (Maude Gonne

herself was a child of Dublin Castle) who sought to retrench their failing energy by alliance with the peasantry and the aristocracy, the two dying but mythologically rich classes of Europe.

In the eighties in Ireland the most potent native literary force was still the Young Ireland of '48, whose leaders in the persons of Sir Charles Gavan Duffy and Lady Wilde ("Speranza") still survived to guide and obstruct the new movement. But the community with which Yeats came to identify himself was given over to the literary culture of the seventies and eighties in England. The shift of interest which we see in Yeats from the Arcadianism of Todhunter to the Ireland of O'Grady, a shift which was general throughout the eighties and nineties, was expressed by W. P. Ryan, who, with the endemic Irish capacity for premature celebration, wrote his history of the movement as early as 1894: "Our Arcadia," he says, "has become Ireland of the four bright seas." [7]

The specific native movement which was to become the successor of *The Spirit of the Nation* and which Yeats transformed and then deserted began as an attempt by Irish expatriates in London to educate their children.[8] The Southwark Literary Society, which was renamed in 1891 the Irish Literary Society, was founded in the early eighties and was visited about 1888 by both Yeats and Wilde, whom the Irish historian of 1894 still delights in calling by his full name, Oscar Fingall O'Flahertie Wills Wilde. The movement which was to eventuate in the imaginative world of Yeats and Synge and which was founded upon the unsubstantial basis of the Southwark Literary Society and its Dublin counterpart, the Pan-Celtic Society of 1888, was not motivated by literary purposes alone.

The increasing political prominence of Ireland augmented by the sympathy of Gladstone created a public interest in things Irish which had not previously existed in England and which made it possible for Yeats and others to enter journalism on the basis of the Irish specialty. The works which became seminal for the Irish literary movement of the late eighties and the nineties had long been in existence without exciting significant literary recognition. O'Grady, who was acknowledged as the spiritual founder of the movement, launched his *History* into obscurity in the seventies, and the sources of Yeats' *The Wander-*

ings of Oisin, as Alspach has noted,[9] lie in publications of the forties and the fifties, such as the *Publications of the Ossianic Society,* the *Kilkenny Archaeological Journal,* the works of O'Curry and O'Donovan commissioned by the Ordnance Survey—all of which O'Leary the Fenian had carefully preserved in his personal collection of Irish books which Yeats consulted. Fenianism bridged the gap between *The Spirit of the Nation* and *The Celtic Twilight* through the mediation of the library of O'Leary and the writing of Ferguson, who was first and last the most influential of the nineteenth-century Irish poets in the mind of Yeats. But while the revolutionary movements of the sixties and the later agrarian movements had little significant influence on the Irish sense of imaginative identity, the age of Parnell and the decade dominated by his career and death were momentous in that they produced a significant image, modeled in large part on Parnell himself, of the idealization and martyrdom of the self by association with the motherland.

By 1891 under the influence of Yeats, then twenty-six years old, the movement which was initiated as a purely national phenomenon under the auspices of the Southwark Literary Society began to dissociate itself from the nationalist background represented by Sir Charles Gavan Duffy, whose purposes were still those of '48.[10] The rift was symbolized by the controversy over the New Irish Library which led to the famous meeting of the Irish Literary Society at the Yeats house in Chiswick in 1891. In the end the London organization sided with Yeats' faction in an unsuccessful attempt to reserve the new national movement for the current literary situation, rather than make of it an echo chamber for the motives and literature of '48. Yeats' ambiguous position with respect to the Nationalist movement at the time of the conception of *The Wind among the Reeds* is reflected in Ryan's history: Ryan expresses the general opinion within the movement when he says that Yeats' "triumph" in 1888 with *Oisin* ranked him "henceforth as the most imaginative of Irish poets"; but he goes on to point out that "critics of late have been concerned to know if he has done his best work, or if there is or will be much in his poetry of an enduring kind." [11] Yeats' *The Countess Kathleen* had been less well received than *Oisin,* and there was a general sense in 1893, as there was in 1899 and for many years thereafter, that Yeats had already done his best work. Yeats himself was troubled by a sense of imaginative "dryness," which was reflected in the slowness with which he composed and in his many passionate attempts to make use of factitious methods such as ceremonial magic for the awakening of the imagination.

That he will be a great poet depends to a large extent on the possibility of his developing other characteristics to the same degree as that already attained by his imaginative faculty and power of vision. He must shake himself free from the passing craze of occultism and symbolism and realize also that the universe is not tenanted solely by soulths and sheogues.[12]

Yeats was confronted by the Nationalist movement with the major crisis of the poet, the choice of a tradition. His literary decision constituted a rejection of the parochial motive and an alliance of imagination with the European tradition of Romanticism, and concomitantly with the most universal of all European traditions, that of occult Wisdom. With this decision the Celtic movement in contrast to the national literary impulse came into being.

At this period in Yeats' early development two distinct motions of mind were in conflict: the first was the turn toward the Irish subject matter, and the second was the transcendence of the Irish style. The first required a certain self-alienation from the tradition of his father, and the second involved a return, not only to the sources of his father's conceptions, but to the sources of "Celticism" itself.

The literary world which Yeats entered when he came to London in 1887 was a world of urban professionalism dominated by the literary journalist. The best and most characteristic products of London in the nineties were the periodicals: the *Century Guild Hobby Horse,* the *Yellow Book,* the *Savoy,* the ephemeral *Pageant,* and the *Dome.* In thirteen years Yeats placed more than two hundred and fifty poems, articles, and reviews in dozens of journals. His first ventures into Irish folklore were of a similar professional character. Under the influence of figures such as Whitley Stokes, Arbois de Jubainville, Andrew Lang, Max Müller, Heinrich Schliemann, and James Frazer, antiquity, and folklore as the gateway to antiquity, had been given currency and imaginative status unmatched since the late eighteenth century. This

together with the emergent political situation made it financially possible for Yeats to undertake a literary career in London without abandoning the Irish commitment. Folklorism, and Irish folklorism in particular, was becoming a recognized professional specialty. Yeats sent
his early Irish folklore books into the world to join such popular works
as D. R. M'Anally's abominable *Ghosts, Giants, Pookas, Demons,
Leprechauns, Banshees, Fairies, Witches, Old Maids, and Other Mar-
vels of the Emerald Isle.* We may therefore make the distinction, in
discussing Yeats' relation to folklorism, between works of purely exo-
teric or professional character and works which have an esoteric intention. *The Celtic Twilight* is Yeats' first work of esoteric folklorism and
is in effect the first book of the Celtic movement.

At a distance of almost forty years, and in the estrangement of old
age, Yeats located the inception of the Celtic movement in 1893, the
year in which *The Wind among the Reeds* was conceived. "The movement began with AE's little verses made out of the Upanishads, and my
Celtic Twilight, a bit of ornamental trivial needlework sewn on a
prophetic fury got by Blake and Boehme." [13] George Russell, who for
some time had been publishing his verse in the *Irish Theosophist,*
brought out in 1894 his little collection, which immediately went into a
second edition in both England and America. In the same year "Fiona
MacLeod" published *Pharais* and dedicated it to the author of *The
Celtic Twilight,* and Nora Hopper plagiarized Yeats' projected title
and brought out her *Ballads in Prose* with a quotation from a poem
called "The Wind among the Reeds" on the cover (see Fig. 1) —a cover
which was later imitated by Althea Gyles.[14]

Although planned for publication in 1894, the order of the poems in
Yeats' *The Wind among the Reeds* came in the end to correspond to the
whole development of Celticism as a poetic movement in the nineties.
"The Hosting of the Sidhe," the first poem in *The Wind among the
Reeds,* was the epigraph of *The Celtic Twilight*. The last poems of *The
Wind* were not ready for publication until 1898 and 1899. With the
Boer War, the dissolution of the symbolist community in London, and
the increasing discipline of objectivity inherent in the rising Irish
theater, the turn of the century saw the disappearance of poetic Celti-

cism as a general phenomenon at the same time that, as a personal obsession, it ceased to preoccupy the mind of Yeats, its creator.

The fact that the actual sequence of poems in *The Wind among the Reeds* follows a historical and biographical rather than a symbolic line of development, and yet is conspicuously organized by a symbolic title, raises the problem of comprehensive structure in Yeats' lyric miscellanies. Yeats' technique of solving the problem of comprehensive structure in the lyric genre by organizing each poetic miscellany under a symbolic title was adopted in his *Collected Poems* of 1895.[15] The titles by which he attempted to organize retrospectively his earliest writing ("Crossways" derived from the predicament of the neophyte in the Golden Dawn, and "The Rose") made their appearance in the *Collected Poems* (1895) about the same time that Yeats conceived *The Wind among the Reeds.*

But the notion that the whole Yeatsian *oeuvre* is ultimately organized symbolically seems to me incorrect. The "symbol" is a magical instrument the proper use of which reveals beneath the secondary world of appearances a primary world to the achievement of which the book, even "the sacred book of the arts," is purely instrumental. The symbol is a "gate," a tool of reverie. It is part of the complexity of Yeats' mind that he never fully accepted the philosophical reality of the literary fact. The most obvious evidence of this is the preoccupation of Yeats' poems with the process of creation itself. It may be said of the poems, as Yeats himself said of his life, that they are a preparation for something that never happens.[16]

Yeats was early trained up to hate all real theories of causality, and yet the most prepossessing single fact about the Yeatsian *oeuvre* is the fact of development. It seems abundantly evident that Yeats conceived of his poetic endeavor, if not from the very first at least from a very early time, as the construction of a single work which ultimately took the form of the posthumously published and carefully edited collected edition of 1949. The basic structure of that work is predominantly autobiographical, insofar as the history of a poet's life can be said to be the history of single man. Since the symbol derives its validity and importance from its relation to an unchanging reality, it can only be integrated into a changing structure as a series of successive discrete closed systems or moments. But in the Yeatsian conception of *the poem,* as has frequently been pointed out, the symbol does indeed become structural, especially in the "pure" poems of *The Wind among the Reeds* with their direct relation to the symbol of the Absolute, the essential characteristic of which is defined by its incapacity to take on new relations. Thus we have the paradox in Yeats' work of a vast, everchanging system of conflicting assertions solved from moment to moment by symbols pitted against the flux.

One evidence of this problem is Yeats' vacillation between the simplicity of the one and the energy and disorganizing power of the many within the self. "The Hosting of the Sidhe" announces the supersession of some prior simplicity by the terrible energy of the multitude. Against this multitudinous energy the prior dispensation of unity can assert itself only in a way so tenuous and ineffectual as to suggest that unity is not really within the competence of the poet. In the early period Yeats cannot conceive of the mind except as multitudinous and cannot conceive of "reality" except as unified. This problem in the end becomes the key to whatever comprehensive structure his total work achieves.

As he was incapable of that stable perception of the One Substance which would have rendered his mystic orientation complete, he was always pre-eminently capable of that continuous personal development which is essentially alien to the achieved mystical consciousness. The key to Yeats' capacity for growth was his reluctance to allow any concept or entity to achieve real metaphysical (that is, ontological) status. By keeping all the phantasms which passed into his consciousness rooted in the emotions he never alienated himself from the vital sources of poetic power.

II

No work of Yeats has more frequently been called perfect than *The Wind among the Reeds,* and yet none of his later books is so heterogeneous in the range of style and influence it reflects. In an attempt to find a larger structure for *The Wind among the Reeds* a recent commentator has suggested "the pattern of a love affair gone wrong, a great passion that after rising to a climax necessarily fades." [17] But the most obvious fact of structure in *The Wind among the Reeds* is the fidelity of its form to the temporal sequence in which the poems it collects were produced.

Of the first twelve poems eight found publication in 1894 or earlier. They are poems which were not included in *The Countess Kathleen* of 1892 and which were not collected in the immensely popular revision of the early published work which came out in 1895. This first section of the book has for its basic style the style of 1892–94. The following is a list of the poems which form the first section of *The Wind among the Reeds* together with the date of first publication : [18]

> The Hosting of the Sidhe   1893
> The Everlasting Voices   1896
> The Moods   1893
> Aedh Tells of the Rose in His Heart   1892
> The Host of the Air   1893
> Breasal the Fisherman   1898
> A Cradle Song   1896
> Into the Twilight   1893
> The Song of the Wandering Aengus   1897
> The Song of the Old Mother   1894
> The Fiddler of Dooney   1892
> The Heart of the Woman   1894

On examination of this first section of *The Wind among the Reeds* the genetic heterogeneity of the book becomes at once apparent. "The Hosting of the Sidhe," Yeats' announcement of a new and terrible energy; "The Moods," his first dogmatic poem analogous to the later "Phases of the Moon"; and "Into the Twilight," an exercise in Irish mysticism, were written under the stylistic influence of George Russell. The second poem of the book, however, bears no stylistic or genetic relation whatsoever to the first and third. Its provenance is Byron, its symbolic content is derived from the Golden Dawn, and its style from the period of the *Savoy*. Between the Ossianism of "The Hosting" and the occultism of "The Everlasting Voices" lie differences of style and iconologic tradition which only Yeats' tendency to prefer the life of the symbol to the life of the poem, and his capacity for seeing symbolic coherence apart from stylistic, could reconcile. In like manner the fourth poem of *The Wind among the Reeds* is a pure example in style and symbol of the philosophical aestheticism of the eighties; the fifth, a tale of folk belief out of Lady Wilde molded by a stylistic and symbolic conception derived from Blake; the sixth, a poem in the latest and most casual style of the early period and founded on an alchemical emblem.

The least congruous stylistic excursions in the first section of *The Wind among the Reeds* are "The Song of the Old Mother" ("I rise in the dawn, and I kneel and blow / Till the seed of the fire flicker and glow.") and "The Heart of the Woman." These poems, despite the transforming power of Yeats' capacity for style, depend on the popular and sentimental tradition of magazine poetry and, beyond some slight occult and spiritualist suggestions, hardly rise above their origins. By contrast, "The Song of the Wandering Aengus," founded implicitly on Irish folklore and explicitly on a translation from Greek folk literature, is one of Yeats' most complex exercises in the mythology of the quest and is dominated by the influence of Morris.

Following from the genetic heterogeneity in the first section of *The Wind among the Reeds,* there is a very wide spectrum of stylistic variation reflecting that struggle for unity of speech which is the problem of a young poet in a complex culture. The style which the book announces at the outset is Ossianic; the diction and metric of manic dream are marked by excited breathing. The threat of uncontrollable energy is indicated by a rhythm based on strong distinction between stressed and unstressed syllables and the division of utterance into breathless ejaculation by caesura. This is the style of "The Hosting of the Sidhe" and "A Cradle Song."

> *The winds awaken, the leaves whirl round,*
> *Our cheeks are pale, our hair is unbound,*
> *Our breasts are heaving, our eyes are a-gleam,*
> *Our arms are waving, our lips are apart.*[19]

Juxtaposed to this style, of the same intensity but of different metrical characteristics, is the style of trance. While the Ossianic style is identified in this period with the state of psychic withdrawal in which the peasant catches glimpses of the sidhe, the "trance style" is associated with the many learned techniques of reverie which Yeats himself practiced with the aid of ceremonial magic for the evocation of symbols. The Ossianic style is dominated by its metrical characteristics, the distinction of stressed and unstressed, the caesura, under the influence of the unsophisticated meters of George Russell; the trance style is an effort at the obliteration of theoretical metrical characteristics. Its special effect is redundance and the absence of the distinction of stressed and unstressed syllables. Every word of the poem bears the same indefinite weight of emotion. This is the characteristic style of English symbolist poetry and is influenced by French syllabic metric. Yeats introduces this style into *The Wind among the Reeds* in the second poem:

> O sweet everlasting Voices be still.[20]

The third important style of *The Wind among the Reeds* is the "aesthetic." Poems in this style lack the irregularity of the Ossianic and the opacity of the trance style.

> I hunger to build them anew and sit on a green knoll apart,
> With the earth and the sky and the water, remade, like a casket of
>   gold
> For my dreams of your image that blossoms a rose in the deeps
>   of my heart.[21]

This is a lucid expositional metric which is almost entirely regular, and which reflects the rebirth of Renaissance models and the occasional archaism of diction of the Pre-Raphaelite movement.

The fourth and most mysterious of the styles of the book is the style in which the predominant influence is Morris. It is the style of personal transformation, in contrast to the transcendence of the tremendous Other characteristic of the Ossianic traditions. We find it in *The Wind* and scarcely anywhere else in Yeats. Primary examples are "The Song of the Wandering Aengus," "The Blessed," and "The Cap and Bells."

> When I had laid it on the floor
> I went to blow the fire a-flame,
> But something rustled on the floor,
> And someone called me by my name:
> It had become a glimmering girl.[22]

Morris, in *The Earthly Paradise* and in his splendid and neglected prose narratives, endeavored to empty discourse of responsibility to personality in order to liberate the mode of romance. The so-called literature of escape as Morris conceived it is a literature of transformation in which the mind disavows its relations to temporality in order to align itself with the noble hypothesis of the ever-troubled but none the less possible happiness of the achieved quest. Yeats took up the style of Morris in this sense, ignoring Morris' canny awareness of the limited capacity for transformation even of those who drink from *The Well at the World's End*. The chief characteristic of this style is the endeavor to dissociate the symbol from history. By this means Yeats attempted to render the relevance of the symbol unlimited while at the same time destroying its relation to all usual conceptual structures. Hopkins drew near to an object until the microscopic clarity with which it was seen destroyed the mind's usual conception of it. Yeats, on the other hand, generalized the object until it had no meaning except in relation to his poetic context.

The fifth style working within *The Wind among the Reeds* is quite different in its implications from the preceding four. The latter have almost no history beyond the nineties and represent the discontinuity of Yeats' early period in relation to what followed. By contrast, however, there was an aspect of Yeats' stylistic ambition which is directly related to all that is excellent in his later verbal conduct. When Lionel Johnson read to the assembled Rhymers his poem on the statue of King Charles, Yeats felt that he had come upon a living style, near enough to common speech to satisfy his desire to reassociate poetry with personal energy, yet sufficiently conventional to assure literary survival.[23]

The reconstitution of poetic language after the Victorian episode was one of the crucial problems of the *fin de siècle*. The simplest consequences of Yeats' concern with this problem can be seen in Symons' exposition of *The Wind,* where he calls attention to the absence of "poetic language," meaning of course the absence of the Victorian imitation of Renaissance conventions. The most important example of this aspect of Yeats' stylistic ambitions in *The Wind among the Reeds* is exhibited in a few poems written in what might be called a casual manner.

> I wander by the edge
> Of this desolate lake
> Where wind cries in the sedge.[24]

> Though you are in your shining days,
> Voices among the crowd
> And new friends busy with your praise,
> Be not unkind or proud.[25]

This style, out of all the possibilities of style in *The Wind among the Reeds*, Yeats selected for development after the *débâcle* of the nineties.

Having established something of the diversity of style in *The Wind among the Reeds*, a diversity the more real because each modulation of the verbal texture of the poems has behind it a temporary alliance with a discrete universe of stylistic models, I shall now proceed to lay out in a preliminary manner the second and third sections of the book. The poems of the second section of *The Wind among the Reeds* cluster about the year of the *Savoy* (1896), the periodical in which they found for the most part their first publication. Whereas Yeats attributed only two of the poems of the first section to the curious surrogates which are one of the book's most obvious mysteries, the second section is dominated by them. These surrogates represent Yeats' attempt to claim for the Celtic movement poems the real provenance of which has nothing to do with the Irish subject matter and at the same time so fully to generalize the Irish reference that no alien teleologies, political or religious, limit its suggestiveness. The second section of *The Wind* consists of the following poems listed in the order in which they appear in the edition of 1899 and followed in each case by the date of first publication:

> Aedh Laments the Loss of Love   1898
> Mongan Laments the Change   1897
> Michael Robartes Bids His Beloved   1896
> Hanrahan Reproves the Curlew   1896
> Michael Robartes Remembers Forgotten Beauty   1896
> A Poet to His Beloved   1898
> Aedh Gives His Beloved Certain Rhymes   1896
> To My Heart, Bidding It Have No Fear   1896
> The Cap and Bells   1894

The Valley of the Black Pig 1896
Michael Robartes Asks Forgiveness
    because of His Many Moods 1895
Aedh Tells of a Valley Full of Lovers 1897
Aedh Tells of the Perfect Beauty 1896

In contrast to the fairly obvious diversity of the first section of the book, the second is considerably more integrated. The specific Irish reference of "The Hosting," "The Fiddler of Dooney," and "Into the Twilight" has disappeared and been replaced by an apparently arbitrary and ahistorical dramatis personae including Aedh, Mongan, Michael Robartes, and Hanrahan. The chief symbolic increment is the emergence of the major symbol of the book, the white woman.

A POET TO HIS BELOVED
I bring you with reverent hands
The books of my numberless dreams;
White woman that passion has worn
As the tide wears the dove-grey sands,
And with heart more old than the horn
That is brimmed from the pale fire of time:
White woman with numberless dreams
I bring you my passionate rhyme.[26]

The salient autobiographical fact of the *Savoy* period, Yeats' affair with Olivia Shakespear, has excited critics (primarily F. R. Leavis) [27] to the perception of a more realistic and integrated sexuality in *The Wind among the Reeds*. However, an examination of the poems produced or completed at the time makes clear that Yeats' response to the relationship in terms of significant fantasy was a characteristic reversion to the prior and subjective soul image of which the type in the literature of the period is Ernest Dowson's "Cynara."

AEDH LAMENTS THE LOSS OF HIS LOVE
Pale brows, still hands and dim hair,
I had a beautiful friend
And dreamed that the old despair
Would end in love in the end:
She looked in my heart one day
And saw your image was there;
She has gone weeping away.[28]

The compulsion, of which this poem is a document, to turn away from the image of the real, or at least the historical, beloved in the direction of the profoundly subjective and timeless image of the woman of romance is the exigency by which both the style and the subject matter of *The Wind among the Reeds* is determined. In the world of this book both the sexual and the creative acts are always incomplete, and for both real acts dream is substituted. In the characteristic image of the book the poet is incapable of weaving the fabric or tapestry of his instinctual destiny and offers therefore to his beloved and muse and to the literary world the alternative of dream.

> Had I the heavens' embroidered cloths,
>
> .   .   .   .   .
>
> I would spread the cloths under your feet:
> But I, being poor, have only my dreams. . . .
> Tread softly because you tread on my dreams.[29]

The profound significance of this reflex of fear in the presence of what Yeats later came to think of as the "real" and "difficult" world of poetry and sexuality can be seen in the prose rehearsal of the just-quoted passage. It occurs in the fable of "The Wisdom of the King." [30] The hawk-headed youth, not yet cognizant of his destiny in the ideal world, mistakenly courts a beautiful young girl, who is the symbol of contemporary Ireland and who prefers Connemara cloth to the tapestries of the Orient. "Day by day the king gave her gifts from oversea, which, though woven with curious figures, seemed to her less beautiful than the bright cloth woven in the Island of Woods [one of the names of Ireland, probably out of Geoffrey Keating's *History of Ireland*]. . . . He lay down his wisdom at her feet." [31] The immensity of the personal ambition which Yeats symbolizes by the hawk-headed youth can be understood by referring to a citation from the *Collectanea Hermetica* of 1896, which was edited by members of the Golden Dawn and which he therefore can be presumed to have seen. There we read, "God is He having the head of a Hawk." [32] The resistance of the Ireland of the nineteenth century and indeed the whole world of contemporary history to the wisdom of the Messianic poet-king is expressed in the rejection of the poetic suitor by his muse. Even in the fantasy of "The

Wisdom of the King," where the poet does in fact possess himself of the
embroidered cloths, the consummation of sexual desire is impossible,
and the poet is forced back into the isolation of his ideal destiny.
Virtually the whole of Yeats' later work is devoted to the attempt to
prepare the way for the reflux of sexual energy which in the early
period was so fatally withdrawn from the consolation of the real object.
The "rough beast" is always about to return to the world, and even so
successful a poem as "Leda" is rendered ambiguous by the final query
already raised by the earlier address of the bird-king to the girl, "Did
she put on his knowledge?"

In the recapitulation earlier in this chapter of the history of the Celtic
Revival, it has been observed that Yeats faced the stylistic problem
raised by the national character of the movement by turning away from
the local and inferior tradition of style governed by the real but
extraliterary teleologies of religious and national interest to the larger
and less limited tradition of Irish ideal self-conception, which had its
origin in European romanticism. As the lover in the poem of "Pale
brows, still hands, and dim hair" is called away from the possible to the
impossible love, so Yeats sought to evade the instant demands of the
Shan Van Voght by transforming her into Sophia. The importance of
the *Savoy* section of *The Wind among the Reeds* to the main line of our
present discussion is that the style which it represents constitutes the
developed image according to which about 1893 he undertook to revise
his earlier work. And that revision represents his attempt to simplify
by a fiat of the imagination both history, which threw up to him the
complexity of styles which we have discriminated in the first section of
The Wind among the Reeds, and the mind, which possessed for him at
this period an equally unresolvable complexity.

The basic technique of the revision is simple. *The Wind among the
Reeds* derives its appearance of redundant unity from the repetition of
a series of symbolic formulas, and these formulas in large part cluster
about and define the person of the white woman. If we turn back to
"The Wanderings of Oisin" we find that Niamh, who was in 1892
"sad," became in 1895 "pearl-pale"; the sea in "The Sad Shepherd,"
which was in 1886 "old," has become in 1895 symbolically "dim"; and

the Virgin herself, who was in *The Countess Kathleen* of 1892 simply "dear Mary," became in the revision significantly "white." [33] The recurrence of certain formulas in the revision of 1895 and in *The Wind*, particularly what Tindall calls the "hair tent," has been noticed and disparaged by Jeffares, Unterecker (following Tindall), and others; [34] but it remains to be noted that this stabilization of the otherwise unmanageable diversity of style and image of his earliest work was, in the dialectic of Yeats' development, in the highest sense constructive, being the first and perhaps most significant response of his mind to the problem of unity.

The confrontation with the white woman and the formulas which establish the pale trance world associated with her is the sign of the transformation of image into symbol by which Yeats in 1908 distinguished *The Wind among the Reeds* from his earliest poetry. The convention of the psychological states expressed by the adjectives "pale" and "dim," by the long-haired woman preternaturally white, is by no means original with Yeats. But the attempt to conform the poem completely to the stylistic demands of this most exacting symbol in its many forms is without parallel in the Romantic tradition. The difference lies in Yeats' capacity to associate the casual image with the historically defined symbol and to comprehend and give life to the symbol in the deepest sense of emotional commitment.

The primary icon in *The Wind among the Reeds* is the "white woman whom passion has worn / As the waves wear the dovegrey sand." She is dead, immortal, and marked by her continuous sexual engagement with the world of the living. From a historical point of view this figure is the fallen aspect of Sophia as she can be found in the early history of Gnosticism. [35] The most vivid image of her available in the period is in Lafcadio Hearn's translation (1895) of Flaubert's *The Temptation of Saint Anthony*, a work which Yeats came to know about this time. In the gnosis of Simon Magus the divine creative thought (*Ennoia*) descends into the world as Helena, reminding us that the Helen of Yeats' later poems is better understood in the Faustian or Simonian sense than in the Homeric.

Here she is Antony; she who was called Sigeh, Ennoia, Barbelo, Prounikos. The spirits who govern the world were jealous of her, and they bound her

in the body of a woman. She was the Helen of the Trojans whose memory
the poet Stesichorus has rendered infamous. She has been Lucretia, the
patrician lady violated by kings. She was Dalilah, who cut off the hair of
Samson. She was the daughter of Israel who surrendered herself to he-
goats. She has loved adultery, lying and folly. She was prostituted by
every nation. . . . At Tyre she, the Syrian, was the mistress of thieves. She
drank with them during the nights and she concealed assassins amid the
vermin of her tepid bed. . . . But she really is the moon. . . . She is
Minerva. . . . She is the Holy Spirit.[36]

Aside from its historical relevance this image, the *Ennoia,* the female
aspect of deity as creator, types of which Yeats found throughout the
mystic literature available to him, correctly anticipates in her transformations as Helen, Delilah, and Holy Spirit the terms of Yeats' long
romance with the Great Mother as muse in the forms of Maude Gonne
and the Shan Van Voght.

It has been suggested that the formulaic nature of the revision of
1893–95, the characteristics of which become predominant in the central or *Savoy* section of *The Wind among the Reeds,* is not merely a
literary device but does in fact serve a purpose in Yeats' complex and
ultimately frustrated attempt to unify the culture of his imagination.
The blocking or negative aspects of the symbol of the white woman, the
unifying term in Yeats' language of archetypal self-finding, are easy to
discern. Like the Shekinah of the Cabalah or the Maid of Law's
Boehme, she is always the bride of God, or, as in the passage from
Flaubert, of some indefinitely potent and alien Other. Thus in *The
Wind* the poet is eclipsed in his suit by the superior potency of the
sidhe, as in "The Host of the Air" and "Aedh Pleads with the Elemental Powers." Creativity is presumptively, if not finally, on the side of
the father. But even in this mythology the primordial woman has also a
countervailing aspect expressed by the formula of the hair tent in
which the poet, protected from the wrath of the father and from the
tyranny of the real, can elaborate his fantasy in uterine safety. Under
the tent of her hair twilight falls upon the lover. The relation of the
hair tent to the liberation of fantasy (creation) can be seen immediately by reference to the opening lines of Browning's "Pauline," an
early and overt example of the tradition of this symbol:

Pauline, mine own, bend o'er me—thy soft breast
Shall pant to mine—bend o'er me—thy sweet eyes
And loosened hair, and breathing lips, and arms
Drawing me to thee—these build up a screen
To shut me in with thee, and from all fear,
So that I might unlock the sleepless brood
Of fancies from my soul.[37]

The concluding section of *The Wind among the Reeds* conveys the
impression of an increase of weight and discursiveness by the grouping
together of the most complex and philosophical poems of Yeats' early
period: "The Blessed," "The Secret Rose," "The Travail of Passion,"
and "Aedh Pleads with the Elemental Powers." Each of these will
require careful scrutiny. This section consists of the following poems:

Aedh Hears the Cry of the Sedge   1898
Aedh Thinks of Those Who Have Spoken Evil of His Beloved   1898
The Blessed   1897
The Secret Rose   1896
Hanrahan Laments because of His Wanderings   1897
The Travail of Passion   1896
The Poet Pleads with His Friend   1897
Hanrahan Speaks to the Lovers   1896
Aedh Pleads with the Elemental Powers   1892–1898
Aedh Wishes His Beloved Were Dead   1898
Aedh Wishes for the Cloths of Heaven   1899
Mongan Thinks of His Past Greatness   1898

This group of poems differs critically from the central and early
sections of *The Wind* by the predominance of what Yeats distinguished
as the intellectual in contrast to the emotional symbol, and any record,
however preliminary, of the general characteristics of the book must
take this distinction into consideration, for inherent in it is Yeats' final
decision with respect to value in the early period.

The sources of Yeats' theory of symbolism are not in the first
instance literary, and its consequences are not confined to the literary
phenomenon. It derives from a once almost universal sense of the
world, a sense of the world common to figures as diverse as Porphyry,
Aquinas, Agrippa, and the authors of the *Upanishads,* which regards
reality merely as the evidence of its own transcendent origin. Its roots

are deep in the religious sense of the real which understands the process of knowing as the reversal of the order of creation whereby man was separated from the Divine Essence. This great process of educing meaning from experience, which constitutes a continuous falsification of history, is in the Yeatsian construction essential to the poetic undertaking because poetry requires a morally intelligible world. Yeats tended to distinguish between himself and the earlier Romantics, primarily Wordsworth, on the basis of the epistemological problem. What was for Wordsworth a real anxiety about the nature of reality and the problem of knowledge was for Yeats, as for Aquinas, a purely exegetical question. Wordsworth had lost what Blake, in his posthumous career, restored to the world, namely, the sense of reality as a "Dictionary of Signs and Symbols." Therefore Yeats, like all mystics, regarded every object in the real world as a potential symbol, a point of view founded upon the presumption of the ideal origin of all things. The function of the artist was to make distinct the relation among these potentially significant events and thus bring them into art.

The symbol mediates between the world of the Divine Essence and the world of temporal accident. It is in the first instance external to the mind and omnipresent in history, but it comes into relation to the mind through the human capacity for emotion, although emotion itself may (it is important that Yeats does not quite know) be *ab extra.*

All sounds, all colours, all forms, either because of their pre-ordained energies or because of long association evoke indefinable and yet precise emotions, or, as I prefer to think, call down among us certain disembodied powers whose footsteps over our hearts are called emotions; and when sound and colour and form are in a musical relation, a beautiful relation to one another, they become as it were one sound, one colour, one form, and evoke an emotion that is made out of their distinct evocations and yet it is one emotion.[38]

At this level the sign of the presence of the symbol and the consequence of the organization of symbols in poetry is the evocation of emotion. Yeats' example of this kind of symbol is well known:

There are no lines with more melancholy beauty than these by Burns

>   The white moon is setting behind the white waves,
>   And time is setting with me, O.

and these lines are perfectly symbolical. Take from them the whiteness of the moon and of the wave, whose relation to the setting of time is too subtle for the intellect, and you take from them their beauty. But, when all are together, moon and wave and whiteness and the setting Time and the last melancholy cry, they evoke an emotion which cannot be evoked by any other arrangement of colours and sounds and forms.[39]

The proper analysis of the poem is no more than the sensibility of the reader to the particular character of the emotion evoked by the poem as distinct from all other emotions. This is the level of response with which Yeats was primarily concerned in the revision of his poetry of which the principal consequence is those poems in *The Wind among the Reeds* published before 1897 (the *Savoy* section). The whole moral problem is absorbed into the capacity to feel in a specific sense, with the understanding that this capacity to feel will extend itself into history.

A little lyric evokes an emotion and this emotion gathers others about it and melts into their being in the making of some great epic; and at last needing an always less delicate body, or symbol, it flows out with all it has gathered among the blind instincts of daily life. . . . I am never certain, when I hear of some war, or of some religious excitement, or of some new manufacture, or of anything else that fills the ear of the world that it has not happened because of something that a boy piped in Thessaly.[40]

In the final section of *The Wind among the Reeds,* however, that is, in the poems written in 1897 and after (of which three found their way into the central section of the book), Yeats developed a somewhat different kind of poem which he identified as deriving its power from the intellectual symbol. The emotional symbol has its effect in history and binds the mind to the world by its dependence on the affective aspect of the self. The intellectual symbol because of its primary relation to an unbodied idea is the more spiritual.[41]

If I say "white" or "purple" in an ordinary line of poetry, they evoke emotions so exclusively that I cannot say why they move me; but if I say them in the same mood, in the same breath with such obvious intellectual symbols as a cross or a crown of thorns, I think of purity and sovereignty; while innumerable other meanings . . . move visibly through my mind and move invisibly beyond the threshold of sleep, casting lights and shadows on what had seemed before . . . but sterility and noisy violence. . . . It is the intellect that decides where the reader shall ponder over the procession of the symbols, and if the symbols are merely emotional he gazes from amid the accidents and destinies of the world; but if the symbols are intellectual too, he becomes himself a part of pure intellect, and he is himself mingled with the procession.[42]

In the desire to mingle with the procession of the symbols in the form of pure intellect we can recognize the structure of a whole series of major poems extending at least from "The Hosting of the Sidhe" and "Sailing to Byzantium" through the hopeless alienation from transcendence in "Crazy Jane on the Mountain" and the strange exaltation of the concluding section of "Lapis Lazuli." Yeats' intellectual symbols are constructed by a very simple process, in later life over and over again repeated. This process we have already described as the comparison of an image in the mind or in the immediate environment with an image in the favored tradition. When these two images coincide, a symbol is born and self-transcendence achieved.

The impulse to free himself from emotion, to pass into the order of the structural in contrast to the purely affective symbol, which emerges at the conclusion of *The Wind among the Reeds,* was necessarily unfulfilled in the context of Yeats' early poetry. The notion of the possibility of complete absorption implied in the desire to join the procession of the gods proved incompatible with life and left as the only resource the objectification of the relation to the symbol which characterizes the shift of point of view from the early to the middle period. Inescapably in the early period, Yeats' canon of the necessary subjectivity of art confronted him with the problem of emotion, the aspect of the self for which he could find no effective mode of transcendence. On the basis of the demand of the emotions he constructed his symbol of the absolute.

In relation to the problem of emotion Yeats generated his symbols of cataclysm. Since, from a conceptual point of view, the Beloved existed only outside time, nothing less than the destruction of the world of time was necessary in order to come to her.

> Until the axle break
> That keeps the stars in their round,

> And hands hurl in the deep
> The banners of East and West,
> And the girdle of light is unbound,
> Your breast will not lie by the breast
> Of your beloved in sleep.[43]

The means of the destruction of time was poetry, which had behind it all the power of the unsatisfied libido. The Black Pig was Yeats' symbol of the imagination which brought the last judgement upon the world by destroying it in its material and accidental mode in order that it might be recreated ideal, essential, and fulfilling.

Chapter II

We have all been taught to look with horror upon Medusa's head with the serpents twisting round its face, the terror of which turned all to stone who gazed upon it. But we must if we would learn to know the secret wisdom of the ages, learn to long for a glance from those wonderful eyes which will bestow upon us the gift of indifference to personal joys and sorrows. For the wise man must be as a precious stone, a center of light to all that approach him, giving joy to others, because he contains the highest joy in himself; desiring nothing from the world, drawing his inspiration from the supernal light—that "Wisdom Goddess" who wears the serpent-crowned head upon her shield.—S. S. D. D. (Florence Farr)

The Muse of Ireland

Y EATS and the lesser poets of his generation in England and Ireland may be said to have been born into one civilization and, under the general license of Celticism and the Decadence, to have created another. The result was an imaginative or "third" culture, organized according to what the poet conceived to be the true needs of the imagination and arbitrarily set over against the given historical constellation of symbols. Having performed this gigantic act, he was ever after troubled by the need of a tradition and by an unremitting anxiety for authenticity.

The shape of Yeatsian scholarship has been determined in large measure by the poet's own method of searching out a labyrinthine path and then leaving in the open or in some ill-concealed place, depending on his measure of certitude, the thread by which it could be found out. In this way Yeats fabricated his poetry, his personal history, and even his personal appearance; and for this reason he continued to make and remake himself until he died.

The need to "Make it new" was by no means exclusively Irish; but the Irish, who had been under the necessity from the end of the eighteenth century of constructing a literature in English where none had previously existed, had a head start on modernity in this matter. Hence the association of some of the best writers of the London group in the nineties with "Celticism," despite the fact that they had no inherited commitment to it.

Throughout the nineteenth century the most crippling and hyperbolic aspects of English Romanticism were attributed to Ireland as ethnic characteristics. The rhetoric of the Young Ireland group was formed on the model of Thomas Campbell, Scott, and Macaulay, and under the pressure of practical hopelessness Irish political poetry constructed an ideal image of Ireland of truly Shelleyan tenuity and toughness. It was against that image that John Synge pitted his genius for lyric realism as late as 1907 and was destroyed. Matthew Arnold, following Renan, found unindustrialized, peasant Ireland quintessentially romantic in contrast to industrialized and imperial England. England was industrial; Ireland was agrarian. England belonged to the future, Ireland to the past. The Englishman was tragically sober; the Irishman was comically drunk. English politics were successful; Irish politics were unsuccessful and therefore Ossianic: "They went forth to battle but they always fell." Ireland is for Arnold "The Palace of Art," and this specialization of Ireland as the true home of the most crippling aspects of Victorian aestheticism had immense weight for Yeats in his reconstruction of his tradition.

Under the influence of the Arnoldian suggestion Yeats as a young man did not attempt as did the great Victorians to break down the barriers between the moral and the aesthetic impulse, but could rather by ethnic right contemplate total withdrawal into the aesthetic mode. He is exactly the "glorious devil" of Tennyson's "Palace," who "large in heart and brain . . . did love beauty only . . . and knowledge for its beauty."[1] This influence was fostered by other Irish writers who founded the movement of which Yeats became the leader, notably Standish O'Grady, and it was the seduction of this image which made so easy the alliance of literary Celticism with English Aestheticism. A striking example of the romantic debris out of which Celticism was refined is the castle on Lough Kay where Yeats planned to found his Irish order of mysteries "like those of Eleusis and Samothrace." "It was not an old castle being but the invention of some romantic man, seventy or eighty years ago."[2]

Characteristically, however, Yeats did not rest in the romantic tradition of beauty but sought out the origin and historical substance of that tradition. To the romantic image he added the occult symbol. The statement of Bowra with respect to the French movement, "Symbolism

. . . was the mystical form of Aestheticism," [3] is directly confirmed by Yeats' understanding of the aesthetic tradition. Symons, when he remarked that *The Wind among the Reeds* "may also seem to be one long hymn to intellectual beauty," [4] pointed to the primary strain of symbolism, well known in the small circle of the initiated, upon which Yeats founded his reconstruction of the aesthetic edifice.

It is by now unnecessary to repeat that a major constituent of Yeats' imaginary culture was the Wisdom tradition; but the relation of Wisdom to the symbolist poem as Yeats came to practice it in *The Wind* remains to be demonstrated. As is well known, he early realized his deep affinities to that tradition and tended to remain unvaryingly loyal only to those aspects of his early work which were founded upon it. The use which he made of that tradition was highly eclectic. His intuitive sensibility to its meaning and artistic consequences far exceeded at the beginning his actual historical command, and his selection of relevant elements tended to be determined by the existence of correlative elements in the Irish background. It was the fact that nineteenth-century Celticism had its foundation in aestheticism and that aestheticism had a fundamental relation to the Wisdom tradition which made it possible for Sophia to become the muse of Ireland.

Symons' reference to intellectual beauty implies the background not only of Shelley's poem, but also of Spenser's "Hymne." The tradition of Sapience as Spenser and everyone else expounds it includes the ineffability of Wisdom's beauty ("The fairness of her face no tongue can tell" [5]). The devotion of symbolist tradition to this beauty, beyond the power of words to describe, tends to demand of the symbolist poet a poem which cannot be written, a poem which is a direct emanation of the impossible beauty that lies outside the characteristics of mortality. Yeats, in his approach to the image of Wisdom in the poetry of *The Wind,* founded as it is on the model of impossible beauty, is confronted with the problem of the absolute poem which must, as it approaches closer and closer to creative realization, destroy itself in its relation to time.

A characteristic expression of that unknowability of Wisdom which has its literary analogy in the cultivated opacity of the poetic text is the fifteenth-century *Idiota* of Nicholas of Cusa.

Wisdom . . . is no otherwise known than that it is higher than all knowledge, and utterly unknowable and unspeakable by all language, and unintelligible by all understanding, and unmeasurable by all measure, and unlimitable by all limit . . . and unfigurable in all figuration . . . and unimaginable by all imagination, and insensible in all sight . . . and because in all speech it is unexpressible, there can be no end devised of these speeches.[6]

Any man who truly loves Wisdom rejoices in her cognitive unattainability just as the poet of *The Wind* deliberately cultivates the unattainability of the sexual object, preferring to imagine her dead and infinite than to imagine her achieved in her mortal and therefore finite body.

If any man should love anything because it were lovely, he would be glad that in the lovely thing there should be found infinite and inexpressible causes of love. And this is the lover's most joyful comprehension, when he comprehends the incomprehensible loveliness of the thing beloved, for he would not so much rejoice to love any second loved object, that were comprehensible, as when it appears unto him that the loveliness of the thing beloved is utterly unmeasurable, undeterminable, and wholly incomprehensible.[7]

Yeats came upon the Wisdom symbol in the form of the Rose, and when in the edition of 1895 it occurred to him to organize his successive volumes with reference to a single talisman it was the Rose which he selected to preside over the poems which prepared the way for *The Wind among the Reeds*. In *The Trembling of the Veil* he recalls his sense of the relation of intellectual beauty and literary hiddenness:

I had an unshakable conviction, arising how or whence I cannot tell, that invisible gates would open as they opened for Blake, as they opened for Swedenborg, as they opened for Boehme . . . [and] that I must . . . on that day when the gates began to open become difficult or obscure. With a rhythm that still echoed Morris I prayed to the Red Rose, to Intellectual Beauty.[8]

A work which Yeats encountered early and which exhibits the relation of the woman Wisdom as she dominated the aesthetic movement is Simeon Solomon's *A Vision of Love Revealed in Sleep*, which Wilde heard read while sitting at the feet of Pater.[9] Solomon describes his encounter with her as follows: "I saw within the glory, one who seemed of pure snow and of pure fire, the Very Love, the Divine Type of Absolute Beauty primaeval and eternal compact of the white flame of youth, burning in ineffable perfection." [10] This was the woman whom Yeats courted in so many forms throughout his life and with such ambition of absolute commitment in the nineties, and it was in her name that he undertook to found his poetic style. Writing in retrospect of the period after 1893, he says:

All poets including Spenser in all but a few pages until our age came, and when it came almost all, have had some propaganda or traditional doctrine to give companionship with their fellows. . . . But Coleridge of the "Ancient Mariner" and "Kubla Khan," and Rossetti in all his writing made what Arnold has called that "morbid effort," that search for "perfection of thought and feeling, and to unite this to perfection of form," sought this new, pure beauty, and suffered in their lives because of it. [11]

After 1893 the search for this "new pure beauty" dominates Yeats' ambitions. In her image, Niamh is transformed and the Countess Kathleen is created; in the person of Mary Hynes she drives Hanrahan to the edge of insanity; and as Maeve, or the Virgin Mary, or the "Rose of Imperishable Beauty" she haunts the pages of *The Celtic Twilight*. In his own life he encountered her embodied in a series of oracular women: Madam Blavatsky, Florence Farr, Maude Gonne, Lady Gregory, his wife, and above all his mother, who first introduced him to the folk as a source of fantasy. [12] But the most important image which Wisdom served to gather within her symbolic frame of reference was the image of Ireland herself, the Shan Van Voght.

Irish nationalism from the time of Daniel O'Connell was Catholic. Under the penal laws secret names for Ireland ("the Black Rose," "the silk of the kine") became current. Irish Catholicism and Irish Nationalism grew to be, because of repeated suppression, occult movements, and their symbolisms did not remain altogether separate. In *The Celtic Twilight* Yeats tells of the Protestant girl who, while walking in the Sligo hills, was taken for the Virgin Mary by a group of children, and we can recognize in his reverie upon that episode the habitual syncretism by which the Virgin becomes the red rose of Ireland, the Mystic Rose of occultism, the Shekinah of Mather's *Kabbalah Unveiled*, the intellectual beauty of Shelley.

Yeats' early sense of the nature of poetry is founded upon poetry's opposition to science, upon the Augustinian distinction between *scientia* and *sapientia*. Ireland, superstitious, unindustrialized, agrarian, quintessentially romantic because existing significantly only in the remote past, was not only the Motherland, but the Muse, Wisdom, the Idea, the Great Mother herself.

Within Ireland, Wisdom is not always kind to her children, requiring of them a renunciation incompatible with moral simplicity, and even with life itself. We have already observed Yeats' comment that those of his generation who "sought this new pure beauty . . . suffered in their lives because of it." As is well known, the nineties proved fatal to the writers who were most characteristic of it and were in the deepest sense its products. Dowson, Beardsley, Johnson, Wilde, Davidson, were all victims of the lethal pathos of aestheticism. On the specifically Irish side, the most important political event of the decade was Ireland's assassination in 1891 of Parnell, which Yeats described twenty years afterward in terms of the myth of Attis: "That woman, the Great Mother imaging / Cut out his heart." [13] In 1897 when Yeats came to publish his long-planned volume, *The Secret Rose,* he described it as having but one subject, "the war of the spiritual with the natural order." The two related traditions of Irish political idealism and English aesthetic idealism concur in involving their followers in a fatal oblation.

II

The basic myth of the early Yeats, and especially of *The Wind among the Reeds,* is the encounter of the suitor of the absolute with its symbol, the Wisdom figure. The resulting mystic experience is the *mysterium tremendum,* [14] that terrible meeting with spiritual fact which leaves the living heart, if life can endure it at all, exhausted with fear. In order to understand the specific meaning of that experience in these poems it is necessary to understand the special matrix of symbolism in which that meaning is displayed.

In *The Wind* the *mysterium tremendum* with its characteristics of awe and terror arises in the heart of the poet in the presence of his muse. Almost everywhere in Yeats the conditions under which poetry comes to exist are a major poetic subject. The living poem, when the circumstances which resist its creation are overcome and in the degree to which they are overcome, is itself the symbol of the moral possibility to which the poetry refers. We have already observed the exactions which the tradition of Wisdom make on the symbolist poem, driving it by the canon of purity away from normal semantic relations; we have yet to observe the effect which the specific vehicle of that tradition, Ireland who presides over the Yeatsian undertaking as muse and fury, has on the poet.

We have found occasion to cite Yeats' reference to Ireland as the *magna mater* who devoured the heart of Parnell. Somewhat earlier in the century Stephen Dedalus described her as "a sow who devoured her own farrow." Yeats' first appearance in an English periodical was in the role of King Goll who, after casting aside all temporal possessions, is visited by a muse which requires of him the destruction of the poetic instrument itself; and this act was carefully represented in an engraving by John Yeats showing his son as Goll tearing out the strings of his harp in a fit of madness (Fig. 2).[15] Ireland in her role as muse followed Ireland in her political identity in that she made impossible demands on her votaries.

According to Yeats' early collections of Irish folklore the Gaelic muse is the vampire, the Leanhuan Shee. "The fairy lives on their life and they waste away. She is the Gaelic muse for she gives inspiration to those she persecutes, and will not let them remain long on earth." [16] In another place he expands the folklore of the Gaelic muse to include that peculiar schizoid characteristic of the Irish peasantry which he so willingly identifies with the creative dream.

Not that those the fairies love are always carried off—they may grow silent and strange and take to lonely wanderings in the gentle places. Such will in aftertimes be great poets or musicians or fairy doctors. They must not be confused with those who have the lianhuan shee, for the lianhuan shee lives on the vitals of its chosen and they waste and die. She is of the dreadful solitary fairies. To her have belonged the greatest of the Irish poets from Oisin down to the last century.[17]

All of Yeats' early poetic self-images were preyed upon by "the dreadful solitary fairy," who symbolizes the terrors of the sublimation
required by Wisdom. Niamh was of the Leanhuan Shee, Cleena who
drives to madness and death Owen O'Sullivan was also, as was Maude
Gonne and Ireland herself.

A most striking example of the *mysterium tremendum* of the Celti-
cists' Ireland occurs in Nora Hopper's *Ballads in Prose,* published in
1894, one of many books made possible by Yeats' *The Celtic Twilight*
of 1893. In 1895 Yeats reviewed *Ballads in Prose* in the London
Bookman [18] in one of a series of articles entitled "Irish National
Literature" and cited at length the following passage describing the
sacrifice of Aodh.

Then the door at which he was striving opened wide and from the dark
shrine swept out a cloud of fine grey dust. The door clanged to behind him,
and he went up the aisle walking ankle deep in the fine dust, and straining
his eyes to see through the darkness if indeed figures paced beside him and
ghostly groups gave way before him, as he could not help but fancy. . . .
At last his outstretched hand touched a twisted horn. . . . With his left
hand clinging to the horn he turned toward the dark temple saying aloud,
"Here I stand, Aodh, with gifts to give the Fianna, and their Gods. In the
name of my mother's Gods, let them who desire my gifts come to me."
"Aodh, son of Eochaidh," a shivering voice cried out, "give me thy youth."
"I give," Aodh said quietly. "Aodh," said another voice, reedy and thin
but sweet, "give me thy knowledge: I, Grania, loved much and knew
little." There was a grey figure at his side and without a word Aodh turned
and laid his forehead on the ghost's cold breast. As he rested thus another
voice said, "I am Oisin; give me thy death, O Aodh." Aodh drew a deep
breath, then he lifted his head and clasped a ghostly figure in his arms, and
holding it there felt it stiffen and grow rigid and colder yet. "Give me thine
hope Aodh." "Give me thy faith Aodh." "Give me thy courage Aodh."
"Give me thy dreams, Aodh." So the voices called and cried and to each
Aodh answered and gave the desired gift. "Give me thy heart, Aodh," cried
another. "I am Maive, who knew much and loved little." And with a
sickening sense of pain Aodh felt slender cold fingers scratching and
tearing through his flesh and sinew till they grasped his heart and tore the
fluttering thing away. "Give me thy love, and I have loved none." "Take
it," Aodh said faintly. [19]

In the Temple of the Heroes the mythical dead of Ireland draw their
substance from Ireland's poet, and the poet withers away. In this way

"Reality" in the Neoplatonic sense, or Wisdom in the occult sense, feeds malignantly on the life of the hero, as art on the vitality of the artist. Given the work, to use the terms of "The Choice," there can be no life.

Among Yeats' earliest poems, "King Goll" declares most clearly the impact on Yeats of the muse of Ireland. The active man runs mad. Abdicating his temporal power, he becomes a poet who finds joy in singing, but is overthrown by the madness which is his inspiration and destroys his instrument. Yeats' poetry of the later nineties represents that terminal point beyond which the further development of style would have meant the destruction of the poem itself. The poet is overshadowed by vast passionate forces to whom he cries out, with the euphemism customary in addressing malignant deities. "O sweet everlasting voices, be still."

III

Celticism and aestheticism are interdependent movements in the latter part of the nineteenth century, both depending in turn on the antecedent symbol of Wisdom, the white woman. The poetic ambition of the London group, with whom Yeats associated himself after 1887, as it was exhibited in the books of the Rhymers' Club, in the *Yellow Book*, and the *Savoy*, was the refounding of poetry in the emotions on the model suggested by the early utterances of Pater and on the analogy of recent developments in French culture. The movement was announced as "subjective" and gave rise to the typical periodical piece of the day, the short psychological prose sketch, and to the brief introspective lyric which expressed by its very shortness and formal particularity the subjective mystery of individuation.

The subjectivity could, however, be regarded in two ways, and concern with it could result in two quite different styles. The self as subject could lead to sensory realism, which seemed in the period to be represented by Zola, and by the current style in the fine arts derivative from realism, Impressionism as practised by Whistler. It could also lead to the literature of "dream," which was the true heir to traditional aestheticism and the last resort of the ideal style in prose.

Relentlessly throughout the period Yeats announced the onset of a new age of subjectivity dominated by moods of the mind and isolated, like Wisdom, from all concern but its own passionate processes. The subjectivity to which Yeats refers is not, however, the environmentally conditioned, individuated, and perishing subjectivity of the post-Freudian self-conception, but rather the ideal inwardness which is eternal in history and which is related to the individual mind as a sojourner. Following Blake and the whole Romantic tradition of Wisdom, which set *sapientia* as the preferred value over against *scientia,* Yeats identifies the valued aspect of inwardness with the passions. The fact that the seat of poetry is the passions and that the passions are solicited not in their real but in their ideal or sublimed character is the source of the paradox and tragedy of the tradition with which Yeats allied himself.

The symbol of the inwardness as a vehicle of Wisdom is Dream. In the last year of the decade "Fiona MacLeod" published a book called *The Dominion of Dream,* and the title is applicable to the entire period. Dream, in the poems of Dowson, Johnson, Russell, Sharp, Symons, and Yeats, signifies the generative aspect of the mind, the unconscious resource, the gate of ideality. But acknowledgment of the dominion of dream leads to preoccupation with its ambiguities.

> They are not long the days of wine and roses:
>   Out of a misty dream
> Our path emerges for a while, then closes
>   Within a dream.[20]

Dream is a symbol of both the birth and the death of consciousness, both the richness and the tyranny of the mind's forces. For Johnson, addressing his Dark Angel, the "land of dreams becomes a gathering place of fears," and for Yeats also Dream commits the mind to the characteristic "despondency and madness" of the poetic role.

> Ah! Druid, Druid, how great webs of sorrow
> Lay hidden in the small slate-colored thing![21]

The Great Mother is jealous of the mortal loves of her children and suitors, setting over against the possible love the obsession with the impossible. Dectora cries out in Yeats' "Shadowy Waters" of 1900:

> O, I would break this net the gods have woven
> Of voices and of dreams. O heart be still!
> O! why is love so crazy that it longs to
> Drown its own image.[22]

This is the predicament of Dowson in his relation to his Cynara, Johnson in relation to the Virgin, Wilde in relation to his own mirror image, and Yeats in relation to Maude Gonne.

Yeats shared with the men of the nineties the complex "Romantic" problem of the refounding of the poetic role on the basis of the restoration to literature of the mind's characteristic of energy. The form the problem took for these men was the difficult act of sustaining a necessary stylistic idealism in the face of the attrition of the real character of the mind itself. The conclusion of their efforts and of Yeats' also was that no sense in which they could possess the symbol of their Ideal compensated for the sacrifice of personal emotion necessary to achieve that possession. The failure of the symbol to compensate the self was the mark of modernity upon the foreheads of the men of the later nineteenth century. The Rose continually threatened to decay from the sublime white to the passionate and terrible red. The paradox which identified the Ideal with the most passionate aspects of the self and found the origin of poetry in "the Dream," inescapably a system of signals from the unconscious (whatever else it may be), proved dangerous to sustain.

In his long tirade against contemporary English culture in *Degeneration,* Max Nordau suggests, with some point, that the prefix of the term Pre-Raphaelitism bears the meaning of psychological as well as historical priority or primitiveness. We may recall in this connection William Sharp's comment which describes the stereotype of the Celtic writer "the temper of whose mind is more ancient, more primitive, and in a sense more natural than his compatriot in whom the Teutonic strain prevails." The Yeatsian use of images (the rose, the cross, the Virgin) inherited from Pre-Raphaelite pseudo-sacramentalism demonstrates how dangerous these powerful signs are when abstracted from the integrity and control of a true sacramental culture and made use of by a poetic culture the foundation of which is essentially psychological. The *mysterium tremendum* which is the chief subject of *The Wind among the Reeds* is the result of a direct confrontation with the mind itself in its beauty and terror.

When Yeats came, sometime after 1917, to locate the nineties in the scheme of *A Vision,* he associated that period and its figures with the fifteenth lunar phase, the phase of total subjectivity, total absorption of consciousness in the natural inwardness, adding further that at the full of the moon as at the dark there is no life. *The Wind* represents, and was to some extent understood by Yeats to have been, an excursion akin to death deep into the subjectivity, from which he returned to an objective art made more passionate by the completeness of his renewed relation to the inwardness. At the farthest reach of the journey away from normal consciousness he encountered the figure of Wisdom whom he had so long sought ("Sero te amavi") and which was the basic motive and symbol of the two strains of literary tradition which he was committed to develop: the Celtic and the aesthetic.

Chapter III

Do you find any meaning yourself though in this mountain air?

Do I? Why, of course I do. I find in it the medium between the beauty of the past and myself. —Edward Martyn, "The Heatherfield"

Luvah is the regent of air and of the breath, whereby the physical body gets the least material, because the least opaque, of its ingredients—the symbol of its wayward feelings, and the vehicle whereby it sighs its sorrows. This correspondence of the emotional life with air is a part of the occult system of Cornelius Agrippa. "The Humours," he writes, "partake of the elements, for yellow choller is instead of fire, blood instead of air, flegme instead of water, and black choller or melancholy instead of earth." Again, air is the symbol of the feelings, because it has no inherent tendency upwards like fire, or downwards like water and earth, but moves hither and thither under the stress of heat and cold as our feelings do, when summoned by instinct on the one hand or imagination on the other. —W. B. Yeats and Edwin J. Ellis in *The Works of William Blake*

Harp of the Ghosts
The Symbols of Wind and Reed

B OTH Wordsworth's Preface to the *Lyrical Ballads* and the early
critical writings of Yeats express the view that the idea of the
poem must be reformed because the preceding literary convention has ceased to be an adequate vehicle of poetic authenticity. Both
poets are concerned with making poetic diction once again faithful to
human reality in terms of emotion. Wordsworth's canon of "vivid
sensation" is analogous to Yeats' "subjectivity" with the difference
that Yeats was obsessed with the problem of rendering emotion transcendental, whereas Wordsworth possessed a fruitful sense of the fac-
tuality of personality. In Samuel Johnson's *Rasselas* the astronomer
cries out:

Hear, Imlac, what thou wilt not without difficulty credit. I have possessed
for five years the regulation of the weather, and the distribution of the
seasons. The sun has listened to my dictates . . . the clouds at my call
have poured their waters. . . . I have restrained the rage of the dogstar
and mitigated the fervours of the crab. The winds alone of all the elemental powers have hitherto refused my authority and multitudes have
perished.[1]

The insanity of Johnson's astronomer is a consequence of "the dangerous prevalence of the imagination," and the symbol of imagination is
uncontrollable wind.

We have observed that the structure of meaning in Yeats' early
poetry is in considerable degree determined by the ambition to overthrow a preceding generation, perhaps in large measure unreal, and to

establish a new dispensation on the basis of a rediscovered relation to
the emotions. Yeats' role is of Messianic proportions ("I was a wise
young king of old"). The spirit liberated by the overthrow of existing
structures brings with it the threat of revenge by the rejected paternal
generation, as well as the novel violence of the newly discovered powers
of the inwardness. No poem of the earlier romantic age is more quoted
by the leaders of the Celtic Revival than Wordsworth's "Solitary
Reaper."

> Will no one tell me what she sings? —
> Perhaps the plaintive numbers flow
> For old, unhappy, far-off things,
> And battles long ago:
> Or is it some more humble lay,
> Familiar matter of today?
> Some natural sorrow, loss, or pain,
> That has been, and may be again?

Consistent with its tendency to reject the more concrete aspects of
Romanticism, Celticism ignored the Wordsworthian alternative of the
"more humble lay" and fixed upon the song of "old, unhappy, far-off
things, / And battles long ago" as the symbol of its inspiration.

The images of the ethnic past ("old, unhappy, far-off things") borne
on the four winds of desire raised for Yeats the problem of control.
How he dealt with that problem is indicated by his use of the Neoplatonic symbol of the demon-laden wind which blows between heaven
and earth, partaking of neither the total sublimation of the spirit nor
the stabilizing concreteness of the flesh.

The symbol carefully delineated by Althea Gyles on the cover of
Yeats' *The Wind among the Reeds* expresses the origin of inspiration.
Yeats' posture is that of the poet in Coleridge's "Dejection: An Ode,"
who seeks to recover a lost harmony between mind and nature through
the mediation of emotion symbolized by the wind rising in the strings
of the aeolian lute, like the "rushing of a host in rout." The mode of
nature is subsumed by the mode of mind just as the ethnic past
becomes the symbol of the personal unconscious. For Yeats as for
Coleridge, the poetic convention of the invocation is not a matter of
ritual certainty, but a chancy and momentous act which preoccupies

and threatens to overthrow the mind and become itself a principal subject of the poetry which it enables. In Yeats' later work the image of the poet is objectified and can be studied within the context of the poetry itself; but in the early poetry, which is our subject, all reference to personality is excluded by the canon of "purity" and the image of the poet must be constructed. That is not to say that the early poetry is any less autobiographical than the later; merely that it is so purely psychological that its processes have been rendered virtually anonymous.

A glance at a first-edition copy of any one of Yeats' books of the later nineties will show that they are not merely books, but talismans or *grimoires*, that they have magical as well as literary significance, and that they express a desire for power and beauty which the literary vehicle alone cannot convey. The book itself, apart from its contents, is a symbolic fact for Yeats, and *The Wind among the Reeds*, as can be seen from its cover (Fig. 3), is not exceptional in this respect. From the time of the publication of *Mosada*, Yeats' first volume, his books reflect an attempt to augment the verbal sign by a plastic correlative, and the artistic aspects of Yeats' earliest books were presided over by his father or members of his father's circle.

The origin of Yeats' self-image as the overthrown artist, the reed bowed by the wind, can be seen in his father's early portraits of him where the son is exhibited either as a youth too effeminate to be in any sense threatening or as a giant destroyed by his own self-destructive power (Fig. 2). From the early portraits it is clear that John Yeats used the aesthetic convention of the disability of the artist as a weapon against his son. William accepted his father's image of him, but attempted to construct a realm of power outside the limits of his father's knowledge and control. This realm of power was magic, the secret sense of the infinite effectiveness of the will of the son. The symbol of this power was the talismanic book. Like Blake, whose dissatisfaction with the existing image of the book led him to reject the conventional modes of printing, Yeats attempted to express his revolt against the imposed image of the sacramental and artistic vehicle and against the paternal image of him by composing a new book and a new self. The talismanic book thus constructed proved to be neither truly sacred nor truly artistic, but it symbolized, like the typographhical experimentalism which became popular two decades later, the deeply felt necessity to reform the tradition in the direction of a newly found subjective organicism.

The advance notice of Yeats' collected *Poems* of 1895 in the London *Bookman* comments that the cover will be done by a young man named "Granville Fell whose water color 'The Virgin Mary's Toumbler' attracted some attention at Mr. Dent's 'Black and White' exhibition last April." [2] In 1904 Yeats commented in John Quinn's copy of the book, "The man who made this cover made a beautiful design, which I saw at an exhibition, but after I saw it Dent had spoilt him, with all kinds of odd jobs, and when he did this the spirit had gone out of him. I hate this expressionless angel of his." [3]

The shadow of commerce which too soon obscured the genius of Granville Fell did not reach to the Theosophical Household in 3 Ely Place, Dublin, where Yeats probably first met Althea Gyles, who in 1899 did in fact create for him the talismanic book for which he was searching. Unlike his previous illustrators, Miss Gyles belonged among the adepts of Yeats' imaginary culture. She was associated with Russell's theosophical circle and was known to Maude Gonne; as late as 1910 Yeats and Aleister Crowley were engaged in a magical battle for the possession of her soul. More important, her designs were the occasion of Yeats' article on symbolism that was printed along with several examples of her art and certain of her poems in the *Dome* for December, 1898.[4] Miss Gyles' designs for the cover of *The Secret Rose* (1897), *Poems* (1899), and *The Wind among the Reeds* provided Yeats with books clothed in effective representations of potent signs.

On the cover of the *Poems* of 1899 Granville Fell's "expressionless angel" gives way to Althea Gyles' emblem of the crucified rose which casts a swirl of beautifully designed petals in the direction of the reader as if to overwhelm him. On the spine, the head of the beloved hangs like a rose on the tree of life, while the hands of the lover reach up hopelessly toward her impassive countenance. The cover of *The Secret Rose* [5] is dominated by the same symbol constructed within the intertwining paths of the sephirothic tree which rises out of the skeleton of a dead warrior of romance whose love is represented as consummated below the three roses of the supernal emanations. On the spine is the spear of Lug, a symbol of everlasting and uncontrollable desire.

These books, *The Wind among the Reeds* included, are not in any simple sense The Sacred Book of the Arts. Unlike Wordsworth's earlier attempt to restore to poetry a lost inheritance of power, Yeats' undertaking is not entirely literary. The magical sign, which served the dual function of awakening and controlling the powers of the emotions, was not wholly assimilated to the concept of the poem which these powers were to serve. In the early period Yeats never fully synthesized the two disparate traditions of poetry and magic, and to the time of his death they had an uneasy relation the significance of which was far more psychological than artistic.

The symbol of the talismanic book as it appears in his prose writings of the period is magical rather than literary. Yeats was, for example, deeply interested, in his characteristically eclectic way, in the moral cosmology of Joachim of Floris. The doctrine of successive "Kingdoms" of father, son, and spirit recapitulated Yeats' sense of his relation as son to the preceding literary generation represented in his mind by his father, and provided authority for the poet's role as forerunner of an apocalyptic reformation of things beyond which he would be united with the eternal Beloved in the form of spirit. In "The Tables of the Law," one of the stories excluded by the publisher from *The Secret Rose*, Yeats describes an occult work of Joachim, banned for somewhat similar motives by the Catholic Church, called *Liber inducens in Evangelium aeternum.*

"I have here the greatest treasure the world contains. I have a copy of that book; and see what great artists have made the robes in which it is wrapped. This bronze box was made by Benvenuto Cellini, who covered it with gods and demons, whose eyes are closed to signify an absorption in the inner light." He lifted the lid and took out a book bound in leather, with filigree work of tarnished silver. "And this cover was bound by one of the binders that bound for Canevari; while Giulio Clovio, an artist of the later Renaissance, whose work is soft and gentle, took out the beginning page of every chapter of the old copy, and set in its place a page surmounted by an elaborate letter and a miniature of some one of the great whose example was cited in the chapter and wherever the writing left a little space elsewhere, he put some delicate emblem or intricate pattern."

"Where did you get this amazing book?" I said. "If genuine, and I cannot judge by this light, you have discovered one of the most precious things in the world." [6]

As Cellini served Joachim of Floris, so, in his imaginary culture, Althea Gyles served Yeats.

And indeed she was well suited to do so. The rose, according to Yeats, was Miss Gyles' central symbol. Speaking of her designs he says,

> One finds in them what a friend, whose work has no other passion, calls "the passion for impossible beauty"; for the beauty which cannot be seen with the bodily eyes, or pictured otherwise than by symbols. Her own favorite drawing, which unfortunately cannot be pictured here, is *The Rose of God,* a personification of this beauty as a naked woman whose hands are stretched against the clouds as upon a cross, in the traditional attitude of the bride, the symbol of the microcosm in the Kaballa; while two winds, two destinies, the one full of white the other full of red rose petals, personifying all purities and all passions, whirl about her and descend upon a fleet of ships and a walled city personifying the wavering and fixed powers, the masters of the world in the alchemical symbolism. Some imperfect but beautiful verses accompany the drawing and describe her as for "living man's delight and his eternal revering when dead." [7]

The unity of culture which Yeats did not find in England and struggled to create in Ireland did exist at least from moment to moment in the artificial cultist subcultures of which as a young man he was sometimes a peripheral and sometimes a central associate. In Yeats' account of this favorite drawing of Miss Gyles we find not only the background of "The Travail of Passion," one of the major poems of *The Wind among the Reeds,* but also an example of the dominant image of his early period, the cabalistic tenth *sephira,* the Shekinah. Althea Gyles' "Rose of God" could not be reprinted in the *Dome* for the same reason that the *Savoy* was banned from railroad stations when Yeats undertook to reproduce in that periodical certain plates of Blake involving nude figures.

The occultist point of view differed from the Neoplatonic in its capacity to tolerate the beauty of the flesh. Although in his early period he was incapable of saying so, it was as true for Yeats then as in 1927 that "all dreams of the soul end in a beautiful man's or a beautiful woman's body." Yeats' early reformation of the self required an emotional *dérèglement* which, under the estranging exigencies of idealization and concealment, involved the onset of the Kingdom of the Spirit in dangerous complexities.

Whatever may have been the degree of collaboration between Yeats and Miss Gyles in other undertakings, the image of wind in reeds belonged to Yeats' own constellation of symbols. He announced the title in the *Irish Theosophist* for November 15, 1893. In 1894 it was plagiarized by Nora Hopper and used as the title of one of the intercalated poems in her *Ballads in Prose,* where she ostentatiously worked the phrase into her cover among the shamrocks which identify the book as part of the rising Celtic movement. As the symbol appeared on Yeats' work, it was not specifically occult, but rather an adaptation of an image deeply involved in the history of the romantic and aesthetic movements.

II

Yeats' image of wind in reeds is a special case of the symbolism associated with the aeolian harp, an instrument which re-entered Europe in the latter part of the seventeenth century and was much discussed and indeed manufactured for sale at the end of the eighteenth. According to William Jones' "Physiological Disquisitions" [8] (1781) Pope, while engaged in his translation of Homer, encountered the device in the Greek commentary of Eustathius of Thessalonica and was sufficiently interested to proceed to have one constructed. If we again consult the "Physiological Disquisitions" we find the following entirely typical descriptions of the sound of the harp:

It very much resembles that of a chorus of voices at a distance, with all the expression of the forte, the piano, and the swell; in a word the harmony is more like to what we might imagine the aerial sounds of magic and enchantment to be, than to artificial music. We may call it, without metaphor, the music of inspiration. [9]

The difference between the romantic instrument here described and Yeats' symbol for the Celtic afflatus lies in the fact that Yeats removed the factor of artificiality: the reed sings in its natural bed on the shore of the lake. As we have already observed, an acknowledged mark of Celticism in contrast to the earlier Romantic movement was its claim to ultimate primitiveness.

COLLEGE OF THE SEQUOIAS
LIBRARY

In 1808 Robert Bloomfield published a pamphlet entitled *Nature's Music* which is a collection of descriptions of the aeolian harp in poetry and prose. In the poems cited the air is filled with faces and voices according to the highly generalized demonology of poetic convention:

> Are ye some fairy . . . ?
> Are ye some nymph of ancient time . . . ?
> Or are ye Ossian's passing voice . . . ? [10]

Further, Bloomfield adds a description of a bamboo wind harp carved from the still living plant which very much resembles Yeats' music of the reed and demonstrates the mutability of the basic image. For "though it has nothing to do with the vibration of a string, [it] is at the same time so strictly nature's music, that it deserves a place where we are following the vagaries of Aeolus." [11] The notion of nature's music was deeply sympathetic to the Celtic Revival, especially when it was conceived as the voice of "some fairy," or "some nymph of ancient time," or of Ossian. The spirit of Ossian and the sound of the wind harp were a habitual association in the nineteenth century: Emerson records in his journals that "if you want Plinlimmon in your closet, Caerleon, Provence, Ossian, and Cadwallan, tie a couple of strings across a board and set it in your window and you have a wind harp that no artist's harp can rival. It has the tristesse of Nature." [12] Celticism was so typically associated with wind mysticism by the time Arnold came to write that he found it significant to repeat a German suggestion that "Gael, the name for Irish Celt, and Scot, are at the bottom the same word meaning wind, and both signifying the violent, stormy people."

But the Ossianic reference has more specific relevance to *The Wind among the Reeds* than merely as one of the associations of the sound of the wind harp. The convention which forms the background of Yeats' "Hosting of the Sidhe" and the major symbol of *The Wind among the Reeds* itself, namely, the presence in the wind of the heroes of the past, derives its currency from Ossian. In Germany, we are told, the aeolian harp was known as the "harp of the ghost," and Macpherson provides us with the specific folk belief that Yeats employs again and again in connection with the symbol of the wind:

It was the opinion of the times, when a person was reduced to a pitch of misery, which could admit of no alleviation, that the ghosts of ancestors *called his soul away*. This supernatural kind of death was called "the voice of the dead" and is believed by the superstitious vulgar to this day.[13]

Such was the death of Ossian himself, and in Macpherson's account of it the wind harp is given its specifically Celtic interpretation.

The winds begin to rise. The dark wave of the lake resounds. Bends there not a tree from Mora with its branches bare? It bends, son of Alpin, in the rustling blast. My harp hangs on the blasted branch. The sound of its strings is mournful. Does the wind touch thee O harp, or is it some passing ghosts . . . ? The aged oak bends over the stream. It sighs with all its moss. The withered fern whistles near, and mixes as it waves with Ossian's hair. . . . The blast of the north opens thy gates, O king! I behold thee sitting on a mist dim gleaming in all thy arms. . . . There is a murmur in the heath! The storm winds abate! I hear the voice of Fingal. Long has it been absent from my ears! "Come, Ossian, come away," he says. Fingal has received his fame. We passed away like flames that had shone for a season. Our departure was in renown. Though the plains of our battles are dark and silent; our fame is in the four grey stones. The voice of Ossian has been heard. . . . "Come, Ossian, come away," he says. "Come, fly with thy fathers on clouds." "I come, I come, thou king of men." [14]

Ossian is omitted from Yeats' description of the hosting of the Shee in the opening lines of *The Wind* because Ossian, as in the above passage, is the speaker of the poem. The cry of the Host in Yeats' lyric is the same, "Come away, come away"; and with the assistance of the Ossianic background the symbol of inspiration (the rising of the wind) becomes explicitly identified with the onset of death.

But the Ossianic reference is only one of the several streams of tradition which mingle in Yeats' speaking wind. As suggested above, Celticism is constructed by the superposition of occultism upon preceding romantic conventions. It might be more properly said as an explanation of Yeats' practice that he reassociated occult motifs already existent in Romantic conventions with their appropriate historical traditions with the intention of rendering them vivid and distinct, for the fairy and demonic voices which Bloomfield and others heard in the aeolian harp have a more than casual history. When in "Leda and the Swan" the god descends upon the girl, Yeats says she is mastered "by the brute blood of the air," which communicates through her to the world not knowledge but violence. This phrase is a somewhat extended translation of the *anima bruta* which Yeats found in the discussion of the powers of air in Kingsford and Maitland's *The Perfect Way*,[15] an early book of the theosophical movement and one which was almost omnipresent in the eighties when Yeats received the most lasting elements of his education. The *anima bruta* is an aspect of the astral body (or *anima mundi*). To this concept the theosophical syncretism of the late nineteenth century assimilated the folk tradition of the powers of the air.

That there is a real relation between Neoplatonism and theosophical structures may be taken on the authority of E. R. Dodds:

The modern mystery religions and especially that singular amalgam of discredited speculations known as theosophy have made us familiar with the theory that mind and body are linked together by a *tertium quid*, an inner envelope of the soul which is less material than the fleshly body and survives its dissolution, yet has not the pure spirituality of mind. This doctrine is popularly regarded as oriental, but it has in fact a very long history in European thought reaching back from the Cambridge Platonists in the seventeenth century, to Porphyry and Iamblicus in the fourth and traceable thence to an origin in the classical period of Greek philosophy.[16]

Yeatsian scholarship is now sufficiently complete for it no longer to be necessary to demonstrate in detail Yeats' early acquaintanceship with Neoplatonism in the texts of Thomas Taylor and in elaborate unscholarly reprints current in the Golden Dawn coterie, such as W. W. Westcott's *Collectanea Hermetica*. It is, however, important to bear in mind that, what the astral body is on the level of the individual, the *spiritus mundi* is to the world as a whole. The wind which blows between heaven and earth is not merely an element; it is a distinctly defined region having its own inhabitants and a special relation to what is above and what is below.

[Air] is a vital spirit, passing through all beings, giving life and substance to all things, binding, moving and filling all things. Hence it is that the Hebrew doctors reckon it not among the elements, but count it as a medium or glue, joining things together, and as the resounding spirit of the world's instrument. It immediately receives into itself the influences of all celestial bodies and then communicates them to the other elements, as also to all mixed bodies. Also it receives into itself as it were a divine looking glass, the species of all things, as well as of all manner of speeches and retains them; and carries them with it and entering into the bodies of men . . . makes an impression upon them, as well when they sleep as when they be awake, and affords matter for diverse strange dreams and divinations.[17]

The air in its many symbolic transformations (*spiritus mundi*, the Host, the Moods) is the Yeatsian concept of tradition and as such will be treated in detail in Chapter IV. Here it is sufficient to make clear that Yeats is deeply involved with this intermediate element which belongs neither to history nor to eternity.

Jewish cabalism, and by affiliation the so-called Christian cabala of Henry More and others which Yeats came to know quite well, is deeply concerned with that mysterious generative event by which the created universe issued from the intact divine unity. One result of this concern is the sephirothic system and a more or less typical preoccupation with the symbols of Genesis when God moved upon the waters in the form of a wind. Yeats too is preoccupied with the "procreant waters of the soul where the breath first moved," [18] and in the symbol of the wind in the reeds he recapitulates the divine act of creation making the first issue of wind on water, the sound of the singing reeds, or poetry. At a time somewhat after our period when images from Spenser and from More's treatise *On the Immortality of the Soul* were more distinct in his mind than the cabala, he transforms the symbol of the reed in water into the *anima mundi* itself, a gigantic mystical plant which is the source not only of poetry but of all life.

I think of *Anima Mundi* as a great pool or garden where it moves through its allotted growth like a gigantic water-plant or fragrantly branches in the air. Indeed as Spenser's garden of Adonis: —

> There is the first seminary
> Of all things that are born to live and die
> According to their kynds.[19]

Throughout his life Yeats meditated on the sexual act, on the fearful apocalyptic consequences of birth, and, under the symbolism of coitus and birth, on the problem of poetry. In the early period the wind, which is the cabalistic symbol of God's desire for the female demiurge on whom he begets the created world, is also the symbol of the poet's own libido. In referring to his desires Yeats' habitual term is "vague," and his habitual symbol is the aimless shifting wind, which "bloweth where it listeth" unassociated with any object. "I use the wind as a symbol of vague desires and hopes." [20] Like the symbolist poem, the symbolist poet can have no commerce with the real world. The philosophy of the pure poem is bound up with the psychology of narcissism, and Yeats' biographers are concerned with his extended physical virginity. (The soul, Yeats says, is always virginal.) Only when individual sexuality recapitulates the primordial sexual act of divinity ("The winds that awakened the stars / Are blowing through my blood") [21] does the poetic speaker become potent, and then the apocalypse is at hand and the Kingdom of the father is recreated by the son in the form of spirit through cataclysm. The creation of the ideal world entails the destruction of the real.

Sexuality in the cabala is the exclusive prerogative of God. In the poems of *The Wind* the host steals away the bride of the poet, and the elemental powers pluck the immortal Rose while the sexual powers of the poet are asleep. Zeus couples with Leda to beget the Kingdom of the father, a world in which the poet "lacks all conviction," while the dominant powers "are full of passionate intensity." One of the basic predicaments in *The Wind among the Reeds* is the competition of father and son for the right of creation, for the white woman on whom the poet meditates hopelessly by the shores of Hart Lake. Under the burden of this exigency Yeats later elaborated the irrational categories involving the mutual exclusiveness of life and work. If life must be abandoned for poetry, then poetry must be wedded to death.

In the period marking his accession to real poetic power, the period of *The Wind among the Reeds,* Yeats solicited violence. Like Blake he early learned that in the matter of gods, as in the matter of politics, it was better to choose the worst. The apocalypse which he did not cease to pursue was his own accession to potency; consequently, it was under the auspices of the wind symbol and at the same time of man as "hater of the wind" [22] that *The Wind among the Reeds* came into the world. The image of the speaking wind, selected out of the general romantic background, was claimed for Celticism by Ossian, given its philosophical structure by Neoplatonism and its fundamental psychological relevance by the cabalistic tradition.

III

The first occurrence of the symbol of wind in reeds in Yeats' poetry is in "Ephemera," assigned by Ellmann to the year 1884. It lies very close to the beginning of Yeats' literary enterprise and to the background of aestheticism. This poem has been affiliated with some probability to Wilde's "Her Voice," though it is sufficiently typical of the poetry of the seventies and eighties so that any of a number of poems by Arthur O'Shaughnessy or Philip Bourke Marston might serve the same genealogical function. The poet and his beloved wander in autumn by the "lone border of the sullen lake" conscious that their love is at an end. Wilde puts their predicament this way:

> And there is nothing left to do
> But to kiss once again and part;
> Nay, there is nothing we should do,
> I have my beauty, you your art —
> Nay, do not start.
> One world was not enough for two
> Like me and you.[23]

In Wilde's poem the absolute character both of beauty and art makes it possible for the lovers to love one another, and both Beauty and the Artist retire into narcissistic isolation without deep regret. Yeats, on the other hand, does not mention art specifically. He attempts to console the beloved for the impossibility of love by projecting his own image of the relationship between the absolute or "poetic" mind and history. The poetic consciousness is transmigrant in time, coming into temporary relation to history without losing its transcendence, through emotion. "Passion," he says, "has often worn our wandering hearts / Earth's aliens. Why so sorrowful? Our souls / Shall warm their lives at many a rustling flame." [24] In the final speech of the beloved, however, an ambiguous but palpable reflex of horror is expressed at the

impersonality of the artist's delight in the eternal relation. The image
she employs is the image of the wind among the reeds.

> The little waves that walked in evening whiteness,
> Glimmering in her drooping eyes saw her lips move
> And whisper, "The innumerable reeds
> I know the word they cry, 'Eternity!'
> And sing from shore to shore, and every year
> They pine away and yellow and wear out,
> And ah, they know not as they pine and cease,
> Not they are eternal—tis the cry." [25]

The predicament which the woman in Yeats' "Ephemera" describes
is that of the "Conclusion" of "The Sensitive Plant" and the style of
that portion of Yeats' poem is Shelleyan. Though the plant may wither,
the ambiguous comfort of the eternity of the ideas remains:

> That garden sweet, that lady fair,
> And all sweet shapes and odors there,
> In truth have never passed away:
> 'Tis we, 'tis ours, are changed; not they.
>
> For love, and beauty, and delight,
> There is no death or change: their might
> Exceeds our organs, which endure
> No light being themselves obscure. [26]

Shelley, who in his "Ode to the West Wind" had cried out "Make me
thy lyre, even as the forest is," was Yeats' first image of the artist, and
in Miss Tynan's memoirs we find Yeats standing in the rain absorbed
in his recital of "The Sensitive Plant." [27] More important, however, is
Miss Tynan's development of the symbol in a poem published in her
volume of 1887 and written at about the same time as "Ephemera." "In
a Garden" is a Catholic version of Shelley's "The Sensitive Plant," in
which the symbol of Christ is substituted for the Lady and the reeds of
the garden sing of Him as Yeats' do of eternity.

> Tall and slender and forlorn
> Frail against the risen morn.
> Lo, across the radiant mists
> Wind that bloweth where it lists,

Taketh them with sudden breath
O'er each reed mouth murmureth
With a mighty quivering
Hark, the reeds begin to sing.

. . . . .

Passionate as though one should take
Some lost heart grown like to break;
Wild with woe and loss and love,
And should make a lute thereof;

. . . . .

So the wind leans over these.

. . . . .

One who standeth by the mere,
Bendeth very low to hear;
Flusheth the wan mere to flame,—
Hush! the sad reeds sob his name.[28]

But the imaginative community in which Yeats and Katharine Tynan rendered the image of wind in reeds available to the Celtic imagination does not quite complete the genealogy of the image.

Reflecting in his *Autobiographies* on the period immediately preceding the stylistic revision which he undertook about 1893, Yeats says, "Arthur Symons brought back from Paris stories of Verhaeren and Maeterlinck and so brought me confirmation, as I thought, and I began to announce a poetry like the Sufi's." [29] Sufism, the esoteric doctrine of Islam, was the religion of the Rubaiyat and of Hafiz. Its doctrine of drunkenness, the ascent to spiritual contemplation through the emotions, and moral passivity lie very close to Yeats' early attitudes, and a major document of Sufi mysticism existed in at least three translations during the 1880's. Edward Henry Palmer, professor of Arabic at Cambridge, published in 1877 certain translations from Rumi's *Masnavi* and other Persian and Arabic poems under the title *The Song of the Reed*.[30] Sufism as represented by FitzGerald and as presented discursively by Palmer's popular *Oriental Mysticism* of 1867 was easily assimilable to the aesthetic attitude as another religion of beauty. The image of the reed as Palmer offers it is an example of the post-Romantic sense of the past as eternally present in the wind, both ideal and alien. The introduction to Palmer's *Masnavi* begins, "List to the reed."

Down where the waving rushes grow
    I murmured with the passing blast
And ever in my notes of woe
    There live the echoes of the past.

My breast is pierced with sorrow's dart,
    That I my piercing wail may raise;
      Ah me; the lone and widowed heart
Must ever weep for bye-gone days.

    . . . .

Though plainly cometh forth my wail,
    'Tis never bared to mortal ken;
As soul from body hath no veil,
    Yet is the soul unseen of men.

So sings the reed, but its mysterious song
No ear attuned to harmony devours;
Music that doth not to the age belong
Dies out symphonious with the dying hours.[31]

    . . . .

In this way or in a way very like this the complex image of wind in reeds became available to Yeats.

By 1894 this symbolism seemed to him indigenous to his own experience. When in that year he went to France with Symons and saw a performance of Villiers de l'Isle-Adam's *Axel,* he ranked the symbols of that play, which he in fact found extremely exciting, as less momentous than others native to his consciousness such as the *chinoiserie* of Whistler, Chapman's Homer, and the vocal reed:

The final test of the value of any work of art to our particular needs is when we place it in the hierarchy of those recollections which are our standards and our beacons. At the head of mine are certain night scenes long ago when I heard the wind blowing in a bed of reeds by the border of a little lake, a Japanese picture of cranes flying through a blue sky, and a line or two out of Homer. I do not place any part of Axel with these perfect things.[32]

From 1887 the wind began to serve Yeats as a symbol of the terror and alienation of the muse of Ireland.

In the eighteenth century, the last century of the old world, the last before the Union, and the last in which the Gaelic tradition of folk poetry was preserved intact, "the poor peasant [the natural poetic speaker] . . . could make fine ballads by abandoning himself to the joy or sorrow of the moment, as the reeds abandon themselves to the wind which sighs through them, because he has about him a world which was steeped in emotion." [33] In the nineteenth century man is a "hater of the wind." From the point of view of Yeats' concept of history, the poet in the modern world is isolated because his consciousness by reason of its relation to the wind is the only old and therefore powerful force in culture. Not only his culture but he himself is incompetent of the rigors of his inspiration, and his sense of alienation within society is constructed by analogy from his sense of alienation within himself. "He who half lives in eternity endures a rending of the structures of the mind, a crucifixion of the intellectual body." [34]

In the development of his mythology of the malign characteristic of the wind, Yeats' use of his tradition is at its most complex. In his notes to *The Wind* he uses the following citation: "Dr. Joyce says, 'of all the different kinds of goblins . . . air demons were most dreaded by the people. They lived among clouds, and mists, and rocks, and hated the human race with the utmost malignity.'" [35] The image of the "Red Wind" was very widely used in the "Celtic" community in the late eighties and nineties, and there is scarcely an author who has not a poem by that name.[36] The meaning of the symbol can be seen by reference to a passage printed by George Russell in the *Irish Theosophist* in 1893.

But most of all dread the powers that move in air, their nature is desire unquenchable; their destiny is—never to be fulfilled—never to be at peace; they roam hither and thither like the winds they guide; they usurp dominion over the passionate and tender soul, but they love not in our way; where they dwell the heart is a madness and the feet are filled with a hurrying fever, and night has no sleep and day holds no joy in its sunlit cup. Listen not to their whisper; they wither and burn up the body with their fire; the beauty they offer is smitten through and through with unappeasable anguish.[37]

This passage, which can scarcely be distinguished from later utterances of Yeats in the same style, emphasizes how dense and interdependent the literary community of the "Celtic" writer was at the outset, and

how presumptively symbols within that community were rendered
psychological. Yeats alludes in his notes to "a very old Arann charm"
which will serve to summarize the sense of the *mysterium tremendum*
with which he invested his symbol of the muse of Ireland:

> Seven Paters seven times,
> Send Mary by her Son,
> Send Bridget by her mantle,
> Send God by His strength,
> Between us and the fairy host,
> Between us and the demons of the air.[38]

Chapter IV

The mind or imagination or consciousness of man may be said to have two poles, the personal and impersonal, or, as Blake preferred to call them, the limit of contraction and the unlimited expansion. When we act from the personal we tend to bind our consciousness down as to a fiery center. When, on the other hand, we allow our imagination to expand away from this egoistic mood, we become vehicles for the universal thought and merge in the universal mood. —W. B. Yeats and Edwin J. Ellis in *The Works of William Blake*

The Moods

Tradition as Emotion

THE archetypal self-finding on which poetic knowledge is based
arises, as we have pointed out, in a single experiment which
Yeats never ceased repeating: the comparison of the imaginal
content of mind as autonomous subject with the imaginal content of
world as the object of mind and the origin of experience. The discovery
to which this experiment leads is that images which arise in the
individual consciousness are also images in the great resource of collective representation which constitutes historical culture. The last and
absolute version of this assertion is that mind and world are symbolically identical. This gigantic assumption was beyond Yeats' intention,
though not beyond his capacity for fantasy. Such a cosmic man would
possess as an account of his origins the origins of being itself. This
would be the absolute or "divine" version of poetic knowledge, and we
have already seen traces of this idea in the course of our exposition. In
the essay on "Magic" Yeats elaborated his notion that "our memories
are part of one great memory." The purpose of this assertion is to
enable the poetic speaker to exercise his traditional powers as the
vehicle of immortal language by declaring that individual experience
and universal or collective experience are the same thing. This is
mutatis mutandis a conventional version of poetic knowledge or what
we have somewhat too formally called archetypal self-finding. The
problem with which Yeats is dealing is a form of the question of
tradition. The essay on magic despite its explicitness is rather a description than a way of working. The major theory which Yeats pro-

mulgated in the nineties to account for the relationship between the content of the individual mind and the content of the collective representations of Western culture was what he called "the Moods."

Yeats' early poetry offers in effect two solutions to the problem of the relation of the mind to history. The first is the transmigrant mind exemplified in Irish mythology by the universal presence of the wonder-working magician.[1] The second is the symbol or multitude of symbols which are themselves omnipresent in history, and which come into relation to the mind of the poet through emotion, the element common to the mind in history and the mind in eternity.[2] Transmigration in one or the other of these forms is necessary to Yeats' conception of the Romantic and post-Romantic worlds, in order to account for the accessibility in the present of the mythologies of the past. Accordingly, the notion of literary tradition as a purely historical phenomenon, that is, as a universe of models for imitation, is alien to Yeats' sensibility.[3]

By and large, he invokes the first of our two alternatives, that of the transmigrant mind, when referring to the ideal poet who is also the ideal man; and the second, that of the transmigrant symbol, when referring to that tradition of symbols which is the exclusive and dangerous resource of humanity in terms of power and beauty. There is no harmony between these two positions. Yeats alternates between the notion that the mind is itself eternal and the notion that the mind, like the reeds which the wind visits, is merely the host of the imagination and suffers inevitably the anguish of the human "amphibion," who is reluctantly man and reluctantly God.

If the whole symbolic resource of the human imagination is equally present at all times in history as a distinct cosmological entity such as the Neoplatonic *anima mundi,* then the significant history of the human mind can be understood as a whole through literature, and the function of literature is to organize and expose the eternal imagination. If on the other hand the mind is itself eternal, the business of the poet is that of the Socratic teacher, namely, the liberation of the eternal from the temporal man. Throughout his career Yeats is concerned, both with the ideal organization of history through poetry, and with the ideal organization of the human mind, which takes place first in the act of creation and then in the experience of art. Both aspects of the enormous poetic ambition suggested by these concepts require the suppression of personality in any recognizable definition of that quality and value the poet insofar as he is a vehicle of something which as a man he is not.

On the whole, Yeats is certain about his symbols but uncertain about their relation to himself. He conceives of them, both as a welcome asylum from the nineteenth century and as a scourge demanding of humanity more reality than it can endure. We see this in his ambiguous treatment of the mythology of the wind. He alternates between the use of the wind as a symbol of the Transcendental in the Neoplatonic sense and its use as an expression of lost but entirely human potentialities of sentiment. His insight demands that, even in the nineteenth century, the psychology of the poet be transcendental, but he is uneasy in the face of that demand as a real moral possibility. As a result his imagination, like Blake's, proliferates entities representative of mind (the host, the fairies, the stars, the everlasting voices) the semantic nature of which is unstable, to some degree dependent on whatever aspect of the poet's real unconscious is at any given moment engaged.

Yeats' first didactic poem is "The Moods." He presents it at the beginning of *The Wind among the Reeds,* as a statement of the problem of tradition. In 1899 "The Moods" appeared as follows:

> Time drops in decay,
> Like a candle burnt out,
> And the mountains and woods
> Have their day, have their day;
> What one in the rout
> Of the fire-born moods,
> Has fallen away?

This poem is not only very slight conceptually but of negligible aesthetic value. It was, however, reprinted by Yeats in all collected editions of his poems after 1899 and, in a somewhat different form, in all editions of *The Celtic Twilight* (1893), in which it first appeared as an epigraph. Further, it is cited in the Tenth Section of *Per Amica Silentia Lunae* (1917) as an illustration of a cosmological system which is still important to him.

"The Moods" exists in at least two discrete versions, the earlier associated throughout all printings with *The Celtic Twilight* and the later occurring in all other contexts. The last three lines in the earlier version are as follows:

> But kindly old rout
> Of the fire-born moods
> You pass not away.

Between the version of 1893 and that of 1899 Yeats disposed though not completely of the trivializing diction of the fairy convention ("kindly old moods") and introduced the terror of a world not susceptible to the control of the mind (his characteristic grammar of query). The superseded convention represents the childhood fantasy of a secret world which supplies the affection that the real world withholds. Yeats valued the supernatural because it gave evidence of possibilities of feeling unavailable to him as a natural man.

The term "Mood" first appears in Yeats' poetry in the poem in question, and an examination of the literary community around 1893 suggests that it had a very limited currency in Yeats' sense. In Edwin J. Ellis' poetic drama "Fate in Arcadia" (1892) we find the moods assimilated momentarily to the fairy convention as impersonal transmigrant emotions.

> *Maid:*   Who lives in Fairyland?
> *Fairy:*   Only the Moods,—a strange and wandering band.
>   They come like travelling maskers for their day
>   And house them here, and grief and laughter play
>   Until their service being done,—on—on
>   They, leaving the heart's door open, are gone.[4]

The irrelevance of this systematic intrusion into the otherwise arbitrary symbolism of Ellis' play suggests that the psychology of the Moods was not indigenous to Ellis' mind.[5] Clearly Yeats and Ellis developed the notion between them in the course of their collaboration on the problem of Blake. In the Yeats-Ellis *Blake* Mary Green is described as a "mood expressed, a State, and as such of more universal importance and artistic significance than an individual." Of *The Book of Urizen,* the editors say,

This is the story of one of the eternal states or moods of man, which are from everlasting. The individual enters these Moods and passes on, leaving them in the Universal Bosom, as travellers leave in space the lands through which they go. The name of the Mood is Urizen.[6]

Whatever the source of the Moods as Yeats understands them, it is clear that he has in this case as in others constructed his symbolism by the addition of an occult to a Romantic attitude. Yeats himself has suggested that nearly all the "popular mysticism" of his youth derived ultimately from Spinoza and that the "modes" of Spinoza are related to the cabalistic *sephiroth* which come into Latin as *affectiones*.[7]

In order to understand Yeats' dependence on the notion of Moods it is necessary to refer to his uncollected contributions in English periodicals, where he deals more extensively than anywhere else with the problem of tradition. In July, 1895, the first of a series of three articles dealing with "Irish National Literature" appeared in the *Bookman*

Englishmen and Scotsmen forget how much they owe to mature traditions of all kinds—traditions of feeling, traditions of thought, traditions of expression—for they have never dreamed of a life without these things. . . . In a new country like Ireland—and English speaking Ireland is very new—we are continually reminded of this long ripening by the immaturity of the traditions which we see about us.[8]

In reviewing the recent past of Irish literature Yeats finds that

the Irish national writers who have bulked largest in the past have been those who, because they served some political cause which could not wait, or had not enough of patience in themselves, turned away from the unfolding and developing of an Irish tradition and borrowed the native English methods of utterance and used them to sing of Irish wrongs and preach of Irish purposes.[9]

From the first half of the century he paradoxically selects Moore, Davis, and John Mitchell, as having dealt substantively with the problem of tradition, although it is only for Mitchell that he has any real admiration.

These were the most influential voices of the first half of the century and their influence was not at all the less because they had not a native style, for the one made himself wings out of the ancient Gaelic music, and the

other two were passionate orators expounding opinions which were nonetheless true because the utterance was alien; and were not poets or
romance writers, priests of those immortal Moods which are the true
builders of nations, the secret transformers of the world, and need a subtle,
appropriate language or a minute, manifold knowledge for their revelation.
John Mitchell, by the right of his powerful nature and his penal solitude,
communed indeed with the great Gods, now and always none other than
the Immortal Moods . . . but he gave them no lengthy or perfect devotion,
for he belonged to his cause, to his opinions.[10]

It is only when he comes to consider William Allingham that he is able
to praise with less qualification.

In him for the first time the slowly ripening tradition reached a perfect
utterance; and the Immortal Moods, which are so impatient of rhetoric, so
patient of mere immaturity found in his poetry this one perfect ritual
fashioned for their honour by Irish hands.[11]

I have quoted from this article at considerable length in order to show
the peculiar complexity of Yeats' attitudes toward the problem of
tradition in general and Irish authors in particular. First of all "tradition" consists in the whole environment of the mind, involving not only
"expression" but also received capacities of "feeling" and "thought."
Secondly, it seems to have nothing to do with a native style in any
comprehensible sense, since if Mitchell did not have it no objective
observer could discover that Allingham did. Thirdly, it involves a
subjectification of reality inconsonant with political cause or with the
arbitrary relation to the external world which Yeats, like Plato, calls
opinion. Although the Moods seem to be universal as they are immortal, the degree to which a writer serves them is the measure of his
achievement with respect to the *Irish* tradition. Tradition therefore is
universal, and "Irish tradition" as Yeats conceived it in 1895 simply
expressed the degree to which Irish writers participated in that universal well of resource. On a psychological level the Moods allowed Yeats
to express his early sense of the infinity of his emotions by translating
them out of the limiting context of time. From a literary point of view
the Moods liberate him from the temporal restrictions of nationality.

The most remarkable thing about the addiction of Irishmen to
Theosophy in the early years of the Celtic Revival is that Theosophy is

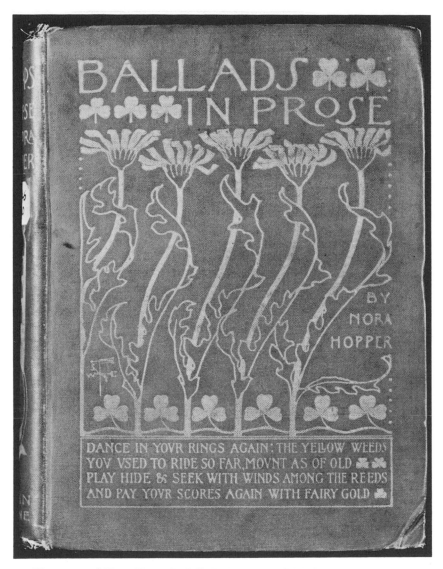

1. The cover of Nora Hopper's *Ballads in Prose* published in 1894. (Reproduced through the courtesy of the Bodley Head Press)

2. John Yeats: "King Goll." This portrait of William was devised by John Yeats to accompany his son's first appearance in an English periodical (*The Leisure Hour,* 1887).

a dogmatically universalist movement. When Mohini M. Chatterjee came to Dublin in 1886, he published an article in the *Dublin University Review* for May of that year called "The Common Sense of Theosophy,"[12] in which he sets forth doctrines basically the same as those which Yeats enunciated fifteen years later in his essay "Magic." In November of that year Yeats published his first critical article in the same periodical showing the effect of theosophical universalism on his aesthetic theories. He is speaking of Ferguson, whom of all the Anglo-Irish writers he seems never to have ceased to admire.

Ferguson's poetry is truly Bardic, appealing to all natures alike, to the great concourse of the people, for it has gone deeper than the intelligence which knows of difference—of good and evil, of the foolish and the wise, of this and that—to the universal emotions that have not heard of aristocracies, down to where Brahman and Sundra are not even names.[13]

Further, without using the term "Mood" he speaks of legends in the sense that was to become his custom ten years later.

Legends are the mothers of nations. I hold it the duty of every Irish reader to study those of his own nation. . . . If you will do this you will perhaps be saved in their high companionship from that leprosy of the modern— tepid emotions and many aims. Many aims, when the greatest of the earth often owned but two—two linked and arduous thoughts—fatherland and song. For them the personal perplexities of life grew dim, and there alone remained its noble sorrows and noble joys.[14]

Ireland is a new country from the point of view of tradition, and the Moods are old. As in the passage above, Yeats frequently equates the Moods with legend. Legends belong to antiquity. Because antiquity in Yeats means virtually the same thing as subjectivity, legends confirm emotions which in the modern world are no longer credible.

Emotions which seem vague or extravagant when expressed under the influence of modern literature cease to be vague and extravagant when associated with ancient legend and mythology, for legend and mythology were born out of man's longing for the mysterious and infinite.[15]

The success of any movement which could give Ireland a tradition in the sense in which Yeats described it in 1895 would be marked by its capacity to come to terms with the past as history and as mind, according to the canons of total subjectivity and extravagant emotion. In the Celtic Revival as characterized by Nora Hopper and George Russell, Yeats felt that he perceived the beginning of such a movement.

Whatever the cause we have for the first time in Ireland and among the Irish in England a school of men of letters united by a common purpose . . . and it is my hope some day in the maturity of our traditions to fashion out of the world about us, and the things that our fathers have told us, a new ritual for the builders of peoples, the imperishable moods.[16]

In Europe the old movement as Yeats conceived it (*In Memoriam,* "Locksley Hall," "Bishop Blougram's Apology," "Les Châtiments," Matthew Arnold) was "scientific and sought to interpret the world"; the new movement (*The Well at the World's End, Parsifal,* "Aglavaine and Selysette," *Axel*) "is religious and seeks to bring into the world dreams and passions which the poet can but believe to have been born before the world and for a longer day than the world's day."[17] For the poet the subjectivity must necessarily be eternal. The agony of the fundamental paradox must be undergone, and though the resources for idealism are as many as the religions of the world, none in Yeats' early verse unified the mind sufficiently to mitigate the pain.

Before 1900 Yeats sought to express his sense of the rising tide of emotion in relation to Ireland through the establishment of a cult of Irish Heroes, after 1900 through the establishment of an Irish theater. But the sources of his poetry were too various, and his emotions too strong, to admit of any successful reassociation of poetry with the Ireland of history under the conditions of his early inspiration. In the notes to his Irish anthology of 1895 he shows his contempt for Tom Moore by praising first a French translation of one of Tom Moore's lyrics and then assigning even higher praise to Bridges' English translation of the French.[18] In this way the poem as Mood passes from country to country seeking a tradition of style competent of it. Similarly when Yeats and George Moore undertook their collaboration on "Diarmuid and Grania," Yeats' program for the development of a stylistically mature product involved a planned transmigration. Moore was to go to Paris and do the scenario in French; thence it was to pass to a second party who would translate it from French into Gaelic; Lady Gregory would translate the Gaelic to vulgar English; and Yeats would "put style on it." Whether or not this is an exaggeration of the fact, the point is clear. The modern literary impulse must undergo a refinement including the discipline of France, where Yeats felt the new movement to have arisen, and of ancient Ireland, from which it derives its power and specificity. Only then could it receive the last mark of transfiguration, "style," and become Irish in the sense that the Moods as a concept of tradition demand.

The Moods are not one, like the Judaeo-Christian deity, but many, like the pagan gods. As a symbol of inwardness they represent a fundamental disunity which Yeats continuously attempts to resolve and yet cherishes as a symbol of mysterious power. The only conventional resolution of the multiplicity of emotions is "abstraction" or the dreaded withdrawal from feeling. The Moods are the "true builders of nations," the source of power both in history and the mind, and to lose through abstraction a direct relation to these powers would be to lose all. In personality the Moods are the sources of motivation. Raised to the level of history (for they are also metaphysical entities), they account for the manner in which poetry, as mediate between eternity and time, forms nations and individuals. But if we pass beyond Yeats' own capacity to comment on his predicament, we must observe that so long as emotional reality remains multiple and unrelated to consciousness, personality cannot emerge. Just as Yeats, in embracing the cosmic psychology of the Moods, disavows true nationality, so also he disavows true identity. Archetypalism, like nonrational psychology, bypasses identity by locating value above or below consciousness. Personal identity was the abstract unity which Yeats felt it necessary to abolish, and the style of *The Wind among the Reeds* is exactly oriented to convey the sense of the extinction of personality in the process of transformation.

Yeats in this period will accord unity neither to deity nor to the self, as if in the dispute for power between God and man, father and son, neither force can be allowed to emerge victorious. Further, the notion of the transcendental character of the Moods literally accords power only to the gods, for clarity is achieved only by the abolition of mechanisms by which time and eternity can mingle. The dispute as to whether the Rose is white or red, the possession of the father or the son—whether reality is occult and generated in the self or Neoplatonic and irrecoverably beyond the self—is one of the irreducible "obscurities" of the Yeatsian text.

The notion that salvation would be achieved by a new resort to the emotions was a common possession of Yeats and his age. In general, it took the contrary form of realism with respect to the external world and the sexual object. The poetry of Symons, Dowson, and Richard Le Gallienne began in the music hall. The new poet like the new woman was undertaking the "larger latitude." Messages were being received from the London East End as well as the Hindu East. Dowson was not only the votary of Cynara but also the lover of Adelaide and the translator of Zola. Edwin Ellis, with whom Yeats seems to have developed the Mood psychology, attracted the young poet by his stories of sexual escapades on the continent as well as by his knowledge of Blake, so that the sexual initiation and the occult became simultaneous. Leonard Smithers, who presided over the *Savoy,* was a notorious publisher of pornography. Decadence in the sense of emotional extravagance was a commonplace.

> Oh! our age-end style perplexes
> All our elders time has tamed.
> On our sleeves we wear our sexes
> Our diseases, unashamed.
> Have we lost the mood romantic
> That was once our right by birth?
> Lo! the greenest girl is frantic
> With the woe of all the earth.

Thus John Davidson, not the least member of the "Tragic Generation," introduces his *Earl Lavender*.[19] The typical solution to the problem was, as in the case of Wilde and Dowson, the complete dissociation of the sexual from the ideal content, a solution worked out in all the bitterness of its moral destructiveness in Hardy's *Jude the Obscure* (1895). But Yeats never allowed his idealism entirely to lose its psychological ambiguity. His symbol of the decadent imagination was the whore who gave birth to a unicorn, "most unlike man of all living things, being cold, hard and virginal," and who cries out after her child in terms of oxymoron expressing the paradox of body and soul, "Harsh sweetness, Dear bitterness, O Solitude, O terror." [20] In *The Wisdom of the King* the hawk-headed youth woos his mortal love (the Ireland of history) with his richest gifts "for he could not believe that a beauty so much like wisdom could hide a common heart." The gift of wisdom which he offers and she refuses are words which tell

How the great Moods are alone immortal, and the creators of mortal things, and how every Mood is a being that wears, to mortal eyes, the shape of Fair-brows, who dwells, as a salmon, in the floods; or of Dagda, whose cauldron is never empty; or of Lir, whose children wail upon the water; or of Angus, whose kisses were changed into birds; or Len, the goldsmith from whose furnaces break rainbows and fiery dew; or of some other of the children of Dana. [21]

The discovery of the hawk-headed youth is that "wisdom the gods have made, and no man shall live by its light, for it and the hail and the rain and the thunder follow a way that is deadly to mortal things."

Chapter V

The chief difference between the metaphors of poetry and the symbols of mysticism is that the latter are woven together into a complete system. The "vexed sea" would not be merely a detached comparison, but, with the fish it contains, would be related to the land and air, the winds and shadowing clouds, and all in their totality compared to the mind in its totality.—W. B. Yeats and Edwin J. Ellis in *The Works of William Blake*

The great matter is to remain positive to all apparitions and to work on the G.D. as far as the 5–6 grade before attempting much or any practical work such as invocation. You should get A.P.S. to send you with your material for examination "The Banishing Ritual of the Pentagram" as you are entitled to it and may find it of importance. It is a great help against all obsession.—Yeats to W. T. Horton, April 13, 1896

The voice that is contagion to the world.
—Shelley, *Prometheus Unbound*

The Wars of Eden

IN the form in which it was first published, *The Wind among the Reeds* was accompanied by a system of notes and mythological elaborations on which Yeats offered the following comment in an undated letter to his French acquaintance and translator Henry D. Davray:

> The notes are really elaborate essays in the manner of *The Celtic Twilight*. They deal with Irish fairy lore and mythology and are in most cases made out of quite new material. They have given me a good deal of trouble, and will probably make most of the critics spend half of every review in complaining that I have written very long notes about very short poems.
>
> I am in hopes, however, that others will forgive me the poems for the sake of the valuable information in the notes. It is a way of getting the forgiveness of the Philistines which may serve as a useful model.[1]

The Celtic Revival, as this comment somewhat evasively illustrates, was almost entirely dependent for its relation to the Gaelic background on scientific and pseudo-scientific researches of the kind represented by John Rhys' *Celtic Heathendom* and Standish O'Grady's histories. Yeats' notes, which offer in fact little if any new material, represent the anxiety for authenticity which haunted him throughout his life. The Celtic literary stereotype promised that the new poetry would be grounded in a superior ethnic reality. Yeats' concern in the notes is to associate himself with this rising convention. In addition, the function of the notes is to reveal the manner in which symbols organize history through the processes of philological and mythological association, and thereby to assure the reader of the relation of the lyric poem to a more than temporary truth. They are not primarily intended to reveal the source of the poem, but to augment lyric reality by reference to the universal substratum, the level at which the finite horizon of the short poem melts into a cosmic whole.

Nonetheless, the notes do not in fact confine themselves to Irish background, but reach outward through Count d'Alviella, Rhys, and Frazer, and through universal magical and folk phenomena, to include in a general way the kind of sources on which Yeats did rely. One class of sources is, however, conspicuously unrepresented, namely, the occult background which is at least as prepossessing in *The Wind among the Reeds* as the Gaelic. For "The Everlasting Voices," Yeats provided no comments. It has no real genetic affinities to the Gaelic background and stands both as an example of Yeats' concern to construct his lyric symbol by assimilating at whatever hazard the occult to the Celtic mode and as a reminder of the fundamental diversity of his imaginary culture. We may recall in this respect his earlier comment on *Oisin,* "The Romance is for readers,"[2] implying that the hidden content is for the adept and the process of reading must be a process of initiation.

Despite the stylistic and genetic dissimilarity of "The Hosting of the Sidhe" and "The Everlasting Voices" the two poems remained associated in Yeats' mind even in old age, reminding us how fully, for him, the true poem lay in the image and not in the literary fact. In his *Diary* for 1930 he writes:

I think that two conceptions, that of reality as a congeries of beings, that of reality as a single being, alternate in our emotion and in history, and must always remain something that human reason, because subject always to one or the other, cannot reconcile. I am always in all I do driven to a moment which is the realization of myself as unique and free, or to a moment which is the surrender to God of all I am. I think that there are historical cycles wherein one or the other predominates, and that a cycle approaches where all shall be as particular and concrete as human intensity permits. Again and again I have tried to sing that approach, "The Hosting of the Sidhe," "O sweet everlasting voices," and those lines about "The lonely majestical multitude," and have almost understoood my intention. Again and again with remorse, a sense of defeat, I have failed when I would write of God, written coldly and conventionally. Could those two impulses, one as much a part of truth as the other, be reconciled, or if one or the other could prevail, all life would cease.[3]

In retrospect the first two poems of *The Wind among the Reeds* seemed to Yeats to announce a dispensation of the "particular and concrete." The limiting clause ("as human intensity permits") is a qualification characteristic of a point of view later than that of *The Wind among the Reeds,* for in the early period it is fundamental to Yeats' sense of "intensity" that it exceed humanity. The cyclical view of history which this passage elaborates resolves itself into a dispute between the dispensation of the son characterized by passion, particularity, multiplicity, and freedom and the dispensation of the father characterized by unity, abstraction, and repression. Early and late Yeats announced the advent of his own emotional liberation, and yet he yearned for the ultimate unification of son and father, the particular and the ideal, which would have made repose possible.

One of the differences between "The Hosting" and "The Everlasting Voices" is that the former poem is an invocation or summoning of power and the latter is a banishing ritual. The occult background, and particularly the ceremonial magic of the Golden Dawn, served Yeats as a technique of control by which trance could be induced and reality recovered according to fixed methods. Therefore ceremonial magic is particularly appropriate as the underlying structure of a poem following the terrified annunciation of "The Hosting of the Sidhe." But the background of ceremonial magic always brings with it into Yeats' early poetry the problem of sexuality, as if sex were the hidden or occult subject. "The Hosting," with which *The Wind* begins, is a projection of the self in terms of the heroic role; "The Everlasting Voices" is a love poem.

"The Everlasting Voices" was published in 1896 and belongs to the period of the *Savoy,* to the London literary environment characterized by Symons, in contrast to the Irish community in which Russell was the chief influence. It is written in the "trance" style which Yeats identified with the French manner and is without Ossianic lapses into the "heavy breathing" and manic gesture of "The Hosting." Like the earlier poem "The Everlasting Voices" is circular and its chief effect

redundance; but now the structure is perfected, and instead of being
the development of an earlier stanzaic arrangement, is a single complex
sentence beginning and ending with the same line and articulated by
only three rhymes.[4]

THE EVERLASTING VOICES

O sweet everlasting Voices be still;
Go to the guards of the heavenly fold
And bid them wander obeying your will
Flame under flame, till Time be no more;
Have you not heard that our hearts are old,
That you call in the birds, in the wind on the hill,
In shaken boughs, in tide on the shore.
O sweet everlasting Voices be still.[5]

The "style" of this poem is continuous and triumphant, making it an
exercise in muteness. Yeats remarks that the "howling" of Blake's
prophetic figures is the shout of desire.[6] This poem is constructed in a
context of the necessity of the concealment of desire. Traditionally it is
Harpocrates, the god of silence, who presides over the mysteries of cult.
The absence of all proper nouns and explicit mythological references
suggests a passage in a lengthy ritual or a brief lyric flight in the course
of a longer narrative; [7] but for Yeats the linear structure and objective
orientation required by narrative are inconsonant with the canon of
purity. Ritual depends for its efficacy on concealment.

Insofar as the poem has internal development, it is divided between
the fourth and the fifth line, the first part of the poem referring to
heaven or a condition of higher organization and the second half of the
poem referring to earth and the disintegration of the will suggested
metrically by the marked caesuras of the sixth and seventh lines. The
speaker of the poem is on earth in the world of history, and his
mortality is signified by his "old" heart, in contrast to the heart of the
immortal which never ceases to be young.[8] Yeats rehearsed this poem in
1893 as part of the fairy culture in a chapter of *The Celtic Twilight*
called "The Golden Age."

I seemed to hear a voice of lamentation out of the Golden Age. It told me
that we are imperfect, incomplete, and no more like a beautiful woven web,
but like a bundle of cords knotted together and flung into a corner. It said

that the world was once all perfect and kindly, and that still the kindly and perfect world existed but buried like a mass of roses under many spadefuls of earth. The fairies and the more innocent of the spirits dwelt within it, and lamented over the fallen world in the lamentation of the wind-tossed reeds, in the song of the birds, in the moan of the waves, and the sweet cry of the fiddle. . . . It said that with us the beautiful are not clever and the clever are not beautiful. . . . It said that if only they who live in the Golden Age could die we might be happy, for the sad voices would be still; but alas! alas! they must sing and we must weep until the eternal gates swing open.[9]

The subject from the point of view of this passage is what Yeats elsewhere calls "the accusation of Beauty." The obscure multiplication of entities involved in the command "Go to the guards" replaces the earlier impossible wish that the undying might die, and the voices become assimilated to the symbol of wind among reeds, the oppression of the Absolute in the form of "the fairies and more innocent of spirits." As in "Who Goes with Fergus?" and most overtly in "Aedh Wishes for the Cloths of Heaven," [10] the poet conceives his overthrow as an unweaving, an incapacity to compose his own destiny, analogous to the difficulty of making poetry. In terms of the immutability of the Absolute, the command "Go to the guards" and the interrogation "Have you not heard . . . ?" become purely rhetorical, confessing by their meaninglessness the presence of a predicament in which all activity is futile. In *The Celtic Twilight* Yeats' symbol for the end of time is the conventional opening of the Eternal Gates, just as his symbol of the lost perfection is the pagan Golden Age, the youth of the world which preceded its decline into culture. In "The Everlasting Voices" such conventional reference has been avoided, the voices are characterized merely by an indefinite omnipresence; and the ultimate cataclysm is rendered ambiguous by the simplicity of the phrase "till Time be no more." Above all we become aware that, like the word "kindly" in the fairy culture, the epithet "sweet" is a euphemism, the complication of speech by fear. Whatever the conception of the poem was in 1893, when Yeats wrote "The Golden Age," it has become something quite different in 1896, and the search for the excluded narrative which will provide the identifying context for "The Everlasting Voices" cannot rest in the fairy culture.

By the time of *Reveries* "The Everlasting Voices" had become associated in Yeats' mind with his father and their early discussions of
works read aloud. Yeats recounts how at a certain point in his life he
"began to play at being a sage or a poet or a magician." [11] Among his
idols were Alastor, Prince Athanase, and Byron's Manfred. His father
read to him from *Prometheus Unbound* and *Coriolanus,* but John Yeats
"did not care even for a fine lyric passage unless he felt some actual
man behind its elaboration of beauty, and he was always looking for
the lineaments of some desirable familiar life. When the spirits sang
their scorn of Manfred, and Manfred answered, "O sweet and melancholy voices," I was told that they could not even in anger put off their
spiritual sweetness." In Byron's poem, Manfred has by his magical
power called up spirits who mock him with their immortality and in
the end destroy him. The spirits ask the magician whether any mortal
gift can satisfy him. He replies:

> No, none: yet stay—one moment, ere we part,
> I would behold ye face to face. I hear
> Your voices, sweet and melancholy sounds,
> As music on the Waters; and I see
> The steady aspect of a large clear star;
> But nothing more. Approach me as you are,
> Or one—or all—in your accustomed forms.
>   *Spirit.* We have no forms, beyond the elements
> Of which we are the mind and principle:
> But choose a form—in that we will appear.
>   *Man.* I have no choice; there is no form on earth
> Hideous or beautiful to me. Let him,
> Who is most powerful of ye, take such aspect
> As unto him may seem most fitting—Come!
>   *Seventh Spirit* (appearing in the shape of a
> beautiful female figure). Behold!
>   *Man.*   Oh God! If it be thus, and *thou*
> Art not a madness and a mockery,
> I yet might be most happy. I will clasp thee,
> And we again will be—
>   [The figure vanishes]
>   My heart is crushed!
>   [MANFRED falls senseless] [12]

Yeats' inaccurate recollection of Byron, a recollection mediated by his
own "The Everlasting Voices," brings us to the fundamental predicament of the Yeatsian seer and poet overshadowed by his own immortal
fancy and in love with the elemental shape changers in the form of "a
beautiful female figure" which disappears. Far from seeking "the lineaments of some desirable familiar life" Yeats devoted himself to the
rejected element in his father's sensibility and developed a lyric style
which cannot "even in anger put off its sweetness."

The mantic role which Yeats founded on the example of Manfred
and Alastor was, as is well known, confirmed by his initiation in 1890
into The Order of the Golden Dawn, an association devoted to the
augmentation of personality by ceremonial imitation of the real order
of the world. The order of the universe in the Golden Dawn is the
sephirothic system, and each stage of personal development corresponds to one of the ten ranks by which reality proceeds toward God,
the lowest being Malkuth or earth and the highest Kether or Crown,
the *sephira* closest to the One Substance of God. Some sense of the
system and its ceremonial equivalents can be gained by examining the
names and grouping of the *sephiroth* and their ceremonial equivalents.
The highest six *sephiroth* are arranged in two triads. No living adept
can in good faith aspire to the ceremonial rank equivalent to the
sephiroth of the first triad, also called the Supernals. The lowest four
are grouped according to the elements in the traditional ascending
order of spirituality.

1. Kether	Crown (Spirit, Ipsissimus)	10–1
2. Chokmah	Wisdom (Magus)	9–2
3. Binah	Understanding (Magister Templi)	8–3
4. Chesed	Mercy (Adeptus Exemptus)	7–4
5. Geburah	Might (Adeptus Major)	6–5
6. Tiphareth	Harmony (Adeptus Minor)	5–6
7. Netzach	Victory Fire (Philosophus)	4–7
8. Hed	Splendour Water (Practicus)	3–8
9. Yesed	Foundation Air (Theoricus)	2–9
10. Malkuth	Kingdom Earth (Zelator)	1–10[13]

This is a vertical system. It serves the adept by bringing the mind's highest and lowest powers into a significant relation. The curious numerical equations by which each grade is identified (Zelator, 1–10, Theoricus, 2–9) express the slow vanishing of the value of the actual personality as the numerical quantity of the sublime or ideal self grows greater. Yeats cherished the hierarchical character of the order, and when the Golden Dawn became disorganized by the bizarre quarrel of MacGregor Mathers and Aleister Crowley, Yeats resisted any democratization. "It was the surrender of freedom that taught Dante Alighieri to say, 'Thy will is our peace.' " [14] Individuals within the order lived at all times in the shadow of the power wielded by the unknown adepts of the highest ranks who were now outside temporal reality. As the reed bends to the wind, so the adept gives himself to the discipline of ceremonial development and to awe of the knowledge to be revealed at each upward advance.

The source of "The Everlasting Voices" belongs to the knowledge revealed in the course of initiation into the Zelator or lowest grade and would become available to Yeats very early in his relation to the Golden Dawn. In the context of this source the drama in which the lyric is spoken is the fall of man.

And Tetragrammaton placed Kerubim at the East of the Garden of Eden and a flaming sword which turned every way to keep the path of the Tree of Life, for He has created Nature that man being cast out of Eden may not fall into the Void. He has bound man with the stars as with a chain. He allures him with scattered fragments of the Divine body in bird and beast and flower. And He laments over him in the Wind and in the Sea and in the Birds. And when the times are ended, He will call the Kerubim from the East of the Garden, and all shall be consumed and become infinite and holy.[15]

The "heavenly fold" is Eden, and its guards are the cherubim whose swords prevent fallen man from reascending to his primal condition. The predicament of Manfred has been systematized and generalized by association with an occult narrative, and the voices become the continual accusation by God of man's primal sin and consequent fall from perfection.

The general structure of this universe can be seen in Fig. 4, an altar glyph belonging to the ritual of the Philosophus grade (4–7) in the Golden Dawn.[16] It will be observed that the upper circle containing the three lesser circles of the supernal *sephiroth* is dominated by the "woman clothed with the sun" of the twelfth chapter of the Apocalypse, who governs the sephirothic world in the primal state and turns aside only to give room to the wrath of God on the occasion of the fall. Despite the fact that the Jewish mystical tradition is overwhelmingly masculine,[17] the supernal *sephiroth* of the Golden Dawn, who constitute the symbol of deity itself, are continuously conceived as feminine. Mathers' preface to his *Kabbalah Unveiled* (1887) announces the attitude toward the feminine aspects of cabala which dominated the Golden Dawn, in which he was for many years the principal figure. "I wish particularly," he says, "to direct the reader's attention to the stress laid by the Qabalah on the Feminine aspects of the deity and to the shameful way in which any allusions to these in the ordinary translations of the Bible have been suppressed." Both Crowley and Regardie put great emphasis on the female divine symbol. A characteristic example of the gratuitous multiplication of the hieratic female image is the description in the Golden Dawn instructional literature of the Seventeenth Key of the Tarot.

A nude female figure which is the synthesis of Isis, of Nephthys and of Athor, . . . Venus, . . . Binah, . . . Aima, . . . Tebunah, . . . The Great Supernal Mother, . . . Aima Elohim pouring upon the earth the waters of creation which unite and form a River at her Feet, the River going forth from the supernal Eden.[18]

According to Regardie, the Supernals,[19] which he identifies with the Jungian collective unconscious and which are the *Aima Elohim*, are symbolized as the First Matter of the alchemists described in Thomas Vaughan's *Coelum Terrae*:

A most pure sweet virgin, for nothing as yet had been generated out of her. . . . She yields to nothing but love, for her end is procreation, and that was never yet performed by violence. He that knows how to wanton and toy with her, the same shall receive all her treasures. First, she sheds at her nipples a thick heavy water, but white as any snow, the philosophers call it *virgin's Milk*. Secondly she gives him blood from her very heart; it is a quick heavenly fire; some improperly call it their sulphur. Thirdly and lastly she presents him a secret crystal, of more worth and lustre than the white rock and all her rosials. This is she and these are her favours.[20]

The Supernals then are the Wisdom figure, the milk-white woman, who feeds her lover and offers him her secret treasures. The *locus classicus* for this woman is the eighth chapter of Proverbs, where she cried out: "The Lord possessed me in the beginning of his way, before his works of old." [21] Thereafter God created the world, and Wisdom becomes the possession of the sons of God.

When he gave to the sea his decree, that the waters should not pass his commandment: when he appointed the foundations of the earth:
Then I was by him, as one brought up with him: and I was daily his delight, rejoicing always before him;
Rejoicing in the habitable parts of his earth; and my delights were with the sons of men.[22]

This is the cosmic drama which forms the narrative event out of which "The Everlasting Voices" is uttered. In the altar glyph the apparition of the face of the father God can be seen rising behind the female Wisdom figure, who is turning away from the created world, giving a vivid representation of the revolution of historical cycles, which, as we have seen,[23] Yeats regards his poems of this period as heralding. The Kingdom of the son, which came into existence at the creation, is giving way to the Kingdom of the father, which preceded the creation, and the lightninglike sword, which, of course, was not present in the glyph of the prelapsarian world, extends itself from the Eden of the Supernals downward toward the four apocalyptic beasts who became the guardians of the now-forbidden place. Hence that curious mixture of seduction and terror which "The Everlasting Voices" conveys.

The occult background of "The Everlasting Voices" well illustrates how "symbolism" in the specific sense in which Yeats used it made the cosmological or epic subject available to him within the confines of the lyric genre. The Miltonic grandeur and equally Miltonic visual indistinctness of "Flame under flame" [24] suggests the larger subject. Unlike Blake, Yeats did not extend his psychological drama into a narrative requiring that objectification of psychic entities which is constantly failing in the Prophetic Books. Instead he undertook to develop a prophetic mode of the lyric, which, without explicitly committing the

poet to a specific cosmological reality, would nonetheless give him all
the scope of primal drama. The human speaker of "The Everlasting
Voices," whose humanity Yeats took the utmost care to preserve by
stripping his speech of all vestiges of "poetic" diction, attempts futilely
to ward off or banish the apocalyptic guardians, God's representatives,
by commanding the *Aima Elohim* [25] to curse *them* as he is cursed with
the endless wandering which in Yeats is the symbol of the hopeless
search for the Beloved. As we read in "The Song of the Wandering
Aengus,"

> Though I am old with wandering
> Through hollow lands and hilly lands,
> I will find out where she has gone.[26]

The energies the onset of which Yeats conceives himself to be announc-
ing are the emotions which he regards as most fully awakened in
exclusive relation to the Wisdom figure. That relation within the context of the poem has been lost, and the flaming symbols of the Father's
omnipotence represent the impossibility for humanity of the once-pos-
sessed immortal love. The door which the sword guards is that "flaming
lute-thronged" gate which, with the onset of love as in "The Travail of
Passion," is opened wide.

Yeats throughout his early life yearned for initiation. He not only
underwent initiation repeatedly as in the case of the I.R.B., the Blavatsky cult, and the Golden Dawn, the ceremonies of which are in fact one
continuous and progressive initiation, he even invented initiation ceremonies as in the case of the abortive Irish Cultus which was to have its
seat at Lough Kay. In the Golden Dawn ritual, a drama fundamental
to the preparation of the initiate is the approach to the guarded place
and the endurance by the candidate of the threats of the ceremonial
officers. That drama is the subject of "The Everlasting Voices." The
meaning of "twilight" from this point of view is the condition of the
uninitiated, the unborn, who awaits in his limbonic state the coming of
the light from within and as preparation must learn to master his
anxiety. The ceremonial chamber, as arranged for the neophyte (o–o)
in the Golden Dawn, was dominated by the Banners of East and West,

symbolizing the morning and the evening twilight respectively (Fig. 5).²⁷ The following is part of the opening of the neophyte ritual.

Hegemon (to blindfolded neophyte): Inheritor of a Dying World, arise and enter the darkness.
Stolises: The mother of darkness has blinded him with her hair.
Dadouches: The father of darkness hath hidden him under His Wings.
Hierophant: His limbs are still weary with the wars that were in Heaven.
Kerux: Unpurified and Unconsecrated, thou canst not enter our sacred hall.

The neophyte is characterized as one newly cast out of heaven, loosely speaking, a follower of Satan who has unsuccessfully disputed with God the right to the Kingdom of Heaven and has, in consequence, fallen into creation. The initiation of the neophyte is the preparation for the reascent through the sephirothic system.

Hierus: (who guards the Banner of the West, and now stands threatening with his sword): Thou canst not pass by me, saith the guardian of the West, unless thou canst tell me my name.
Hegemon (answering for the neophyte): Darkness is thy name, thou Great One of the Paths of the Shade.
Hierus: Thou hast known me now, so pass thou on. Fear is failure, so be thou without fear. For he who trembles at the Flame and at the Flood, and at the Shadows of the Air, hath no part in God.²⁸

"The Everlasting Voices" represents the fallen condition of man, tempted and afraid. Building on the situation of that poem, *The Wind among the Reeds* presents a series of lyrics, corresponding to ascending grades in the Golden Dawn, which reproduces unsystematically the process of initiation. Indeed, the poems of *The Wind* represent in general a ceremony of initiation from which Yeats emerged with increased power in the first decade of the twentieth century, as if born for the first time into the real world. The program of the poems is ritual transformation based on heroic, alchemical, magical, and ceremonial symbols, bridging the gap between the human candle and the divine flame, between the peasant and the sidhe, the Irishman and the idealization of the self in the native land, man and his Supernal Bride.

The passage in the ceremonial drama cited above finds its development in *The Wind among the Reeds* in a poem called "To My Heart,

Bidding It Have No Fear." [29] In *The Celtic Twilight* Yeats had rehearsed an anecdote about a sea captain:

> "Sur," said he, "did you ever hear tell of the sea captain's prayer?"
> "No," said I; "what is it?"
> "It is," he replied, " 'O Lord, give me a stiff upper lip.' "

To which Yeats adds, "Let us look upon him with wonder, for his mind
has not fallen into a net of complexity, nor his will melted into thought
and dream. Our journey is through other storms and other darkness." [30]
Forty years later, speaking as though from his grave in "Under Ben
Bulben," he praises a similar capacity for facing life and death with a
"cold eye." The result of the transformations of initiation is emotional
integration, leaving the heart fearless and the eye clear. The version of
this process in *The Wind among the Reeds* is as follows:

> TO MY HEART, BIDDING IT HAVE NO FEAR
> Be you still, be you still, trembling heart;
> Remember the wisdom out of old days:
> *Him who trembles before the flame and the flood,*
> *And the winds that blow through the starry ways,*
> *Let the starry winds and the flame and the flood*
> *Cover over and hide, for he has no part*
> *With the proud majestical multitude.*[31]

This poem served Yeats in 1907 as an epigraph to his essay "Poetry
and Tradition," where it is further explained. The conquest of fear
becomes a condition of style. As we have seen in earlier chapters, men
in more favorable cultural conditions sang joyfully under the burden of
the same Moods, the eternal tradition, which now fill them with fear
and hopelessness.

Three types of men have made all beautiful things. Aristocracies have
made beautiful manners, because their place in the world puts them above
the fear of life, and the countrymen have made beautiful stories and
beliefs, because they have nothing to lose and so do not fear, and the
artists have made all the rest because Providence has filled them with
recklessness. All these look backward to a long tradition, for, being without
fear, they have held to whatever pleased them initially.[32]

The ritual of the Golden Dawn makes it possible for the poet to suffer
and ultimately to become part of the "proud, majestical multitude" by

the conquest of fear, which raises him ceremonially through the august grades of Zelator, Theoricus, Practicus, Philosophus, to the Supernals, where man is quintessentially himself, the Ipsissimus. The antagonists are the volatile elements in their occult forms—air, fire, and water— which like the guardian cherubim of "The Everlasting Voices," stand between man and his desired identity. In *The Wind among the Reeds* the elements are hostile. They symbolize the competing reality of the external world and of the father, which keeps man from his true inwardness and his destined marriage. As a symbol, they also include, as we have seen, the medial condition in which the tempest of the actual emotions coerces and overshadows the mind because it is unsimplified by successful idealization.

The Banners of East and West symbolize for Yeats the process of initiation. Beyond that process is the last judgement of the imagination when body and soul are reunited like lovers in the work of art outside time. The song of the wind in "Aedh Hears the Cry of the Sedge" represents the necessity of transcending the condition of "becoming," symbolized by the great banners of the morning and evening twilight, in order to achieve the Beloved.[33]

AEDH HEARS THE CRY OF THE SEDGE

I wander by the edge
Of this desolate lake
Where the wind cries in the sedge
Until the axle break
That keeps the stars in their round
And hands hurl in the deep
The banners of East and West
And the girdle of light is unbound,
Your breast will not lie by the breast
Of your beloved in sleep.

This is the end of initiation, signified by the destruction of the natural order, the dispersal of the twilight, and the unbinding of celestial illumination.

For the authors of the Yeats-Ellis *Blake* the effect of mystic thought was to mature the mind and give steadiness to character.[34] One of the underlying aspects of structure in *The Wind among the Reeds* is the attempt to conquer by ceremonial techniques the unborn condition of the poet whose consciousness is complicated by the shadows of twilight. The Order itself was under the presidence of Venus,[35] and the entrance to the sacred vault, guarded by the symbolism of the cherubim, was called the Venus gate. In order to come to her the problem of twilight, the subjectification of the real, had to be solved; otherwise man remained isolated from the Beloved, who is in the occult sense and under many symbols his own reality.

The only technique which Yeats would admit for the objectification of the self in the nineties was total idealization of the emotions. The source of the ambiguous gesture of command in "The Everlasting Voices" ("Go to the guards") is Blake, but Yeats' conception of the event which Blake also anticipates is different from that of the earlier master:

The ancient tradition that the world will be consumed in fire at the end of six thousand years is true, as I have heard from Hell.

For the cherub with his flaming sword is hereby commanded to leave his guard at the tree of life, and when he does, the whole creation will be consumed, and appear infinite and holy whereas it now appears finite and corrupt.

This will come to pass by an improvement of sensual enjoyment.

But first the notion that man has a body distinct from his soul is to be expunged.[36]

Yeats and Ellis deal with this passage as follows:

When man ascends wholly out of "the wheel of birth" into "the imagination that liveth forever," a last judgement is said to pass over him. He is done with the opacity of corporeal existence and has attained that state which Blake announced or rather summoned in "The Marriage of Heaven and Hell" with the words "The Cherub with his flaming sword is hereby commanded to leave his guard. . . ." The interpretation of the flaming sword in this passage is the same as that in the Jewish Kabala. When the Last Judgement has passed over a man he enters that community of Saints who "are no longer talking of good and evil, or of what is right and wrong, and puzzling themselves in Satan's labyrinth; but are conversing with eternal realities, as they exist in the human imagination." [37]

The community of saints referred to here is of course analogous to the Yeatsian sidhe and its many symbolic correlatives, but the notion that "this will come to pass by an improvement of sensual enjoyment" is alien to Yeats' sensibility if taken in the tactile sense Blake here intends. The occult doctrine to which Yeats and Ellis assent,[38] namely, that "man has no body distinct from his soul," means, for Yeats, when he attempts to conceive of the two elements in harmony, not the assimilation of soul to body, but of body to soul. In the first decade of the twentieth century Yeats attempted to reverse this aspect of his sensibility, but in the period under consideration Yeats resolved the conflict of the occult and Neoplatonic traditions, of the Rose and the Cross, in favor of the absolute point of view. Occultism matured the mind by objectifying and rendering inevitable the process of sublimation.

Yeats was obsessed in the period of *The Wind among the Reeds* with the fantasy of that apocalypse, the consequence of the *fiat* of the son, which would undo the initial *fiat* of the father by which He created the physical world. We have already commented on the example from "The Everlasting Voices."

> Go to the guards of the heavenly fold
> And bid them wander obeying your will
> Flame under flame till Time be no more.

In "The Secret Rose" the poet cries out:

> When shall the stars be blown out of
>   the sky
> Like sparks blown out of a smithy,
>   and die? [39]

This image Yeats derived from his reading in MacGregor Mathers' translation of Knorr von Rosenroth's *Kabbala Denudata*. Yeats was attracted by a series of paragraphs dealing with the destruction of prior worlds.[40]

#421   And therefore were the prior worlds destroyed for the prior worlds were formed without conformation.

#422   But these which existed not in conformation are called vibrating flames and sparks. Like as when a worker striketh sparks from the flint with his hammer, or as when the smith smiteth the iron and dasheth forth sparks on every side.

#423   And these sparks which fly forth flame and scintillate but shortly
       and are extinguished. And these are called prior worlds.

#429   From a Light-beam of insupportable brightness proceeded a Radiat-
       ing Flame, dashing off like a vast and mighty hammer those sparks
       that were prior worlds.[41]

The importance of this image, which for Yeats meant the end of time in
the form of astrological fatality and the onset of eternity, consists in
the fact that it signifies destruction through creation. As the smith
labors at the anvil, so the poet labors at his art, to bring about a new
world which will supplant the old and restore the son to that Eden
from which he was expelled at the beginning of history and which is so
jealously guarded by the ministers of God.[42] From this follows in part
the intense resistance to creativity which Yeats records in *The Wind,*
where the attempt to make the perfect poem is overthrown not only by
the temptation to sexuality but by the host itself.[43]

Alternating with the son's conquest of the world of the father is the
father's conquest of the world of the son, demanding, as Yeats says,
"the surrender to God of all I am." [44] On the lid of the *pastos,* or
innermost chamber of the vault of the Golden Dawn ritual temple, is an
image of Christ the judge, modified from Dürer's "Apocalypse" so that
the sword of judgement includes the whole of the sephirothic system
(Fig. 6).[45] In "The Valley of the Black Pig" Yeats takes up the subject
of the wars of Eden and represents the defeat of the son by the father.
The poem concludes:

> We who still labour by the cromlec on the shore,
> The grey cairn on the hill, when the day sinks
>   drowned in dew,
> Being weary of the world's empires, bow down to
>   you
> Master of the still stars, and of the flaming
>   door.[46]

Here God, in Dürer's image, sustains the order of nature and remains
master of the gate of Eden. Yeats had a great deal to say about this
battle in his notes. This poem is one of his peasant visions and is, he
says, founded on "prophesies of the coming rout of the enemies of
Ireland, in a certain Valley of the Black Pig." The Black Pig is the

boar that killed Attis and "Dearmod," the powers of fertility so potent that they have become dangerous; it is winter contesting the dominion of the earth with summer; finally, "for the purposes of poetry" he believes it is "the darkness that will at last destroy the gods and the world." [47] The "Black Boar" is one of those symbols which, like "Clooth-na-Bare," Yeats feels called upon to augment and complicate. The important thing about the poem is that the anticipated cataclysm does not take place. Although the armies of Ireland perish and its horsemen faithful to the Ossianic convention fall, the confused conflict of potencies which Yeats feels to be suggested by "The Valley of the Black Pig" remains unresolved. In the end the impulse to throw off the burden of mortality is abandoned, the speaker sinks back into the paralysis of twilight, and the pre-existing order of things as we have described it in terms of "The Everlasting Voices" is reasserted. The complexity and presumptive subjectivity of "the matter of Ireland" is resolved by the use of Golden Dawn symbolism, which always provided Yeats with a stable hierarchy by reference to which he was protected from the violence of his desire to overthrow all order.

The ends of the earth are swept by the border of his Garments of Flame—from Him all things proceed and unto Him all things return. Therefore, we invoke Him. Therefore, even the banner of the East falls in adoration of Him.[48]

But at least once in *The Wind among the Reeds* the guarded door of the Supernal Eden does swing open. In 1896 Yeats published in the *Savoy* "Two Love Poems," of which one was "The Travail of Passion." [49] Whatever the general literary consequences of Yeats' sexual episode with Olivia Shakespear, it provided him with the motive for a poem representing the union, insofar as that was possible in Yeats' mind, of the upper and lower elements of reality.

THE TRAVAIL OF PASSION

When the flaming lute-thronged angelic door is wide;
When an immortal passion breathes in mortal clay;
Our hearts endure the scourge, the plaited thorns,
    the way
Crowded with bitter faces, the wounds in palm and
    side,

> The hyssop-heavy sponge, the flowers of Kedron stream:
> We will bend down and loosen our hair over you,
> That it may drop faint perfume, and be heavy with dew,
> Lilies of death-pale hope, roses of passionate dream.[50]

Despite its biographical motive, the event which this poem records is the entrance into mortality of the immortal Moods by the process of incarnation. The origin of all real passion from the point of view of this poem is in eternity, and man truly loves only by the consent and participation of what he is not, that is, only "When an immortal passion breathes in mortal clay." The experience of love is an agony, like the crucifixion, the end of which is the death and consequent purification of the lover. This basic situation is described in conceptual terms in the Yeats-Ellis *Blake:*

Therefore when the Imagination enters experience to turn it into symbol and release the mind from its domination, that is to say when Christ is born of Mary, he puts on, through his maternally derived portion, a body for the express purpose of putting it off.[51]

In this construction Christ is the imagination which enters "mortal clay" for the purpose of purifying it, rendering it symbolic. In "The Travail of Passion" the Supernals, which are the imagination, become Christ. The specific mood of emotion by which the relation of higher and lower is symbolized is "Passion," which connotes both ultimate suffering and intense sexual feeling. In a story, also published in 1896, Yeats rehearsed the basic predicament of this poem in a more specific context. Costello the Proud is one of Yeats' early heroes, one of his hawk-headed men, for whom the effort to consummate love in this world is little more than a painful discipline preparing them for the love which is not compatible with life.

He was one of those ascetics of passion who keep their hearts pure for love, or for hatred as other men for God, for Mary and for the saints, and who, when the hour of their visitation arrives, come to the Divine Essence by the bitter tumult, the Garden of Gethsemene, and the desolate Road ordained for immortal passion in mortal hearts.[52]

The real motive of Costello's love was his desire to merge with the Divine Essence, and the hour of its consummation was the hour of death. Then and then only "the flaming lute-throated angelic door is wide." The speakers of this poem are the Supernals themselves, "The Everlasting Voices," which now render explicit the terrible demands in the face of which humanity must learn to put off fear or remain forever isolated from its supreme identity.

One of Yeats' retrospective comments on his early use of the rose symbol is that "the quality symbolized by the rose differs from the Intellectual Beauty of Shelley and Spenser in that I have imagined it as suffering with man and not as something pursued and seen from afar." Despite these protestations Yeats' sense of the Ideal was in the nineties something "pursued and seen from afar"; [53] but he is right in saying that it included a factor which participated in the suffering it enforced. Yeats also suggests that this was a conception characteristic of his generation and in this he is right also. In "The Travail of Passion" it is hard not to feel that the sufferers of lines three, four, and five are in some sense quite different from the comforters of lines six, seven, and eight. Yeats had conflated the roles of the suffering Christ and the consoling Marys without rendering them quite identical. For the general notion that the Ideal is crucified when the artist suffers on its behalf Yeats had the authority of George Russell, who declared that "those who were of the hosts of Beauty wore each one a crown of thorns on his brow." [54] For the image of Christ comforting those who suffer on his behalf he had the very striking confirmation of Burne-Jones' "The Merciful Knight (Fig. 7). The comfort which the Supernals administer is Yeats' symbol here of the sexual relation, and that relation is conceived by him in this period in pregenital terms. As in Blake's plate of the reunion of soul and body the Beloved ministers delight from above. But in contrast to Blake, Yeats emphasizes the protective and compassionate aspect of the relation, so that the care of the Beloved effects a shrouding of the sufferer, a withdrawal of the mind from the real world, which in its imperfection is the conventional crucifixion of the aesthete.

The importance of this posture is emphasized by the fact that in other poems Yeats attempts to reverse the relationship, to make up the desired role out of his own heart lest he be destroyed by a world in which it is absent. In "Aedh Tells of the Rose in His Heart" [55] the poet yearns to destroy the nature of things in order to create a place where Beauty will no longer suffer; in "Aedh Pleads with the Elemental Powers"[56] he undertakes to mitigate the violence of elemental forces who have utterly usurped the Beloved and made it impossible for her to help him. The curious sixth line of "The Travail of Passion" is itself an ironic veiling or mitigation of the suffering which is the subject of the poem. In later versions, as we have noticed, "hyssop," which is a conventional decadent orientalism, becomes "vinegar"; Kedron is the garden where in the Gospel of Saint John Jesus was betrayed.[57]

Yeats used the Tarot pack constantly during the nineties and after; in the Golden Dawn he learned that the Hanged Man signifies the submergence of the higher in the lower in order to sublimate the lower.[58] Further, the Golden Dawn had required him to place himself exactly in the position of the Hanged Man. In 1893 he underwent the ceremonial initiation of the grade Adeptus Minor (5–6), the first grade of the inner order corresponding to the lowest of the two upper sephirothic triads. This ceremony, which has been described at length by Virginia Moore, required that the aspirant be bound to the cross and there recite an elaborate oath avowing humility, secrecy, and purity.[59] When released from the cross, he received symbolically the stigmata, and only then was he allowed to penetrate the mysteries of the vault and the *pastos*, the tomb of Father Rosencross guarded by the sword and image of God, which Yeats identified with the imagination itself.[60] These were the conditions under which the imagination in its absolute form was to be sought by Yeats in the nineties, and it is to his consummation that "The Everlasting Voices" calls the artist.

The last line of "The Travail of Passion" describes the mortal lovers who have initiated the cosmic drama of these poems. The lily "of death-pale hope" is the male predicament; the rose of "passionate dream" the female. In *The Shadowy Waters*, which Yeats elaborated concurrently with *The Wind among the Reeds*, the lily is embroidered on the breast of Forgael and the rose on the bosom of Dectora. In the curious emotional dialectic of *The Wind among the Reeds* the rose is a creation of the lily, the woman is that of which in the ideal sense the poet passionately dreams. To become worthy of her he must become morally competent of the demands of his own imagination. In the introduction to *The Shadowy Waters* Yeats asks of "the immortal, proud, high shadows" whom his myth presents to him,

> Is Eden far away, or do you hide
> From human thought, as hares and mice and coneys
> That run before the reaping-hook and lie
> In the last ridge of the barley? Do our woods
> And winds and ponds cover more quiet woods,
> More shining winds, more star-glimmering ponds?
> Is Eden out of time and out of space? [61]

The answer that these poems give is unequivocal. Eden is in the self; the only proper metaphor of that self is the timeless and absolute Ideal; the only moral act equivalent to the greatness of the self so conceived is death. From the profundity of the inwardness of this book there is no way out but up, and after the nineties Yeats must be said to have ceased to be a mystic and become a philosopher. But the greatness of the speaking voice which finally emerged would have been inconceivable without this prior confrontation. Yeats was the last English poet to confront the ideal basis of poetry directly. What later poets could not in any real sense imagine, he could with some right mourn for.

Chapter VI

The fiery soul, pure as clear gold, and tested in the fire of God, is the husband of the noble *Sophia*. . . . If the tincture of the fire is perfectly pure, then will Sophia be united with it, and thus *Adam* receives again the most noble bride that was taken away from him during his sleep. . . . But how the bride receives her groom in his clear and bright fire-quality, and how she gives him the kiss of love, this will be understood only by him who has been at the marriage of the Lamb. To all others it will be a mystery.–Boehme, *Mysterium Magnum*

3. The cover of *The Wind among the Reeds*. (Reproduced through the courtesy of George Allen & Unwin)

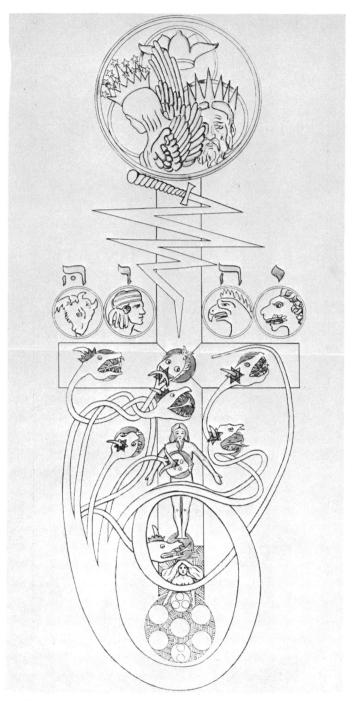

4. The altar glyph of the postlapsarian world in the ritual of the
Golden Dawn. (From Israel Regardie, *The Golden Dawn*, 1937–40)

The Triplicities of Fire
Aedh, Hanrahan,
and Michael Robartes

THE conclusive act in the creation of a tradition is the capacity to serve it. In his *Reveries* we find Yeats as a young man struggling with his father toward a tolerable definition of the voice of the artist. His description is not without pathos. Yeats had been reading in a newspaper "verses describing the shore of Ireland as seen by a returning, dying immigrant." He says, "My eyes filled with tears and yet I knew the verses were badly written—vague, abstract words such as one finds in a newspaper."

They had moved me because they contained the actual thoughts of a man at a passionate moment of life, and when I met my father I was full of the discovery. We should write out our thoughts in as nearly as possible the language we thought them in, as though in a letter to an intimate friend. We should not disguise them in any way; for our lives give them force as the lives of people in plays give force to their words. Personal utterance, which had almost ceased in English literature, could be as fine an escape from rhetoric and abstraction as drama itself.

At this moment the poet had discovered a conception of style consonant with his natural and freely expressed self-image. His father, the portrait painter, would not sanction in his son the expression of emotion through direct self-representation.

But my father would hear of nothing but drama; personal utterance was only egotism. I knew it was not, but as yet did not know how to explain the difference. I tried from that on to write out of my emotions exactly as they came to me in life, not changing them to make them more beautiful.

"If I can be sincere and make my language natural, and without becoming discursive like a novelist . . . ," I said to myself, "I shall, if good luck or bad luck make my life interesting, be a great poet; for it will no longer be a matter of literature at all." Yet when I reread those early poems which gave me so much trouble, I find little but romantic convention, unconscious drama. It is so many years before one can believe enough in what one feels even to know what feeling is.[1]

The young Yeats was certainly able to feel and "know what feeling is," but the pre-emptive definitions of art imposed by his father drove him, as he explains, into secrecy. The personae of Yeats' early poetry (Kanva, Nicholas Flamel, Owen Ahearne, Aedh) are at the farthest remove from true dramatic occasions. They are deliberately the very opposite of the kind of persons his father recommended as proper poetic speakers. They are occult in the sense in which the profoundly personal is occult. They represent the creative in the self, the anonymous passions of inner being, acting out in hidden forms unconscious dramas of emotion in relation to art and experience.

In another sense, however, these flame selves are a revelation, obscure and unaccommodating because direct, of an enormous moral ambition with which the young man informed a poetry that seemed even to the poet himself at fifty merely "romantic conventions." They are the psychic components of the universal red man, the cosmic Adam, a magnificent anthropomorphic world picture of man as the totality of the real and of the real in man as the capacity to feel emotion. In the period of *The Wind among the Reeds* Yeats was continually secreting accounts of his predicament in the interstices of his pseudo-historical fantasies:

Joachim of Flora acknowledged openly the authority of the Church, and even asked that all his published writings, and those to be published by his desire after his death, should be submitted to the censorship of the Pope. He considered that those whose work was to live and not to reveal were children and that the Pope was their father; but he taught in secret that certain others, and in always increasing numbers, were elected, not to live, but to reveal that hidden substance of God which is colour and music and softness and a sweet odour; and that these have no father but the Holy Spirit.[2]

Yeats as a young man was among those elected not to live but to reveal. It is now our business to explore the allegory under which that revelation took place. The question was, "What self-image should the poet-messiah of the new order of reality entertain, what man is competent to speak the ultimate word and at last become the accepted lover of the Absolute?" Over and over again Yeats sought the proper surrogate: Kanva, Nicholas Flamel, Owen Aherne, King Goll, Aedh, Michael Robartes, the Hawk-Headed King, the Virgin's Jester, Owen O'Sullivan. None of these figures are truly individuated because each is designed to symbolize Man at the center of his reality. None is intended to be anyone in particular because all are essays toward the image of the ultimate, creative inner being, the self as flame.

The reader, for obvious reasons, is not greatly helped by Yeats' deliberately evasive explanations:

These are personages in "The Secret Rose"; but, with the exception of some of Hanrahan's and one of Aedh's poems, the poems are not out of that book. I have used them in this book more as principles of mind than as actual personages. It is probable that only students of the magical tradition will understand me when I say that "Michael Robartes" is fire reflected in water, and that Hanrahan is fire blown by the wind, and that Aedh, whose name is not merely the Irish form of Hugh, but the Irish for fire, is fire burning by itself. To put it in a different way, Hanrahan is the simplicity of an imagination too changeable to gather permanent possessions, or the adoration of the shepherds; and Michael Robartes is the pride of the imagination brooding upon the greatness of its possessions, or the adoration of the Magi; while Aedh is that myrrh and frankincense that the imagination offers continually before all that it loves.[3]

A glance at *The Variorum Edition* will make clear that most of the poems assigned to this set of personae in *The Wind among the Reeds* were initially published under other titles or attributed to other speakers. But the contexts provided by the stories of *The Secret Rose* ("The poems are not out of that book") offer no stable identification. The chief hero of those stories as they appeared in periodicals was the eighteenth-century Jacobite poet Owen O'Sullivan, the Red. Yeats' treatment of him does not differ greatly from that of O'Daly and Walsh in their *Reliques of Irish Jacobite Poetry*.[4] According to Walsh, O'Sullivan's downfall resulted from his love of one Mary Casey, whom he celebrated in an English song called "Molly Casey's Charms." Yeats' O'Sullivan suffers similarly because of Molly Casey, who be-

comes in *The Secret Rose* Maive Lavell. To this figure Yeats assimilated various stories, such as "The Twisting of the Rope," which he
found in Douglas Hyde's *Love Songs of Connacht,* in Hardiman's *Irish
Minstrelsy,* and other popular Irish sources. The Jacobite poet in
eighteenth-century Ireland reflected, in his role as a champion of a
suppressed language and religion and as an adept in the secret names of
Ireland, much of Yeats' sense of his own predicament. But the persona
of O'Sullivan was too overt and subject to limitation by historical fact,
and the Jacobite position was, though colorful, excessively specific.

Between their first periodical publication and their subsequent appearance in *The Secret Rose,* to which Yeats refers the reader of *The
Wind,* the stories of O'Sullivan became the tales of Hanrahan. In
addition, many of the other proper names in these stories were transformed more or less obviously after the generalized pseudo-antique
manner of William Morris' romances. *Shawn Bui* becomes "Yellow
Shawn," Copes Mountains becomes "The Steep Place of the Strangers,"
Crug-na-Moonach becomes "The Rock of the Bogs," *Eri* becomes "The
Woods." [5] But the important thing about "Hanrahan" is that it is a
modern name without historical specificity in the mind of the Irish
reader.

Red Hanrahan is an imaginary name—I saw it over a shop, or rather part
of it over a shop in a Galway village—but there were many poets like him
in the eighteenth century in Ireland.[6]

Yeats makes the appropriate point with force and pride twenty years
later in "The Tower": "And I myself created Hanrahan." [7] Yeats
developed *The Secret Rose* by the process of rendering his poetic
surrogates subject to the mind, rather than to history. They are the
universal creative Moods, who have no father but the Holy Spirit.

THE TRIPLICITIES OF FIRE

Much comment has been devoted to Yeats' declaration "that 'Michael
Robartes' is fire reflected in water, and that Hanrahan is fire blown by
the wind, and that Aedh, whose name is not merely the Irish form of

Hugh, but Irish for fire, is fire burning by itself." [8] The structure on which Yeats built this identification is what in occult terms is called the Triplicities of the zodiac. These he found in a volume codifying all the mystic equivalences of the Golden Dawn called *777,* one of the unauthorized publications of the heretical Aleister Crowley released by him in 1909.[9] According to the Triplicities, each of the signs of the zodiac is associated with one of the four elements and each of the elements themselves exists in three additional elemental phases (corresponding to air, fire, and water) to make up the zodiacal number of twelve. The Triplicity of Fire is as follows with the Yeatsian equivalents:

Fire of Fire. Aries, Lightning—swift violence of onset.

Aedh

Air of Fire. Leo, Sun—steady force of energy.

Hanrahan

Water of Fire. Sagittarius, Rainbow—fading spiritualized reflection of the image.

Robartes [10]

The general characteristics of these three phases of the elements are described by Crowley as follows: "In each case the cardinal sign represents the birth of the elements, the Kerubic sign its life, and the mutable signs its passing over toward the ideal form proper to it, i.e., Spirit." [11]

Since Yeats applied this systematization to the poetic speakers of *The Wind* in most cases after the composition and publication of the poems to which they are assigned, it is hardly remarkable that it is difficult to determine the appropriateness in each case of the speaker to the poem. It is clear also that in the case of the "Air of Fire" Yeats differs from Crowley in conceiving it as a vexed and troubled condition. In "Aedh Pleads with the Elemental Powers" Yeats refers to "windy fire," which in fact reflects another form of reference to "The Triplicities." [12] Between 1893 and 1902 W. W. Westcott edited a series of magical and alchemical texts with the assistance of members of the Golden Dawn, including Florence Farr, called *Collectanea Hermetica,* in which the *Somnium Scipionis* appeared in 1894 as Volume V. There we read, "Thus the fiery signs, viz. Aries, Leo, and Sagittarius were all considered to transmit the influence of subtil fire, but in three different conditions—the Fiery, Watery, and Airy degrees of aetheric Fire." [13] In this way Yeats establishes his symbolic speakers in the flame self, giving them relations to universal causality by way of the zodiacal signs.

Aedh, the pseudo-heroic figure, is the birth of the element, Fire of Fire, fire burning by itself; Hanrahan, founded on the violent Jacobite O'Sullivan, is Air of Fire, the life of the element, or fire blown by the wind; Michael Robartes, the modern Rosicrucian adept, is the passing of the element over toward the Ideal, Water of Fire, the fading spiritualized reflection of the image. Fire is an attribute of the sidhe in its masculine form and of God the Father in the mythology of Eden. As a poetic speaker Yeats plays the Promethean role. He is the antinomian thief of fire for whom occult discourse serves as a form of protective hiddenness necessary to the poet who would set his face against the created world. In Law's edition of Boehme we read, "This folly caused King Lucifer to aspire, desiring to be an artist, and absolute Lord like the creator." [14]

Beyond their occult relations these figures have relevance to the myth of the birth of the Christ child. The birth of the Christ is for Yeats that rebirth of the self which is the consequence of initiation. This event is anticipated throughout his poetry, and it is this event that the imagination serves. In 1890 Yeats discussed with Katharine Tynan the possibility of a "little 'Mystery Play' on the 'Adoration of the Magi.' " He says, however, that he "could not get on without knowledge of the Catholic tradition on the subject." [15] The tradition which he did know was the theosophical tradition as represented by the writings of Madam Blavatsky, who had no hesitation in declaring that "the three magi, also denominated Kings, that are said to have made gifts of gold, incense and myrrh to the infant Jesus, were fire-worshippers like the rest, and astrologers; for they saw the star." [16] In Yeats' story "The Adoration of the Magi," privately printed in 1897, the Magi become "three brothers, who had lived in one of the western islands from their early manhood, and had cared all their lives for nothing except for those classical writers and old Gaelic writers who expounded an heroic and simple life." [17] In the presence of the prostitute who gives birth to the unicorn of the new dispensation one of them becomes possessed by Hermes and in a trance declares:

When the Immortals would overthrow the things which are today and bring the things that were yesterday, they have no one to help them, but one whom the things that are today have cast out. Bow down and very low, for they have chosen this woman in whose heart all follies have gathered, and in whose body all desires have awakened; this woman who has been driven out of Time and has lain upon the bosom of Eternity. [18]

This is the birth at which Aedh, Hanrahan, and Michael Robartes attend, and among them are distributed three of the postures of the imagination. The Hanrahan-O'Sullivan figure is assimilated to the adoration of the shepherds, representing "the simplicity of the imagination too changeable to gather permanent possessions," an appropriate description of the lowborn, gay, obsessed, itinerant hedge poet. Michael Robartes, the adept, becomes the Magus whom Madame Blavatsky associated with astrological practice and fire worship; his "possessions" are the Moods of the past which occult invocation makes available to the mind. Aedh is the sacrifice merely, "the myrrh and frankincense that the imagination offers continually before all that it loves."

AEDH

Of all the avenues inward which Yeats attempts to identify by means of the symbol of fire Aedh is the most complicated and fully developed. We have previously observed that Yeats' concept of history is founded on the succession of cycles in which the son alternately rules and is enslaved. In the version of "The Wanderings of Oisin" which Yeats published in 1889, Niamh and the poet-warrior, in the second book of their wanderings, encounter a maiden chained to the feet of two ancient eagles. She is enslaved to a demon. Approaching her, Niamh cries out, "I bring thee a deliverer." [19] The maiden inquires of Niamh whether or not he is a spirit, that is, supernaturally powerful. Upon receiving a negative reply, the maiden despairs:

> Then get ye
> Once more unto your flowers, for none may fight,
> With hope, mine enemy. As he by night
> Goes dropping from his eyes a languid light,
> The demons of the wilds and winds for fright
> Jabber and scream. Yet he for all his bold
> And flowing strength, with age is subtle-souled.
> None may beguile him, and his passion's cold.[20]

In Yeats' revision of "Oisin" for the collected *Poems* of 1895, the revision which created the poem we now have, the reply of the maiden is as follows:

> Neither the living, nor the unlabouring dead,
> Nor the high gods who never lived, may fright
> My enemy and hope; demons for fright
> Jabber and scream about him in the night;
> For he is strong and crafty as the seas
> That sprang under the Seven Hazel Trees,
> And I must needs endure and hate and weep,
> Until the gods and demons drop asleep,
> Hearing Aed touch the mournful strings of gold.[21]

This in contrast to the earlier version is the world of *The Wind among the Reeds*. The age of the tyrant has been suppressed as well as the bitter sexual suggestion of "passions cold"; the demon is still unconquerable by Oisin, but Aed is introduced who will herald his downfall. The following is the identity of Aed according to Yeats' note in his edition of 1895:

Aed. A God of death. All who hear his harp playing die. He was one of the two gods who appeared to Cuhoollin before his death, according to the bardic tale.[22]

Sometime between 1887 and 1895 Yeats had read or reread O'Grady's *History* and been struck by a passage dealing with this supernatural poet whose song meant death to the greatest of the Irish heroes. In his early treatment of Cuchullain Yeats does not, as later, identify with him, but rather makes war upon him as son upon father.[23] The predicament of Oisin and the captive maiden in the second book of "The Wanderings of Oisin," the book of "vain battles," is the same as that which we have described in Chapter V, "The Wars of Eden."

In O'Grady's *History* Cuchullain, having been informed that "Mac-Manar" will sing when his death is at hand, asks, "What is the form of MacManar?" O'Grady explains that the real name of MacManar is "Aed Orphid, Aed of the golden harp" and that his harp was given him by "Efeen, a fairy princess." Then in direct reply to the hero's question he says:

To thee and to those like thee he is young and very beautiful, and like a tender girl in feature and in limb. But they say that to others he appears like a demon, more frightful and horrible than aught, which the eye of man awake or in a dream hath seen. He carries a harp of pure gold; and against the melody of that harp they say that not even the gods themselves are secure, and it is said too that he is the strongest of the gods and in the end will slay them all, for he alone is really immortal, nor was he made so by eating of the herd of Mannanon, but he is immortal in his own right, and while things endure he will endure. And there is no singing so sweet as his and no music like the music of his harp, suggestive of things never seen or heard, beauty beyond all beauty, and nobleness to which the knighthood of earth may not be compared, and visions of love and bliss and of worlds fair and good.[24]

This is the Aed whom Yeats introduced in "The Wanderings of Oisin" as the ultimate agent of the destruction of the demon, which (like the cherubic guardians of the sephirothic woman) stands between Oisin and the liberation of the maiden. Aed is the poet-youth whose power exceeds that of "the unlabouring" dead "and the high gods," and whose immortality is his possession "in his own right" and not as a contingency of the immortality of the father god. He is "fire burning by itself." The Aed described by O'Grady is a positive image of the Aedh of *The Wind among the Reeds,* the consummation of whose love requires the destruction of the whole real world.

Aedh is by far the most important single poetic surrogate in *The Wind among the Reeds*. To him are assigned nine of the thirty-seven lyrics in that volume, while Hanrahan and Robartes have six between them. He is a god of death in the form of a poet obsessed with cataclysm. But the representation of him is always negative. He is referred to in the notes merely as the sacrifice, "the myrrh and frankincense that the imagination offers continually before all that it loves."

The source and development of this negative image of Aedh can be traced by observing that after the *Poems* of 1895 and before *The Wind among the Reeds* of 1899 Yeats never refers to this figure as Aed or Aedh but as *Aodh*. Aodh entered the world of "Celtic" discourse with Nora Hopper's *Ballads in Prose* (1894), where, as we have already seen (see p. 38), he offers himself as a sacrifice together with his beloved to the gods of Ireland who drain his life in order to augment theirs. After the appearance of Nora Hopper's story Yeats wrote his "The Binding of the Hair," in which he presents the bardic poet Aodh as the hopeless lover who dies at the hand of "The nations with ignoble bodies and ragged beards," and thereafter sings to his beloved as a disembodied head.[25] "Singing" in this context is a symbol expressing the completion of a sexual relationship the condition of which is the death of the poet-lover.

While chanting of ancient battles, the poet conceives his love lyric. Before he can utter it, the antagonists of his queen's people attack, and the poet is killed. The frontispiece of *The Secret Rose* in which "The Binding of the Hair" is the leading story is a vague picture by the poet's father representing the following situation:

Of a sudden, a sweet, tremulous song came from a bush near them. They hurried toward the spot, and saw a head hanging from the bush by its dark hair; and the head was singing, and this was the song it sung:

> Fasten your hair with a golden pin,
>   And bind up every wandering tress;
>   I bade my heart build these poor rhymes:
> It worked at them day out, day in,
>   Building a sorrowful loveliness
>   Out of the battles of old times.
>
> You need but lift a pearl-pale hand,
>   And bind up your long hair and sigh;
>   And all men's hearts must burn and beat;
> And candle-like foam on the dim sand,
>   And stars climbing the dew dropping sky
>   Live but to light your passing feet.

And then a troop of crows, heavy like fragments of that sleep older than the world, swept out of the darkness, and, as they passed, smote those ecstatic lips with the points of their wings; and the head fell from the bush and rolled over at the feet of the queen.[26]

The notion that the heart must found its love and its songs of love on Wordsworthian "battles of old time" is characteristic of *The Wind among the Reeds*. It means, in general, that all energy is in the past. Songs thus constructed are "sorrowful" because all real experience is as impossibly distant and as hopelessly lost as memory. There is the suggestion that the past of the mind experienced a vague and hopeless battle and that the process of composition is the process of coming by way of dream into significant relation to this past event. The music of heaven, Yeats was fond of suggesting, is a "continual clashing of swords." [27] Unlike the stereotype of the succoring woman who engulfs the lover with her odorous tresses, Dectira of "The Binding of the Hair" fastens them up, making emphatic the hopelessness of the poet's address and constructing a typical symbol of a condition of order beyond human achievement. In *The Secret Rose* we read that the poet's "tale, and its songs, . . . were like the foam upon the wave." Symbols expressing the condition of mortality are images of the dispersal and futility of energy, the "candle-like foam," and the wandering stars. Dectira, the queen, recapitulates the predicament of the captive Wisdom figure. Death attends this love and conquest. Whether it be the lover, the Beloved, or the cosmos which is destroyed, Aedh is a god of death.

This is a poetry the processes of which are represented as sunk below the agency of consciousness:

> I bade my heart build these poor rhymes
> *It* worked at them day out, day in.

The woman addressed is pearl pale, reflecting the affinities to death of the poetic impulse of which she is the presiding spirit. The convention of the poet mutilated in this fashion preoccupied Yeats late in life as well as in his youth and became the subject of "The King of the Great Clock Tower" and of "A Full Moon in March," where the head sings in the simple later style:

> I sing a song of Jack and Jill
> Jill had murdered Jack;
> *The moon shone brightly.*[28]

We will deal in another chapter with the fatal moon woman; from the point of view of this discussion it is sufficient to comment that the aspect of the poetic self here represented requires the complete separation of head and heart before the claims of the heart can be uttered. As John was served by Salome, so Aodh is served by the guardians of the white woman. And like John, Aodh is the prophet of a new historical cycle.

Yeats' effort to reorganize the basis of poetic authority in terms of a renewed relation to the inwardness led him to attempt to objectify the central principle of personal energy as flame. That flame can be seen flickering about his own name on the cover of *The Wind among the Reeds*. Of the three surrogates, Aedh, Hanrahan, and Robartes, Aed, the ancient name, led him closest to the impulse to die and to destroy which represents his dominant fantasy both about the sexual relation and about the poetic act. Hanrahan and Michael Robartes are redheaded men closer to the surface of history. Aedh is flame itself.

MICHAEL ROBARTES

Michael Robartes is assigned three poems in *The Wind among the Reeds*: "Michael Robartes Remembers Forgotten Beauty," "Michael Robartes Bids His Beloved Be at Peace," "Michael Robartes Asks Forgiveness because of His Many Moods." As the modern alchemical adept, the Mood of Michael Robartes is the third of the fiery Triplicities, "the passing over of the sign toward the ideal form proper to it." We first encounter him in "Rosa Alchemica," one of the stories Yeats wrote after leaving Dublin "in despondency." The speaker of "Rosa Alchemica" is a decadent aesthete cut from the cloth of Des Esseintes, who has created an imaginary culture but has withdrawn from "the call" which demands total commitment and is drifting in the direction of Catholic monasticism.[29] Michael Robartes appears to him as what we shall define in the next chapter as "the figure at the center."

I shuddered as I drew the bolt. I found before me Michael Robartes, whom I had not seen for years, and whose wild red hair, fierce eyes, sensitive tremulous lips, and rough clothes, made him look now, just as they used to do fifteen years before, something between a debauchee, a saint, and a peasant.[30]

Michael Robartes is the vehicle for Yeats' transformation in terms of occult doctrine of the concept of Celtic tradition. Above all he comes as a personification of "the call" to bring the protagonist of the story to initiation and thus liberate him from the twilight of the unborn. He recapitulates the call to reality of "The Hosting of the Sidhe," but in more generalized cultural terms:

"They have come to us; they have come to us," the voice began again; "all that have ever been in your reveries, all that you have ever met with in books. There is Lear, his head still wet with the thunderstorm, and he laughs because you thought yourself an existence who are but a shadow, and him a shadow who is an eternal god, and there is Beatrice, with her lips half parted in a smile, as though all the stars were about to pass away in a sigh of love; and there is the mother of the God of humility, He who has cast so great a spell over men that they have tried to unpeople their hearts that He might reign alone, but she holds in her hands the rose whose every petal is a god; and there, O, swiftly she comes! is Aphrodite." [31]

Michael Robartes possesses direct relation to the Moods; his will is perfected. In the end he dies by the hands of the enraged Irish fishermen whose orthodoxy will not countenance Robartes' heterodox beliefs. The violence of his death is much more explicit in the *Savoy* version of the story than in that published in *The Secret Rose;* but the conclusion is in both cases clear: Robartes' will is incompatible with life.

   "Michael Robartes Remembers Forgotten Beauty" was in the first instance assigned to "O'Sullivan Rua" and addressed to "Mary Lavell," but the specificity of the reference to the Irish hedge poet exceeded the broad relation which Yeats had developed to the spectrum of styles in *fin-de-siècle* England. The style assigned to Robartes does not lie in the direct line of development represented by the Aedh poems, many of which form the background of Yeats' later achievement, but rather represents a special style which he chose not to develop—"wavering, meditative, organic rhythms, which are the embodiment of the imagination that neither desires nor hates, because it has done with time and only desires to gaze on some reality, some beauty." [32] The text of "Michael Robartes Remembers Forgotten Beauty" is as follows:

When my arms wrap you round I press
My heart upon the loveliness
That has long faded from the world;
The jewelled crowns that kings have hurled
In shadowy pools, when armies fled;
The love-tales wove with silken thread
By dreaming ladies upon cloth
That has made fat the murderous moth;
The roses that of old time were
Woven by ladies in their hair,
The dew-cold lilies ladies bore
Through many a sacred corridor
Where such gray clouds of incense rose
That only the gods' eyes did not close:
For that pale breast and lingering hand
Come from a more dream-heavy land
A more dream-heavy hour than this;
And when you sigh from kiss to kiss
I hear white Beauty sighing, too,
For hours when all must fade like dew
But flame on flame, deep under deep,
Throne over throne, where in half sleep
Their swords upon their iron knees
Brood her high lonely mysteries.[33]

As in "The Binding of the Hair" all true energy lies in the past, and true emotion is not with respect to the present object but moves by way of the present object in the direction of the lost absolute reality.

And when you sigh from kiss to kiss
I hear white Beauty sighing, too.

The origin of the defeated world of "Beauty," which is here represented under images of a highly generalized but nonetheless distinctly chivalric character, is dream (the "more dream-heavy land" and "more dream-heavy hour").

The convention in which Yeats is working can be illustrated from Beardsley's "Under the Hill," his unfinished prose contribution to the *Savoy*, which appeared in the same issue with Yeats' "Rosa Alchemica" and constitutes a parody of it. The role of the alchemist in Yeats is played in Beardsley by the cosmetician, a figure much admired among those who, like Wilde and Symons, affected to prefer art to nature. Beardsley's hero, the Abbé Fanfreluche, one of the products of the cosmetician, is more overtly narcissistic than Yeats', and upon waking in the morning engages in a parodic reverie:

"How sweet it all is," exclaimed the Abbé, yawning with infinite content. Then he lay back in his bed, stared at the curious patterned canopy above him and nursed his waking thoughts.

He thought of the "Romaunt de la Rose," beautiful but all too brief.

Of the Claude in Lady Delaware's collection.

Of a wonderful pair of blonde trousers he would get Madame Belleville to make for him.

Of a mysterious park full of faint echoes and romantic sounds.

Of a great stagnant lake that must have held the subtlest frogs that ever were, and was surrounded by dark unreflected trees.

Of Saint Rose, the well-known Peruvian virgin. . . .

He thought of the splendid opening of Racine's "Britannicus."

Of a strange pamphlet he had found in Helen's Library, called "A Plea for the Domestication of the Unicorn."

Of the "Bacchanals of Sporion."

Of Morales' Madonnas. . . .

Of Rossini's "Stabat Mater" (that delightful *démodé* piece of decadence with a quality in its music like the bloom upon wax fruit).

Of love, and of a hundred other things.[34]

The Abbé Fanfreluche dreams not of nature but of art, or of nature in one of its many conventional Romantic transformations. Like Michael Robartes, though in a satiric sense, he is a master of the Moods which replace the real past of the poet and give up to memory instead a congeries of impersonal images which constitute his past insofar as he is an artist.

The structure of "Michael Robartes Remembers Forgotten Beauty" is fundamentally the same as that of Yeats' later superb poems which have the order of memory, such as "The Tower." In the early period the memory of the artist is the *anima mundi*. He has or will acknowledge no real inwardness. In the later poems the mind possesses real memories, mostly of men such as Dowson and Johnson, Mathers and Horton, who gave themselves up to the alienation of the unreal and grew momentous as a consequence. The predicament of the "white beauty," which Robartes comes to by way of the defeat of kings in forgotten nameless battles [35] and the destruction of mortal beauty by time in the conventional symbolism of the moth, is the same as that of the captive maiden whom we have discussed in connection with the Aedh surrogate. At the end of the temple corridors through which ladies for indefinite reasons bear the symbols of the son ("dew-cold" lilies) as offerings are the gods (in later editions God), who unlike mortals do not sleep ("Where such gray clouds of incense rose / That only the gods' eyes did not close."). The kisses of the mortal lovers create the ideal beloved who awaits the apocalyptic dawn. The last five lines of the poem are ambiguous. They represent the transcendental worshipers of Beauty in the form of the hierarchy of the angels who, as we have seen, are Yeats' way of referring to the cherubic guardians of the Heavenly Eden. All will "fade" at the anticipated Last Judgement but the celestial guardians. They remain:

> Flame on flame, deep under deep,
> Throne over throne, where in half sleep
> Their swords upon their iron knees
> Brood her high lonely mysteries.

Yeats is always least clear where the problem of conflict with the paternal phantasm is most acute. In "Rosa Alchemica" Robartes is quite explicit about the necessity of commitment in the form of submission to the Moods:

You have shut away the world and gathered gods about you, and if you do not throw yourself at their feet, you will always be full of lassitude, and of wavering purpose, for a man must forget he is miserable in the bustle and noise of the multitude in this world and in time; or seek a mystical union with the multitude who govern this world and time.[36]

The process in "Michael Robartes Remembers Forgotten Beauty" draws the mind inward through images of defeat to the archetype of the "white beauty," and then generates the image of the protective male hierarchy which arrests the process of self-possession and renders it futile by resisting the dissolution, through reverie, of the real. Submission as a form of commitment, the only form of commitment possible in the face of the demands of the sidhe, is an act which Yeats continually contemplates and is seldom capable of representing.

Yeats' capacity to conceive of an ideal poetic speaker exceeded his capacity to devise poems from the point of view of the projected role. Hence the importance for the student of seeking to define the role, even where the poems do not sustain it. The Robartes poems in general are characterized by the arrest of that cataclysm the consummation of which as fantasy we have observed again and again in the Aedh poems. But unlike the Robartes of "Rosa Alchemica" the Robartes of the poems, while suppressing the song of death which is the role of Aedh, is incapable of the commitment to hierarchy which is the ideal role of Robartes as a poetic surrogate.

Michael Robartes is "fire reflected in water." Water is the origin of images. Accordingly, two of the three poems assigned to Michael Robartes are constructed on the process of "reflection." "Michael Robartes Asks Forgiveness because of His Many Moods" [37] is another expression of the defeat of commitment, either to the self or the other. It is dominated by Yeats' diction of defeat of which we have already seen several examples. The determining words are expressive of arrested activity: "murmuring," "glimmering," "longing," "wandering." Motion within the poem is utterly defeated. The central address which the poet speaks for the Beloved despite its extended reference has no verb. Although the occult meaning of "reflection" is "the transmission of power," the sense in which that word is active in this poem is narcissistic, the evocation of the self-image. The poem is utterly self-referent. It is an act by the poet of self-comforting in the face of the indefinite oppression of the eternal, an act which we have alluded to in our discussion of "The Travail of Passion" (see p. 98). The suppressed narrative out of which this poem is an utterance is the same as that in "The Everlasting Voices," but here the indefiniteness of the emotion is increased by the exclusion of the cause of the disturbance.

The subject of "Michael Robartes Asks Forgiveness because of His Many Moods" is the failure of initiation. It was first published in 1895 in the *Saturday Review* under the title, "The Twilight of Forgiveness," and the first five and last three lines of the poem deal with the poet's fantasy of a comforter. The dynamic aspect of twilight is the access it affords to vision, the beginning of ideal self-definition; its negative aspect, here exhibited, is the mere confusion of the unborn.

The central portion of the poem consists of the words which the poet would have the Beloved speak. Their function is the definition of the disturbance which the poet feels:

> O Hearts of wind-blown flame!
> O Winds, elder than changing of night and day,
> That murmuring and longing came,
> From marble cities loud with tabors of old
> In dove-grey fairy lands;
> From battle banners fold upon purple fold,
> Queens wrought with glimmering hands;
> That saw young Niamh hover with love-lorn face
> Above the wandering tide;
> And lingered in the hidden desolate place,
> Where the last Phoenix died
> And wrapped the flames above his holy head;
> And still murmur and long:
> O piteous hearts, changing till change be dead
> In a tumultuous song.[38]

Michael Robartes here defines himself as a victim of the wind in the form of the *anima mundi*. Yeats uses a special diction, itself symbolic of the Romantic background, to suggest the futility of the reverie. The important thing about this diction is that in it there is no augmentation of the Romantic convention by an occult substratum and consequently no development. The poet is surrounded by gods but can commit himself to none. Being isolated from the significant aspects of his mind, he is also incompetent of the heroic aspects of the past.

In "Rosa Alchemica" Michael Robartes appears as a figure out of the center of energy and invites the speaker of the story to commit himself to the self-development of initiation by which he would come into a real relation to the gods who surround him. The speaker of the story fails of that commitment, and Michael Robartes as a consequence of his success is destroyed. Whatever Yeats' intention in this poem, its effect is negative. It declares that "the imaginary culture" only becomes real when the highest powers of the mind commit themselves to it. Death is the desired end, and the speaker of this poem, unlike the Robartes of the story, is unable to achieve that last transfiguration.

Change will end in a "tumultuous song," and for that song we must look elsewhere.

HANRAHAN

The poems assigned to Hanrahan are the easiest to identify in terms of the surrogate.[39] They were all initially associated with O'Sullivan and they all reflect the context in which Yeats imagined his peasant-poet. The poems of Robartes are pseudo-aristocratic and reproduce the environment and failure of Des Esseintes; the poems of Hanrahan are peasant, colored with references to the curlew, to Maurya, and to the Colleen. In contrast to the Robartes poems they are more or less overtly sexual, and they are love poems bearing traces of the Catholic symbolism which Yeats explored and abandoned repeatedly.

In order to provide a context for "Hanrahan Reproves the Curlew" we must turn to a story of "Fiona Macleod" (William Sharp) published in *The Dominion of Dreams* in 1899 and called "The Crying of the Wind."[40] The inevitable Aodh, having lost his beloved Oona at "the terrible Battle of the Field of Spears," now wanders obsessed by "the crying of the wind":

"In that crying I hear the baying of the two wolves whom ye saw. They are Death and Life. They roam the dark wood."
"Is there a wolf or hound here now, Aodh-of-the-Songs?"
Aodh answered nothing, for his head was sideway, and he listened as a hart at a well.
Barach the Blind rose and spoke.
"There is a white hound behind him, O King."
"Is it the hound Love?"
"It is the hound Love."
There was silence. Then the King spoke.
"What is it that you hear, Aodh-of-the-Songs?"
"I hear the crying of the wind."[41]

The evil on the wind is the emotional trace of the lost sexual relation.

HANRAHAN REPROVES THE CURLEW

O, Curlew, cry no more in the air,
Or only to the waters in the West;

> Because your crying brings to my mind
> Passion-dimmed eyes and long heavy hair
> That was shaken out over my breast:
> There is enough evil in the crying of the wind.[42]

In the early Yeats he who listens to the cry of the birds listens to the complaint of his own inwardness. The birds are the symbols of Aengus' perfect love that man desires but cannot emulate, or more explicitly: "The passions of Adam, torn out of his breast became the birds and beasts of Eden." [43] Like "The Everlasting Voices," "Hanrahan Reproves the Curlew" is a banishing gesture, an attempt to restore a protective condition of dream by committing the voice of the infinite emotion to the West, "the place of sunset" and "fading dreaming things." [44] The suggestion that the cry of the first line of the poem and the cry of the last pertain to two different kinds of love is born out by the complex situation which Yeats developed for Hanrahan in *The Secret Rose.*

Hanrahan is beloved of Cleena of the Wave, who is his "Leanan Sidhe," or fairy mistress. She induces him to invoke her, and he through the ritual obtains an image of her and falls in love with it. When she assumes human form in order to become his lover, he remains obsessed with her lost ideal image and rejects her. In her anger she curses him, and he is thereafter always unsuccessful with mortal women, whom he continues to desire, and forever unsuccessful also in his search for the divine love for which he cannot cease to yearn. The cry of the bird signifies the seduction of the lost Eden (the Wisdom figure) and the cry of the wind represents the obsession of the lost mortal love. This sexual paralysis and concomitant hopeless excitement is evident from time to time throughout Yeats' life and work, and the Hanrahan surrogate characteristically exposes it.

In the candor of his middle years Yeats wrote about the restlessness of Hanrahan in his "Beggar to Beggar Cried":

> "Time to put off the world and go somewhere
> And find my health again in the sea air,"
> *Beggar to beggar cried, being frenzy-struck,*
> "And make my soul before my pate is bare."

"And get a comfortable wife and house
To rid me of the devil in my shoes,"
Beggar to beggar cried, being frenzy-struck,
"And the worse devil that is between my thighs." [45]

In "The Twisting of the Rope," which Yeats composed initially in
1892, Hanrahan enters the house of a girl to whom he unsuccessfully
makes love muttering, "There is a devil in the soles of my feet." [46] The
reference to the worse devil is covertly supplied by a poem which, in
The Wind, became "Hanrahan Laments because of His Wanderings":

O where is the Mother of Peace
Nodding her purple hood?
For the winds that awakened the stars
Are blowing through my blood.
I would that the death-pale deer
Had come from the mountain side,
And trampled the mountain away,
And drunk up the murmuring tide;
For the winds that awakened the stars
Are blowing through my blood,
And our Mother of Peace has forgot me
Under her purple hood. [47]

Like all the poems of Hanrahan the subject of this is sexual excitement.
As in "The Travail of Passion" the force which symbolizes the emotion
is cosmic rather than personal and involves the usurpation by the
mortal lover of the same energy by which God created the world. In the
face of the sexual demand the poet yearns for the pregenital Wisdom
figure, here under the awkward guise of the Virgin. Simultaneously, he
invokes the apocalyptic "death-pale deer," which is to come from Slieve
Gullion and put an end to the arrested condition of the lover by
putting an end to the symbols of obstruction and confusion, among
which is the familiar "murmuring tide." [48] Slieve Gullion, according to
Yeats, is the place of Hanrahan's tomb; thence comes his death in the
form of an all-consuming hunger for reality.

Chapter VII

The hero is he who is immovably centered.–Emerson

Yet I am certain that there was something in myself compelling me to attempt creation of an art as separate from everything heterogeneous and casual, from all character and circumstance, as some Herodiade of our theater, dancing seemingly alone in her narrow luminous circle.–Yeats, *Autobiographies*

> *A little Indian temple in the Golden Age.*
> *Around it a garden; around that the forest.*
> —Yeats, "Anashuya and Vijaya"

But God is He having the Head of a Hawk.–*The Chaldean Oracles*

The Figure at the Center

Aherne, Finivarach, Mongan

THE speaker in *The Tables of the Law* (1897) describes Owen Aherne as follows:

The impression of his face and form, as they were then, is still vivid with me, and is inseparable from another and fanciful impression of a man holding a flame in his naked hand. He was to me, at that moment, the supreme type of our race, which, when it has risen above, or is sunken below, the formalisms of half-education and the rationalisms of conventional affirmation and denial, turns away, . . . from practicable desires and intuitions toward desires so unbounded that no human vessel can contain them, intuitions so immaterial that their sudden and far-off fire leaves heavy darkness about hand and foot. . . . For such there is no order, no contentment, no finality in this world.[1]

Yeats' "fanciful impression of a man holding a flame in his naked hand" derives from a passage in Browning's essay on Shelley in which he distinguishes the objective and the subjective poet; the following is a description of the latter:

He, gifted like the objective poet with the fuller perception of nature and man, is impelled to embody the thing he perceives, not so much with reference to the many below as to the one above him, the supreme Intelligence which apprehends all things in their absolute truth—an ultimate view ever aspired to, if but partially attained by the poet's own soul. Not what man sees, but what God sees—the Ideas of Plato, seeds of creation lying burningly on the Divine Hand—it is toward these that he struggles.[2]

Yeats' Aherne is not only the image of the "subjective poet" who attains his power by a relation to the Divine essence, but he is himself that God in whose hand the seeds of creation lie. Further, the divine poet whom Yeats embodies in Aherne is the apotheosis of the Irish ethnic identity ("the supreme type of our race"). Recourse to the subjectivity of which Ireland is the symbol always leads to the Idea, and the Idea drives the poet out of the world.

Yeats' early notion of the Absolute is personal. The vision of a figure who possesses true archetypal identity moves in many forms among his early stories and poems. Each of these is a version of "the figure at the center," the lost hero of Yeats' mind whose origins are the same as the universe itself. These figures are the possessors of Wisdom. There is a pathos about them which testifies to the total sincerity with which they were conceived. Of the three with which we here deal, it is Mongan who is the most momentous because his drama is the drama of poetic knowledge itself.

Yeats' preoccupation with his role as "the figure at the center" can be traced from the earliest recollections recorded in his autobiographies. Scott's *The Lay of the Last Minstrel,* he says, "gave me a wish to turn magician."[3] All things interested the young Yeats insofar as they pertained to his image of himself as "wise." Natural science, which seems to have been Willy Yeats' first passion, became for him in retrospect a symbol of ultimate authority. Some of his earliest reading was done in a "small, green-covered book, an account of the strange sea creatures the man of science had discovered among the rocks of Howth, or dredged out of Dublin Bay." "When I read it," he recalls, "I believed I was growing very wise."[4] He read Browning, who moved him "by his air of wisdom," and Thoreau, who inspired him likewise to conquer his "bodily desire" and live "seeking wisdom." We have already commented on his identification with those hungry figures Alastor and Athanase, Manfred and Prometheus. The most striking and pertinent additions to this body of alternately desperate and powerful self-images were the heroes of the philosophical romances of Balzac: *Seraphita,* with its image of the bisexual Swedenborgian saint; *La Recherche de l'absolu,* the portrait of a victim of the alchemical quest; *La Peau de chagrin;* and above all *Louis Lambert,* the image of the great man destroyed by his fidelity to an inward relationship. In a late comment Yeats goes so far as to say that the whole shift of intention between the early version of "Oisin" and the "Rosa Alchemica" was due to a passage in *La Peau de chagrin,* "but because I knew no other ally but Balzac I kept silent about all I could not get into fantastic romance." [5]

By contrast to Balzac, Yeats may be said scarcely to have read Pater, whose Marius is made quite explicitly to reject the orientation which Yeats was developing. Nothing could have been further from Yeats' instincts than Pater's account of the crucial moment in the development of his hero:

[Marius] might have fallen prey to the enervating mysticism, then in wait for ardent souls in many a melodramatic revival of old religion or theosophy. . . . But it was to severer reasoning, of which such matter as epicurean theory is born, that, in effect, he now betook himself. Instinctively suspicious of those mechanical *arcana,* those pretended "secrets unveiled" of the professional mystic, . . . for Marius the only possible dilemma lay between the old ancestral Roman religion, now become incredible to him, and the honest action of his own unassisted intelligence.[6]

Pater, who invented Marius during the years of Yeats' adolescence, is referring specifically to Blavatsky's *Isis Unveiled* (1877), which was then becoming for Yeats evidence of the possibility of the identity to which he aspired. The real relation of Yeats to Pater, aside from the generalized climate of style in the *fin de siècle,* derived from the fact that Pater's Marius, Leonardo, and Pico were the products of transitional cultures like the Irish and communed with ancient sources of power as did the young Irishman for whom the active subsistence of an elder mythology beneath the cold ash of the contemporary dispensation seemed a matter of everyday experience.

Throughout the nineties Yeats came to be known in the occult subcultures as D[emon]. E[st]. D[eus]. I[nversus]., a title which he found in the first volume of Blavatsky's *The Secret Doctrine.*[7] Not only is the demonic or satanic role godlike, but it is in fact an aspect of god himself. According to Madame Blavatsky the wars in heaven were unreal. The Absolute did not in fact extend itself into division, and it is the everlasting self which is the binding dynamism in the universe.

One cannot claim God as the synthesis of the whole Universe, as Omnipresent and Omniscient and Infinite, and then divorce him from evil. As there
is far more evil than good in the world, it follows on logical grounds that
either God must include evil, or else surrender his claims to absoluteness.
The ancients understood this so well that their philosophers—now followed
by the Kabbalists—defined evil as the lining of God or Good: *Demon est
Deus Inversus,* being a very old adage. Indeed evil is but an antagonizing
blind force in nature; it is *reaction, opposition,* and *contrast. . . .* There is
no *malum in se:* only the shadow of light, without which light would have
no existence. . . . Everywhere the speculations of the Kabbalists treat of
Evil as a force, which is antagonistic but at the same time essential to
Good, giving it vitality and existence, which it could not have otherwise.[8]

The *Demon* has the same right to an absolute identity within the
order of things as the *Deus;* in terms of the Deus-Demon dynamism
the very existence of God is contingent on the existence of the demon.
The role of the demon is "reaction" and "opposition," and its gift to the
real is "vitality." As we have seen, this is the role of the poet in Yeats'
fantasy and this was the identity which occult discourse allowed him at
once to assume and to conceal. It was a dangerous role, and it was in
this role that Yeats cast himself as the poet-lover of Wisdom.

In the section of *The Secret Rose* called "The Wisdom of the King"
(when it first appeared in Henley's *New Review* in 1895 it was called
simply "Wisdom"), Yeats records the birth of the wise youth with
whom he identified himself. He is the son of a queen who died in
childbirth. To his cradle come the "crones of the grey hawk," who sing
over him with voices "like the wind blowing in the great wood." They
are the sidhe who have been hungry since men ceased to sacrifice at
their altars. They curse the prince with their hunger letting a drop of
their blood, "grey as the mist," fall on his lips. In this way they create
the demon. The hawk feathers which he grows instead of hair, like the
flaming tresses of Caolte, like the red hair of Hanrahan and Robartes,
and like the flame of Aedh, mark him as an aspect of God himself.
Thereafter he is Yeats' image of the figure seeking the center, and his
hunger is the mark of his identity.

The sidhe are the demonic phase of Yeats' God, as the pagan gods are
the hidden and violent aspect of the Christian deity. In the text of his

early poems Yeats generally exposes the negative aspect of his aspiration as *deus inversus,* sequestering the positive face of his infinite ambition to the occulted fantasy of the poetic speaker. Only in a single unreprinted story do we see Yeats in his positive role as the hero of achieved wisdom, as the *deus inversus* directly presented.

In 1896 Yeats published a story called "The Cradles of Gold" in a short-lived London periodical, the *Senate.*[9] The basic situation is that struggle for possession of the pale woman in the role of mother which is everywhere in Yeats' work of this period. The story takes place near Yeats' mother's birthplace "on one of the more Easterly of the Ox Mountains looking to the Sligo and Balina road." Whinny Hearne, having married one of the "violent and grim" Hearne brothers and given birth to a child, is gone among the sidhe.

She had been queer, distraught, low-voiced and pale-faced for the three years of their married life, and went often, and particularly when the moon was up, to the edge of the Lough and lingered there, whispering ancient songs to herself, and gazing out over the water. . . . One night she came in and said she had seen cradles of gold hanging between the trees and bushes on a little island that is under Sleuth wood.[10]

The principal figure of the story is Michael Hearne, Whinny's brother-in-law, who is solitary and surly "because of the many scars left by the fights at patterns and on fair days." Through a hole in the bone of a hare the veteran fighter, with the assistance of "the wise man of Cairns," gets a glimpse of Whinny "sweeping over the water among the Shee, tossing out her hair, and laughing at her image in the water." As is common in these stories, the abducted mother returns to nurse her mortal child. Michael waits for her and lays hold of her. She cries out:

"Let me go, Michael Hearne, for I am nurse to the child of Finivarach, the King, and it will cry if I do not go." [11]

Then Finivarach appears. We know him as the figure at the center by his flame crown and by the fact that he has drunk the mystical draught, of which Michael Hearne is now threatening to deprive him. The description has all the marks of Yeats' self-image. But now he is the god, competing with the mortal child for what might appease the hunger of the host and lessen their paleness. Finivarach enters.

"Did I not tell you to be silent that I might meditate upon the wisdom that Mongan raved out after he had drunken from the seven vats of wine. . . ?"

Finivarach, a tall person with a pale proud face and eyes which seemed to burn with some unquenchable desire, wearing a much-pointed and flame-like crown of red gold and looking all of fire in his straight robe of saffron, was standing in the door against the dark and vaporous blue of the lake. . . .

"I am Finivarach, the King, and understand many things that even the archangels do not understand and out of my knowledge bid you let her go. There are those in the world for whom no mortal kiss has more than shadowy comfort, nor the rocking of any mortal cradle a fragile music and she is of them. But now when the moon has crumbled a little longer, the last affection will die out of her heart and she will become a crowned flame dancing on the bare hills.[12]

This is Yeats' self-image, both pathetic and powerful, whose claim to strength is the wisdom which from childhood he had hoped would place him at the center of the universe. The gesture by which he attempts to dismiss Michael Hearne is the same which we have analyzed in connection with "The Everlasting Voices." It is this situation, an attempt to interpret the psychotic withdrawal which his mother suffered in her later years and a reflection of his response to the birth of his brother Robert, which excites the most passionate expression of Yeats' early poems.[13] The hero of the absolute endeavor is the spoiled child of the universe competing with the realities of time and physical limitation for acknowledgment of the cosmic centrality of his identity. But Michael Hearne, a trained fighter and named for the warrior archangel whom Finivarach exceeds in wisdom but not in strength, wins back the mother. In the sense of this loss Yeats allows "The Cradles of Gold" to come into *The Wind among the Reeds.*

The text of "A Cradle Song," later renamed "The Unappeasable Host," is as follows:

> The Danaan children laugh, in cradles of wrought gold,
> And clap their hands together and half close their eyes,
> For they will ride the North when the ger-eagle flies,
> With heavy whitening wings, and a heart fallen cold:
> I kiss my wailing child and press it to my breast,
> And hear the narrow graves calling my child and me.

> Desolate winds that cry over the wandering sea;
> Desolate winds that hover in the flaming West;
> Desolate winds that beat the doors of heaven, and beat
> The doors of Hell and blow there many whimpering ghost;
> O heart the winds have shaken; the unappeasable host
> Is comelier than candles before Maurya's feet.[14]

This poem, like others which we have analyzed, is divided between the mortal and immortal condition. The speaker, who is Whinny Hearne, has suckled both her own mortal child and also the children of the sidhe. She knows the distinction between time and eternity, and the terrible oppression and magnificence of the sidhe. In the story "The Cradles of Gold" this poem is given a complex context which expresses much of Yeats' deep sense of the extraliterary affinities of poetry.

Then she [Whinny] looked at the child . . . and pressed it passionately against her breast, and did this again and yet again, and then she laid it in the cradle, and began rocking the cradle and singing. He [Peter Hearne] recognized the air and words of "The winds from beyond the world," a very ancient cradle song, made for her only child by the wicked wife of that wizard Garreth, who rides hither and thither over the hills of Munster, awaiting the time when the shoes of his horse, now thin as a cat's ear, shall be worn through and the deliverance of Ireland be at hand. He listened with a shudder to the wild air, at whose sound all wholesome desires and purposes were thought to weaken and dissolve, and to the unholy words which pious mothers had ever forbid their daughters to sing.[15]

The effect of poetry is to induce the trance that loosens the bonds of reality. Further, this poetry is associated with the liberation of Ireland, which will come when the material culture that shoes the horse is worn away by the attrition of magical forces always violently at work. The reader overhears the poem as he would something occult and forbidden, something which does not belong to the order of God's world.

The children of the sidhe possess that autonomy of self-delighting energy which is only the possession of those who need no longer desire; hence their hearts have fallen cold, and Yeats assigns to the description of them the manic style which we have remarked in connection with "The Hosting of the Sidhe" and a metrically long line which exhausts the breath in speaking it. The apparition of the sidhe reminds the

mortal woman of death and elicits one of Yeats' extended and various
uses of the wind symbolism. The sidhe are the rising wind, and as
Michael Hearne awaits the apparition he does so in "that mysterious
stillness which falls upon the exterior when the interior world is about
to open its gates." The apparition of the sidhe is a mental event. The
wind from the inwardness, when conceived in relation to the conscious
mind, is characterized by the privations which it requires of consciousness, itself a symbol of mortality. From the point of view of mortality
it is "desolate," requiring either the total sublimation that would open
the "doors of heaven" or total reduction, the opening of "the doors of
Hell."

The last two lines of the poem are one of Yeats' many exercises in
irony or euphemism in referring to the sidhe.

> O heart the winds have shaken; the unappeasable host
> Is comelier than candles before Maurya's feet.

The meaning of these lines is that the presence of the host makes
impossible the desired relation to the symbol both of comfort and of
order which is embodied in Maurya, Gaelic for Mary. The presence of
the host invalidates the prayers of the mortal, symbolized by the
votarists' candles. The exclamation of awe embodied in these two lines
expresses the impossibility of drawing near to the Wisdom figure, an
impossibility which arises from the presence of the host, expressing the
superior potency of the pagan over the Christian symbol. The key word
is "unappeasable." The "wailing child" of the world competes with the
insatiable children of the host for the possession of the source of life
and is ultimately baffled by the complexity of the inwardness symbolized by winds which blow both East and West, both up and down,
frustrating by their conflict the transformation of mortal into immortal. Even as Finivarach, Yeats cannot command exclusive possession of
the source of the magical drink which would render him the only child
of the universe. Yeats conceives the alternatives of identity as total
actualization or total extinction, and Finivarach, like Aherne and Aedh,
are his attempt to project into reality the former possibility.

In his anger Finivarach cries, "Did I not tell you to be silent that I
might meditate upon the wisdom that Mongan raved out after he had

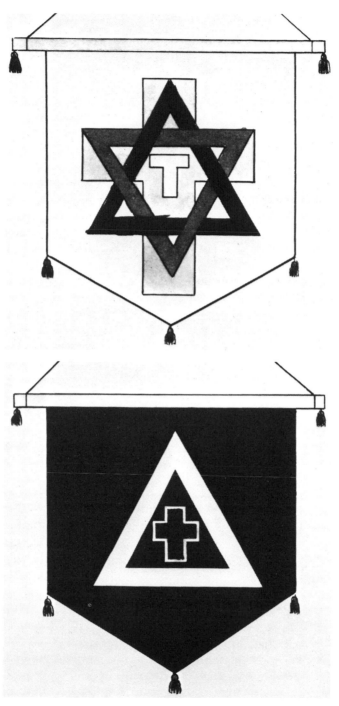

5. The Banners of East and West, symbols of the two twilights separating lover and beloved in "Aedh Hears the Cry of the Sedge." (From Israel Regardie, *The Golden Dawn,* 1937–40)

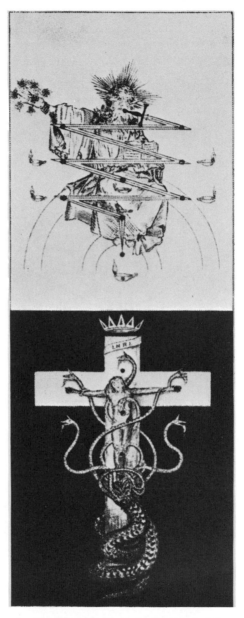

6. **The lid of the Pastos in the ritual of the**
Golden Dawn showing the paternal guardian
of Eden and the crucified son. (From Israel
Regardie, *The Golden Dawn,* 1937–40)

drunken from the seven vats of wine?" This Mongan, Yeats represents as reflecting the consequences of total insight. Mongan is Yeats' symbol of the achieved relation. Unlike the other surrogates which we have studied, Mongan retains in Yeats' writing his historical identity in the old Celtic poetry as "a famous wizard and king who remembers his past lives." [16] In "Mongan Laments the Change That Has Come upon Him and His Beloved and Longs for the End of the World" [17] Mongan meets the god of love directly as does no other figure in the drama of Yeats' early poetry. The result is both mournful and illuminating.

The poem which Yeats assigns to him and with which he concluded *The Wind among the Reeds* in 1899 is "Mongan Thinks of His Past Greatness."

> I have drunk ale from the Country of the Young
> And weep because I know all things now:
> I have been a hazel tree and they hung
> The Pilot Star and the Crooked Plough
> Among my leaves in times out of mind:
> I became a rush that horses tread:
> I became a man, a hater of the wind,
> Knowing one, out of all things, alone, that
>   his head
> Would not lie on the breast or his lips on
>   the hair
> Of the woman that he loves, until he dies;
> Although the rushes and the fowl of the air
> Cry of his love with their pitiful cries. [18]

Mongan drinks the "ale from the Country of the Young" and thereby comes upon his identity.

The symbol of absolute personal identity, the identity of the poet, is the knowledge of the past transformations of the self. Unlike the predicament of the speaker of the Robartes poems, who is only the victim of the past, Mongan is also a part of it. The history of the past of the self recapitulates the progressive degradation of man in time, and Mongan becomes successively the tree of life itself, a rush in a great hall of the middle ages trampled by horses, and finally the reed, man, whose oppression is the wind. In 1885 Mohini Chatterjee came to Dublin and introduced Yeats to the notion of metempsychosis as a formal concept, which was then reflected in his "Quatrains and Aphorisms" (1886), written in the style of William Watson's *Epigrams*, and his "Kanva on Himself" (1889).[19] But long before the appearance of Mohini Chatterjee in Dublin, Matthew Arnold had associated transmigration with the Celtic imagination, using as his source Lady Guest's translation of *The Mabinogion,* and it is in the chants of Taliesin and the "Song of Amergin" that the real analogies to Yeats' poem lie.[20]

Each time Taliesin is asked what he is, "whether man or spirit," he replies by recounting his past transformations. Arnold puts emphasis on Taliesin's boast: "I obtained my inspiration from the Cauldron of Ceridwen." [21] As with Mongan so also with Taliesin, the magical drink was the beginning of life. Ceridwen, who had borne an ugly and unpromising child to Tegid Velo, her husband, undertook to prepare for the infant a magic drink that would achieve his transformation.

So she resolved, according to the arts of the books of the Fferyllt, to boil a cauldron of Inspiration and Science for her son, that his reception might be honorable because of his knowledge of the mysteries of the future state of the world.[22]

Three drops of this "charmed liquor" are accidentally drunk by Gwion Bach, who is pursued by Ceridwen in the form of a hawk. He changes himself into a seed and is swallowed by Ceridwen, who has transformed herself into a chicken. She carries him for nine months and gives birth to a child who is Taliesin.

Taliesin's account of his previous incarnations is thus a recapitulation of the drama by which he came to be a man, and it is in this sense that Yeats is using the convention. At the end of his long account of his past states Taliesin sings:

> Then I was for nine months
> In the womb of the hag Ceridwen;
> I was originally little Gwion,
> And at length I am Taliesin.[23]

The descent of the self from its primal identity as the magical "hazel tree" to the condition of man "hater of the wind" is Yeats' account of his own sense of the personal transformations involved in the development of the mind from infancy to maturity. This is the knowledge which characterizes the artist. By drinking again of the Cauldron of the Inspiration of Ceridwen, the poet comes upon the irreversible

descent of his identity from the condition of the child who possesses
both himself and the universe unconsciously to the self-knowledge of
the adult troubled by the winds of sexual emotion.[24] The last act of
"the figure at the center" is the realization of the hopelessness of the
desire to recover the lost absolute relation to the breast of the mother,
of which he is reminded each time he experiences desire.

The ultimate act of consciousness is the realization of the irreversibility of time in terms of personal growth. Since time has deprived the
poet both of the personal integrity of the child and of the source of all
poetic inspiration, time, which entered the world with the creation and
which belongs to the dispensation of the father, must end. Either the
poet or the world must be destroyed, and in this poem Mongan anticipates his own death as the restoration of the relation to Ceridwen.

> I became a man, a hater of the wind,
> Knowing one, out of all things, alone, that his head
> Would not lie on the breast or his lips on the hair
> Of the women that he loves, until he dies.

Repeatedly in the later poems Yeats comes upon this infant self who is
"the figure at the center," the child of the romantic Idea, presided over
by Ceridwen, Maeve, Clooth-na-bare, Aefe, Cybele, or the Shan Van
Voght. In "The Hour before Dawn" (1914) the incomplete man, the
mature objectified sensibility ("A one-legged, one-armed, one-eyed
man") comes upon the infant identity in the cave of Cruachan, the
capital of ancient Connacht where Maeve nursed her nine children.[25]

> But while he fumbled with the stones
> They toppled over; "Were it not
> I have a lucky wooden shin
> I had been hurt"; and toppling brought
> Before his eyes, where stones had been,
> A dark deep hollow in the rock.
> He gave a gasp and thought to have fled,
> Being certain it was no right rock
> Because an ancient history said
> Hell mouth lay open near that place
> And yet stood still, because inside
> A great lad with a beery face
> Had tucked himself away beside

> A ladle and a tub of beer,
> And snored, no phantom by his look.
> So with a laugh at his own fear
> He crawled into that pleasant nook.[26]

The drunken sleeper is awaiting the Last Day, the last judgement of the imagination. From the rigors of this expectation the mature man turns away:

> The other shouted, "You would rob
> My life of every pleasant thought
> And every comfortable thing
> And so take that and that." Thereon
> He gave him a great pummeling.[27]

The posture of the poems of *The Wind* is the posture of the sleeper whose metaphor of impersonal consummation is death.

Yeats acquired O'Curry and D'Alviella in his preparation for the Irish cult. From D'Alviella came his sanction for the association of the magical hazel tree of the Irish with the Tree of Life.[28] This was one of the symbols which, like Clooth-na-bare, Yeats was concerned with expanding. His note to the poem in question states that "the Hazel tree was the Irish tree of Life or of Knowledge, and in Ireland it was doubtless, as elsewhere, the tree of the heavens." This tree which "had sometimes the stars for fruit" and which bears at its top the lotus or the rose, the flowers of life, is the primal condition of man, inhuman, comprehending in its identity both knowledge and life, mother and son. To the status of this symbol Yeats' hawk-headed youth attempts to come. There man is no longer at war with the world; the stars are part of his being; and the whole cosmos is comprehended in his nature. "Mongan Thinks of His Past Greatness" represents the realization of the impossibility of that identity.

Yeats is in search of a concept of grace. The ceremonial magic of the Golden Dawn promised to place him at the center of the universe by assimilating him to the tree of the *sephiroth*. The ultimate book, the characteristics of which we discussed in Chapter II, was to have provided the power of absolute transformation. The pure poem, with its scorn of contingency, was to have been the sign. The function of the poem was the symbolization of the self leading to a restoration of a lost relation to the timeless origins of the human psyche. But neither alchemy, nor ceremony, nor poetry provided the process of transformation. The search for the reality at the center, being unmediated, remained futile. The figure at the center which Yeats attempted to project in the surrogates of Aedh, Hanrahan, Michael Robartes, Finivarach, and Mongan was to be the poet. But Yeats could not utter the poem which belonged to this authority. Eternity was incompatible with identity. The poem proved to belong to the real world. Only with the acknowledgment of the reality of the self in time could the world and the poem expand in a productive mimetic relation one to the other.

One of the meanings of "decadence" is the attempt to internalize the totality of the real. Although the decadent abandoned time as an environment in which the value of the self could emerge, he had no stable concept of eternity. The withdrawal from the actual left the poet with no viable relation to the real, except by way of poetry itself; and if poetry was to serve as a daemonic or mediating phenomenon it required to be liberated from the stress of the Absolute.

Chapter VIII

I cast off traditional metaphors and loosened my rhythm, and recognizing that all criticism of life known to me was alien and English, became as emotional as possible but with an emotion which I described to myself as cold. It is a natural conviction for a painter's son to believe that there may be a landscape that is symbolical of some spiritual condition and awakens a hunger such as cats feel for valerian.–Yeats, *Autobiographies*

> For if I triumph I must make men mad.
> —Yeats, "The Tower"

The Example of Majesty

Symbolism and Didacticism

THE correlative of Yeats' enormous ambition for the poetic speaker was the equally enormous demands which, in his view, poetry makes on reality. Despite his protestations of affiliation to an aesthetic and symbolist culture in reaction against the explicit didacticism of Victorianism, the whole moral import of the "epic-lyric" genre as Yeats constructed it in *The Wind among the Reeds* would be lost if it were not understood that Yeats' ambition for art lies directly in the tradition of Ruskin and constitutes a reconstruction rather than an obliteration of the Victorian concern for the relations of beauty to civilization. For the didactic rhetoric which in his mind seemed to vitiate the fundamental poetic qualities of Shelley, Wordsworth, Tennyson, and Arnold, Yeats substituted a prophetic rhetoric founded on different aesthetic principles, but tending to the same end. The whole array of Yeats' sources, which constituted for him the very soul of history, Neoplatonism, alchemy, occultism, and ceremonial magic, without being ethical in the categorical sense, are fundamentally and exclusively moral. While Victorianism attempted to reach man by rational persuasion, the Yeatsian ethic undertook to transform him by awakening his unconscious powers. Beauty was the paradigm of human reality, and the loss of it to the world meant the loss of the possibility of salvation.

The Horatian categories of the relation of art to the mind, *prodesse* and *delectare,* define in a general way Yeats' sense of the possible effect of art. Victorianism emphasized the artistic *prodesse,* or the rational and instructive aspects of poetry. Symbolism was founded on *delectare,* or the delight of the artistic experience. In the process of the reduction of the effect of poetry to the experience of delight the category of instruction was not lost. Rather it was subsumed under the category of Beauty, which is the stimulus in response to which delight arises in the mind. Since the rational man was not in Yeats' mind the real man, true instruction could only take place at a level of being other than the understanding.

"The Blessed" derives its special place in Yeats' early work as an image of the true pedagogic community. Neither Cumhal nor Dathi possesses the condition of being of the drunken musician, nor does Dathi articulate the nature of that being, and yet initiation takes place. Blake's Proverb of Hell, "The tigers of wrath are wiser than the horses of instruction," without being a didactic statement, is none the less part of a prophetic rhetoric the function of which is the transformation of sensibility. The notion of Art for Art's Sake proposes a self-referent system in which energy circulates endlessly without outlet. That apparently fruitless circularity is reflected in the structure of many of the poems of *The Wind among the Reeds.* The positive aspect of this wholly internal process is the achievement of a superior relation to the inwardness, an archetypal self-finding, a reascent to Eden in the self which takes place when the mind, like the poem, abandons all illegitimate relations to the external world.

In the occult construction the imagination is the perfected instrument of the will, and correlatively the instrument of the perfected will. The alchemical transformation of matter is a contingency of the moral condition of the alchemist, demanding perfection of the worker before perfection of The Work becomes possible. In Agrippa and the writers of the Christian cabala, among whom in Yeats' mind Henry More was the most prominent, there is a convention which vividly illustrates the occult sense of the powers of the imagination. According to what More calls the Signatures of the Foetus, the mother's imagination shapes the infant in the womb. Hence come genetic monstrosities, both in men and animals. The significant experience of the mother is generally one of fear; therefore chickens are born with hawk's heads and men in the form of terrifying animals.[1] This convention attracted Yeats; hence

Seanchan in "The King's Threshold" utters the following threat with much tradition to enforce it:

> If the Arts should perish,
> The world that lacked them would be like a woman
> That, looking on the cloven lips of a hare,
> Brings forth a hare.[2]

With even more force and with the increment of the biblical story Seanchan's pupil makes the same point:

> I said the poets hung
> Images of the life that was in Eden
> About the child-bed of the world, that it,
> Looking upon those images, might bear
> Triumphant children.[3]

In this way the imagination is powerful beyond rational discourse, and the poem by its relation to Beauty transforms the world virtually as from the womb. It was in this sense, though without so concrete a tradition, that Ruskin, Rossetti, Whistler, and Wilde cared for the aesthetic aspects of the physical environment and attempted to be worthy of the cathedrals and white porcelain which Beauty, according to their various preferences, inhabited. Further it was in this way that aristocracy served the mind of the people; and Yeats' later brutal interest in eugenics follows directly from the occult tradition.[4]

Symbols in their nonliterary form had for Yeats a power over the mind analogous to hypnotic suggestion, because they communicated with the real motive forces of personality. On the analogy of the magical Yeats constructed the effectiveness of the literary symbol. Hence the necessity of unifying the cultural environment. Just as the man who imagined his bed protected by four great animals at its four corners would be safe as long as he sustained the image, so the artist who was capable of imagining a unity of culture could in fact create it. Even in physical matters the perfect imagination was effective to save the imperfect. One evening in the nineties George Pollexfen was ill, and the doctors were of no use.

I sat down beside his bed and said, "What do you see, George?" He said, "Red dancing figures," and without commenting, I imagined the cabbalistic symbol of water and almost at once he said, "There is a river running through the room," and a little later, "I can sleep now." I told him what I had done and that, if the dancing figures came again, he was to bid them go in the name of the Archangel Gabriel. Gabriel is the angel of the moon and might, I considered, command the waters at a pinch.[5]

Yeats' prose is full of his experimentation, much of it trivial, with the power of mind to command mind through symbols.[6] Since the reality to which the symbol corresponds lies outside the mind, the function of the magical practitioner and of the poet is to render the mind susceptible to the highest influences of which it is capable.

The Moods are the "mothers" or "creators" of nations, and the poet is their priest, the conduit by which they become effective in the world. The poet as daemonic servant of the Moods (though he does not quarrel with humanity as did Wordsworth and Tennyson) nonetheless commands, by the images which he makes available to the world, its transfiguration. Art creates reality, and the God in whose image art creates the world is a terrible and passionate being.

The ambition of Yeats for his lyric verse cannot be better illustrated than by a passage which we have already cited in part in another context:

A little lyric evokes an emotion, and this emotion gathers others about it and melts into their being in the making of some great epic; and at last, needing an always less delicate body, or symbol, as it grows more powerful, it flows out, with all it has gathered, among the blind instincts of daily life, where it moves a power within powers, as one sees ring within ring in the stem of an old tree. This is maybe what Arthur O'Shaughnessy meant when he made his poets say they had built Nineveh with their sighing; and I am certainly never certain, when I hear of some war, or of some religious excitement, or of some new manufacture, or of anything else that fills the ear of the world, that it has not all happened because of something that a boy piped in Thessaly.[7]

Virtually all the poems of Yeats' early years, either explicitly or regarded from the point of view of their sources, are cosmological in scope. They are "epic-lyrics" which assert that the whole nature of things is involved in human feelings. True emotion is a cosmic event, and there is no trope or image large enough to express the real nature of humanity except eternity. The function of the lyrics of *The Wind among the Reeds* is to provide an example of the real majesty of the human symbol, and thereby to set man at war with all trivial images of himself.

The lyric genre, which Yeats practised even while writing drama, troubled him by its incompleteness as a total statement about reality. In his early reading Yeats was always in search of the man speaking, the human symbol who would provide a unified authority for poetic statement by the example of his own commitment to the images he proposed. Of Browning he writes in 1890:

I like to think of the great reveries of the Pope in *The Ring and the Book,* with all its serenity and quietism, as something that came straight from Browning's own mind, and gave his own final judgement on many things. But nearly always he evades giving a direct statement by what he calls the dramatic method. It is hard to know when he is speaking or what is only one of his *dramatis personae.* An acquaintance of mine said once to him: "Mr. Browning, you are a mystic." "Yes," he answered, "but how did you find out?" [8]

In sorting out his tradition, both Irish and English, Yeats constantly listened with the ear of a metaphysician for the voice of a speaker whose authority was established in a commitment to a total image. Of Allingham he writes in 1888 that he lacks "central seriousness," that he is the poet of "isolated artistic moments," [9] and therefore disqualified from the burden of lyric prophecy.

With respect to the lyric genre Yeats had two attitudes. First of all, the lyric was the sign of that return into the self which was the only avenue by which the mind could recover its relation to the Idea.

A new poetry, which is always contracting its limits, has grown up under the shadow of the old. Rossetti began it, but was too much of a painter in his poetry to follow it with a perfect devotion; and it became a movement when Mr. Lang and Mr. Gosse and Mr. Dobson devoted themselves to the most condensed of lyric poems, and when Mr. Bridges, a more considerable poet, elaborated a rhythm too delicate for any but an almost bodiless emotion, and repeated over and over the most ancient notes of poetry, and none but these. [10]

The process of contraction was necessary to rid the lyric of the irrelevant relations which rendered Browning, Tennyson, Swinburne, and even Shelley impure. Symons had brought from France Mallarmé's notion that there would never be again, and perhaps had never been, a long poem. As metaphysics was dying in England, so was the poem of the whole view. Yeats could not rest in such a position.

I think there will be much poetry of this kind [lyrics], because of an ever more arduous search for an almost disembodied ecstasy, but I think we will not cease to write long poems, but rather that we will write them more and more as our new belief makes the world plastic under our hands again.[11]

But the epic (the *Odyssey* as interpreted by Porphyry is Yeats' example) remained beyond his scope. One of the functions of the later Vision is the adaptation of a total view of reality to the lyric genre. In the early period Yeats undertook to find within himself a speaker capable of "central seriousness" who could bear the tremendous moral burden of the meaning. From first to last, the only poetry which in Yeats' mind would serve culture in any way appropriate to the dignity of the poetic mode required as its foundation a totally intelligible world. The function of the poet was to create culture, and in doing so to make it possible for mankind through poetry to create itself.

In old age Yeats took to keeping birds. His letters and *Autobiographies* are full of descriptions of them, and especially of their capacity for nest building. In his later philosophical reading he had discovered that Henry More in defiance of Locke considered the birds' instinct in nest building to "prove the existence of the *anima mundi*, with its ideas and memories." [12] In constructing a myth of authority for his *A Vision*, Yeats not only resurrected his early images of absolute occult authority (Aherne and Robartes) but also invented his tale of John and Mary Bell. John Bell, being at leisure, had undertaken as an act of philanthropy to teach the cuckoo to build a nest. But he succeeded as little in awakening that stubborn and unteachable bird to its heritage in the soul of the world as Yeats did in awakening the Irish, of whom the cuckoo is a symbol. Yeats had hoped in making the stories of *The Secret Rose* and the poems for which they provide the matrix to augment the sensibility of Ireland by providing it with new examples of majesty.

Lady Gregory and I wanted a Gaelic drama, and I made a scenario for a one act play founded upon an episode in my *Stories of Red Hanrahan;* I had some hope that my invention, if Hyde would accept it, might pass into legend as though he were an historical character.[13]

But Yeats never taught Ireland to make her soul, and he was continually worried after 1916 that Ireland had caught from him, as Leda did from the bird-god, not knowledge but power in the form of meaningless violence.

This was a speculation not without foundation in Yeats' fantasy. When Aherne appears to the speaker of "The Tables of the Law," he does so as a prophet of the didactic role of art in its extreme form. The crucial discovery of Aherne was this:

That the beautiful arts were sent into the world to overthrow nations, and finally life herself, by sowing everywhere unlimited desires, like torches thrown into a burning city. This idea was not at the time, I believe, more than a paradox, a plume of the pride of youth; and it was only after his return to Ireland that he endured the fermentation of belief which is coming upon our people with the reawakening of their imaginative life.[14]

The demands upon culture of the ultimate speaker for whom Yeats sought and of the ultimate book which he hoped to write were revolutionary in the total sense. For Yeats, poetry, like the song of Mac-Manar which announced the death of Cuchullain, was the true weapon. In "The Shadowy Waters" we find Forgael using the harp as if it were a sword.[15]

If the world were external from the mind, then, insofar as Yeats was concerned, it was unintelligible. Yeats' artistic canon of subjectivity was an attempt to reassociate meaning and experience in a way which would make a true didacticism once more possible. The authority of his speakers was their relation to the real rather than the actual, and the final passing of the world into its real identity was its destruction. Magic provided an extraliterary analogy of the relation of art to society but was never fully assimilated by Yeats to the artistic fact. The example which was the legacy of the early imagination of Yeats was incompatible with life. In the early period Yeats mourns the loss of the life which the Wisdom figure demands as the price of sublimation; in the later poems he mourns the loss of the perfection which the decision for life rendered impossible.

Insofar as the symbolist tradition exists in English it is didactic. The mode of instruction can be compared to irony, for such didacticism awakens the sense of unlikeness which leads either to reformation or absurdity. The ultimate image to which men are called is Wisdom. Since Yeats was not a systematic writer, the theory of the relation of poetry and civilization is lacking. It may be said, however, to be a call from the abyss of the poem to the abyss in the self through the sleep which it is the function of meter to induce. It is this call to poetic knowledge of lost identity which Blake represents at the beginning of the "Songs of Experience."

> Hear the voice of the Bard!
> Who Present, Past, & Future, sees;
> Whose ears have heard
> The Holy Word
> That walk'd among the ancient trees,
>
> Calling the lapsed soul,
> And weeping in the evening dew;
> That might control
> The starry pole,
> And fallen, fallen light renew!
>
> "O Earth, O Earth, return!"

"The Holy Word," or Logos, is one of the many traditional surrogates of the Sophia.

Chapter IX

COLLEGE OF THE SEQUOIAS
LIBRARY

The joy of woman is the death of her most beloved,
Who dies for love of her
In torments of fierce jealousy and pangs of adoration.

—Blake, *Vala*

Strange is thy pallor! strange thy dress!
Strange, above all, thy length of tress,
And this all solemn silentness!

—Poe, "The Sleeper"

The Prior Love

WHEN Edgar Allan Poe declared that the death of a beautiful woman "is unquestionably the most poetical topic in the world, and equally is it beyond doubt that the lips best suited for such topic are those of a bereaved lover," he reflected the sacramental necrophilia which became a convention when the Christian lover abandoned the physical for the metaphysical body of the Beloved and came, like Dante, to love her in her "second life" with better right than when she lived.[1] The Yeats of our period was, like Poe, a lover of Beauty. The dead beloved is his image of the maternal figure who confers both Wisdom and passion, and who can be recovered only at the cost of all relations to the external as real. From a historical point of view she is, as we have suggested, the ascended Logos, the maid of Boehme, the cabalistic bride of God to whom Yeats seeks to come by the processes of initiation. It was characteristic of Symbolism as a movement that it tended to restore the otiose theological and psychological substratum of romantic conventions and, by re-evoking lost relations to historical and affective origins, render its symbol autonomous and vital.

The white woman of Yeats' poetry in the nineties, like the Idea of which she is the symbol, is beyond life. The convention of the dead love was an integral part of the metaphysical background of the Symbolist notion of beauty. It can be observed in a "pure" form in Symons' *Images of Good and Evil*.

> I spoke to the pale woman, and said:
> O pale and heavy-lidded woman, why is your cheek
> Pale as the dead, and why are your eyes afraid
>   to speak?
> And the woman answered me: I am pale as the dead,
> For the dead have loved me, and I dream of the dead.[2]

The white woman is so fully part of the mind that she continually
solicits desire. Like the soul she is both virginal and promiscuous.

> But I see in the eyes of the living, as a living
>   fire,
> The thing that my soul in triumph tells me I have
>   forgot;
> And therefore my eyes are heavy, and I raise them
>   not,
> For always I see in the eyes of men the old desire,
> And I fear lest they see that I desire their desire.[3]

This last phrase, of which both Symons and Yeats were fond, is out of
Coleridge. "The desire of man is for the woman, the desire of woman is
for the desire of the man." The pale woman like the work of art is
absolutely "self-delighting," demanding love but not returning it and
therefore terrible, an occasion of sacrifice.

During an illness on the continent in 1890 Maude Gonne received
from Yeats a poem called "An Epitaph."[4] In her autobiography she
reports, "I was getting steadily better and was greatly amused when
Willie Yeats sent me a poem, my epitaph, which he had written with
much feeling."[5] This poem (an imitation of Wilde's "Requiescat"
which was later called "A Dream of Death") represents, within the
convention, a strong reflex of feeling on Yeats' part. The death of the
Beloved renders her so essentially an aspect of the reverie of her lover
that the individuating complexities of emotion and will no longer
separate them.

This formula is represented in *The Wind* by a poem called "Aedh
Wishes His Beloved Were Dead," published in April, 1898, one of the
latest poems included in the volume.

AEDH WISHES HIS BELOVED WERE DEAD

Were you but lying cold and dead,
And lights were paling out of the West,
You would come hither, and bend your head,
And I would lay my head on your breast;
And you would murmur tender words,
Forgiving me, because you were dead:
Nor would you rise and hasten away,
Though you have the will of the wild birds
But know your hair was bound and wound
About the stars and moon and sun:
O would beloved that you lay
Under the dock-leaves in the ground
While lights were paling one by one.[6]

The environmental drama here is the passing of evening into night. The poem's structure possesses that circularity which we have so frequently remarked, the last lines recapitulating the first. The rhyme scheme exposes an irrationality characteristic of Yeats' poetry in the late nineties. It is the formal correlative of the syntactic design of the poem, an elaborate condition contrary to fact.[7] The poem turns on the central line ("Nor would you rise and hasten away"), which introduces a new rhyme element and a new syntactic unit, though the poet is reluctant to admit an interruption of the single extended arc of speech.

The key to the identity of the Beloved lies in the ninth and tenth lines. Years later Yeats remembered in *A Vision* the image of the beard of Macroprosopus which he had encountered in his early studies of Mathers' *Kabbalah Unveiled*. In *A Vision* he defends his use of occult structures. They are, he says, the "hard symbolic bones under the skin."

One remembers the six wings of Daniel's angels, the Pythagorean numbers, a venerated book of the Cabbala where the beard of God winds in and out among the stars, its hairs all numbered . . . the diagrams in **Law's** *Boehme*, where one lifts a flap of paper to discover both the human entrails and the starry heavens. William Blake thought those diagrams worthy of Michael Angelo, but remains himself almost unintelligible because he never drew the like.[8]

The Macroprosopus, whom Yeats calls God, is the mystical gigantic countenance in the likeness of which the created world was formed. The translation of the male into the female symbol was, as we have seen, normal in circles influenced by Mathers, and the Beloved considered in connection with the occult background takes on the status of the tree of life, that half-remembered primordial condition which we have explored in our comment on "Mongan Remembers His Past Greatness." If the Beloved were dead, Yeats is saying, she would no longer wonder at the nature of his devotion, but would become aware of the identity in relation to his own past which he attributes to her, and therefore be able to respond in the sense in which he solicits her. The whole character of the contrary-to-fact condition implies two competing identities of the Beloved. The first and éxcluded one is that of the living woman who cannot respond to the nature of the poet's address, which is at a level beneath or beyond conscious sexual relation. The identity which the process of the poem invites the Beloved to acknowledge ("If you were dead, then you would know") is the primitive maternal identity which, as we have seen, is part of the past self, consciousness of which is the special psychic possession of the artist. Then the Beloved would forgive and feed him, and his hunger for reality and compassion would be satisfied:

> And I would lay my head on your breast;
> And you would murmur tender words,
> Forgiving me, because you were dead.

This was the transformation which Yeats required of Maude and which she resisted to the end of her life and his. The occult substructure which seemed to Yeats to give distinctness and historical autonomy to his images is also the gateway to the psychological reality of his fantasy. This poem is late in terms of *The Wind among the Reeds* and exhibits a candor of desire of which he was incompetent in the *Savoy* period.

We must now proceed to examine the tyranny of this prior love, which requires the death of the proximate relation. Idealist philosophy, from Plato to F. H. Bradley, posits the subjective character of the real.

Yeats' pursuit of the white woman, Wisdom, recapitulates in mythical terms the idealist transformation of personal energies into philosophic attitudes.

The poem which most simply exemplified the experience of the prior love in terms of the suffering it imposed is "Aedh Laments the Loss of Love." The subject of this poem, exactly portrayed in Burne-Jones' "The Baleful Head," is expressed by the title (Fig. 8). The confrontation with the Wisdom figure involves the impossibility of the objective relation and leads to the loss of love. The basin into which Burne-Jones' lovers gaze is the heart of the poet. There the gorgonic face is discovered, the face which is the symbol of the poet's self-conquest and from which the mortal beloved must ultimately flee. The first line of "Aedh Laments the Loss of Love" is an address to the dead woman.

> Pale brows, still hands, and dim hair,
> I had a beautiful friend
> And dreamed that the old despair
> Would end in love in the end:
> She looked in my heart one day
> And saw your image was there;
> She has gone weeping away.[9]

The synecdochic formulas of the first line define, as nearly as Yeats is capable, the female symbol of the Absolute. We have seen that the special mark of this poet is his capacity to recover this image as an account of personal origins. The special sorrow of the poet is the cost of the relation which drives not only the poem but also the poet out of time.

Yeats returns to the situation of this poem again and again, beginning in the earliest of his writings. It is the predicament in "Ephemera," and it even haunts the little Indian romance "Anashuya and Vijaya," where the hero compulsively cries out the name of someone other than his Beloved ("My mother's name"). In "The Shadowy Waters," the most complex of Yeats' early works, Forgael and Dectora sail into the land of the dead together in search of the mystic third who is his destiny. For the sublimely oblate man the temptation of physical sexuality is an agony. In this vein Forgael cries out to Dectora:

> I will have none of you.
> My love shakes out her hair upon the streams
> Where the world ends, or runs from wind to wind
> And eddy to eddy. Masters of our dreams,
> Why have you cloven me with a mortal love?
> Pity these weeping eyes! [10]

In *John Sherman* the mortal woman is associated with the city, while Ireland and the native town hold Mary Carton, the true love of the hero. She is the national image and the symbol of archetypal personal origin.

Such is the background in Yeats of "Aedh Tells of a Valley Full of Lovers."

> I dreamed that I stood in a valley, and amid sighs,
> For happy lovers passed two by two where I stood;
> And I dreamed my lost love came stealthily out of
>   the wood
> With her cloud-pale eyelids falling on dream-dimmed eyes:
> I cried in my dream *"O women bid the young men lay*
> *"Their heads on your knees, and drown their eyes with*
>   *your hair,*
> *"Or remembering hers they will find no other face fair*
> *"Till all the valleys of the world have been withered*
>   *away."* [11]

Deep in dream the poet comes upon a "Valley of Lovers" which is threatened by the approach of his love described in terms of the formula of the eye turned away from all objective relation. She is dead; as long as the women of the valley are alive they will never recover the fidelity of their young men.

The gorgonic strangeness of the white woman loved of the poet is enhanced by the formulaic character of his reference to her. The recurrent synecdoches of eyes, hair, brow, and hands as they accumulate throughout *The Wind* convey the impression of an unspeakable and unchanging mystery. The source of the narrative situation of this poem is unclear, but Miss Gurd's suggestion of Spenser, though it does not solve the poem, nonetheless draws the appropriate relation within the context of Yeats' work.[12] Yeats' earliest poems, which were influenced by Spenserian pastoralism and chivalry, make frequent reference

to valleys of happy lovers or shepherds upon which, as in the case of
"Anashuya and Vijaya," the dead woman or her minion intrude as
another and more complex reality. Synge saw fit to use the "Aran"
dialect for the translation of Petrarch. The symbolist attitude toward
the white woman, as Synge detected, was a perverse transfiguration of
the courtly convention.

The dead woman is Yeats' symbol of his sense of special identity in
the early period. In philosophic poetry, which is always in one way or
another love poetry, the identity and relations of the lover are defined
by the nature of the Beloved. Before Yeats discovered the fairly stable
mythology of Sophia, he entertained the white woman under many
factitious disguises. In "The Two Titans" of 1886 she oppressed the
white-haired Shelleyan youth under the allegory of England oppressing
Ireland. In "The Seeker" a happy pastoral valley is troubled by the
arrival of an obsessed knight, who enters a deadly and terrible wood
nearby in search of his identity. Before a ruined palace presided over
by a "motionless Figure" the knight confesses the effect upon him of
his quest.

> Thou madest me
> A coward in the field; and all men cried:
> "Behold the knight of the waterfall, whose heart
> The spirits stole, and gave him in its stead
> A peering hare's": and yet I murmured not,
> Knowing that thou hadst singled me with word
> Of love from out a dreamless race for strife
> Through miseries unhuman ever on
> To joys unhuman, and to thee—Speak! Speak! [13]

The confrontation with the source of his obsession is simultaneous with
the death of the seeker. This is the description of her appearance:

> A bearded witch, her sluggish head bent low
> On her broad breast! Beneath her withered brows
> Shine dull unmoving eyes. What thing art thou?
> I sought thee not.

Figure.   Men call me Infamy.
  I know not what I am.
Knight.   I sought thee not.
Figure. Lover, the voice that summoned thee was mine.

Knight.   For all I gave the voice, for all my youth,
   For all my joy—ah, woe!

> [*The Figure raises a mirror, in
> which the face and the form of
> the Knight are shadowed. He falls.*] [14]

Such is the terror of the Wisdom figure in one of its primitive negative transformations.

The seeker, a type of the Irish aesthetic artist, is disabled from physical battle because of his devotion to the inward image. Although Yeats from the beginning regards the artist as an outcast and an alien, this attitude precedes the impact on him of the social position of the artist in the nineteenth century and is a function of his sense of himself and not of the attitude of society toward him. The apparition of the white woman is a consequence of the intrapsychic affinities of the poetic enterprise itself and is not a socially determined disease of consciousness.

In 1898 Yeats published another poem about the white woman under the title "Breasal the Fisherman." The figure of Breasal is associated in the first edition of "The Hour Glass" with the magical fool who has right knowledge about the nature of the real. The poem assigned to him in *The Wind among the Reeds* is about quest.

BREASAL THE FISHERMAN
Although you hide in the ebb and the flow
Of the pale tide when the moon has set,
The people of coming days will know
About the casting out of my net,
And how you have leaped times out of mind
Over the little silver cords,
And think that you were hard and unkind,
And blame you with many bitter words.[15]

The time of this poem is the intertidal twilight after the moon has set and before the rising of the sun. The moon woman is associated with the tidal characteristics of the sea which participate in the power of the moon, but the quest of the aesthetic fisherman is undertaken at the time when the moon is hidden. For the construction of the love relation on the analogy of the fisherman and the fish we need look no further than Hyde's *Love Songs of Connacht*.

> Dear God! were I fisher and
>   Back in Binédar
> And Nelly a fish who
>   Would swim in the bay there,
> I would privately set there
>   My net there to catch her,
> In Erin is able no maid to match her.[16]

But the folk tradition provides no stable background for any of Yeats' poems in this period, and the fish he seeks is no more "Nelly of the Top Knots" than it is in any recognizable sense Maude Gonne, as Marion Witt has suggested.[17] The effective tradition of "Breasal the Fisherman" is alchemical, in accordance with which Yeats changed the title of the poem in his collected edition of 1908 to "The Fish." If we confine ourselves to sources which Yeats is known to have handled, we may refer with most relevance to Westcott's edition of the *Hermetic Arcanum* which appeared as the first volume of his *Collectanea Hermetica* in 1893. There we read,

Philosophers have their sea also, wherein small fishes plump and shining with silver scales are generated; which he that shall entangle, and take by a fine and small net shall be accounted a most expert fisherman.[18]

The fish is the *prima materia*, the *lapis philosophorum*, the ultimate identity of the self, and Yeats is in search of it the more hopelessly because the moon, symbol of the subjectivity, has set, and the creature of the moon is not to be found elsewhere.[19] Like the sidhe, the white woman, whose whiteness here is not only that of the moon but also of the symbolic mercury, is "hard" and "unkind."

The process of the alchemical "work" in its relation to the development of the self is analogous to the ceremonial initiation which we discussed in Chapter V, "The Wars of Eden," and it will be well to have an authoritative statement before us. All of the processes here referred to were available either in Westcott's *Collectanea Hermetica* or in *The Hermetica Museum*, translated by A. E. Waite and published in 1893.[20]

The alchemists call the first stage, or Blackness, Putrefaction. In it the three principles which compose the "whole man" of body, soul, and spirit are "sublimated" till they appear as a black powder full of corruption, and the imperfect body is "dissolved and purified by subtle Mercury"; as man is purified by the darkness, misery, and despair which follows the emergence of this spiritual consciousness. As psychic uproar seems part of the process of mental growth, so *"Solve et Coagula"* —break down that you may build up—is the watchword of the spiritual alchemist. The "black beast," the passional element of the lower nature, must emerge and be dealt with before anything further can be done. "There is a black beast in our forest," says the highly allegorical *Book of Lambspring*, "his name is Putrefaction, his blackness is called the Head of the Raven; when it is cut off, Whiteness appears." This Whiteness, the state of Luna, or Silver, the "chaste and immaculate Queen," is the equivalent of the Illuminative way: the highest point which the mystic can achieve short of union with the Absolute.[21]

This is the whiteness of the white woman in its personally constructive meaning. The search for this condition is projected in "Breasal the Fisherman." Beyond union with the chaste and immaculate queen is "The Marriage of Luna and Sol," the fusion of the human and divine spirit.

Aside from the symbolic processes represented, "Breasal the Fisherman" introduces an element which we have not previously observed in these poems. In his appeal from the impossibility of the quest to the counter immortality of art ("The people of coming days will know/ About the casting out of my net"), the speaker of the poem objectifies the role of the artist. In this way he dissociates himself from the acknowledged hopelessness of the enterprise. One of the conventions of the Gaelic poetic role which Yeats brings into his stories of Hanrahan in *The Secret Rose* is the bardic curse, which is fatal because it sets the powers of earth against the object of the poet's wrath. Fear of the curse led the Abbot to crucify Cumhal; when Raftery cursed the thorn tree it withered. The speaker of "Breasal the Fisherman" in effect curses the Beloved with the bad immortality which the artist can confer and, in doing so, for the moment breaks the spell of the obsession. When Yeats begins to refer to himself as an artist, he ceases to be a mystic. This reliance on an immortality other than personal transformation is one of the strains of development which leads out of the early period into Yeats' later style.

In an earlier chapter we identified the white woman with the Logos of the Simonian gnosis, the beloved of god descended into history, transmigrant and endlessly promiscuous. As such she is the muse.

A POET TO HIS BELOVED

> I bring you with reverent hands
> The books of my numberless dreams;
> White woman that passion has worn
> As the tide wears the dove-gray sands,
> And with heart more old than the horn
> That is brimmed from the pale fire of time:
> White woman with numberless dreams
> I bring you my passionate rhyme.[22]

Her affinities are, as in the Breasal poem, to the sea, and she is passionate. We have seen in our citation from Symons above that "The Pale Woman" cries out, "The dead have loved me, and I dream of the dead." Insofar as she is ascended or heavenly Logos, Wisdom is the bride of God; insofar as she is the Simonian or descended Logos she is, as in the poem above, the bride of the dead in history. As we have seen repeatedly, she is never the bride of the poet; for time and eternity do not mingle until the Last Judgement. Hence Yeats' realization in his later verse that wisdom belongs to the dead:

> Wisdom is the property of the dead,
> A something incompatible with life; and power,
> Like everything that has the stain of blood,
> A property of the living.[23]

For the coital relationship which as a lover the poet seeks, he substitutes his "dreams"; poetry is the sexual act of the impotent man. Only as a result of his address to the white woman do the poet's "rhymes" become in the last line of the poem "passionate."

From the relationship of the Wisdom figure to someone other than the poet comes Yeats' interest in the theme of "The Stolen Bride." Denis Saurat emphasizes the role in occultism of sexual life within the deity.[24] As we have seen, Yeats regards this as an exclusive relation. In one of the earliest poems which came to be included in *The Wind among the Reeds,* "The Host of the Air," Yeats represents O'Driscoll, the poet, singing by the shore of Hart Lake or Heart Lake, that mysterious place of the mind which is the site of "Ephemera" and "Aedh Hears the Cry of the Sedge," as well as many later poems. As night falls O'Driscoll begins to dream of his bride Bridget, the name, as Rhys informs us, of the Irish goddess of poetry. As the dream which constitutes the rest of the narrative comes upon him, he hears above his own singing the singing of the sidhe. "The Host of the Air" was written sometime before 1893, and at the height of Yeats' preoccupation with Blake; the song of the fairies recalls the "piping" of the poet who meets the child-muse in Blake's Introduction to *Songs of Innocence:*

> He heard while he sang and dreamed
> A piper piping away,
> And never was piping so sad,
> And never was piping so gay.[25]

The juxtaposition of "sad" and "gay" informs us that we are in the presence of that mystic morality which transcends the normal conditions of human emotion. The fairies are sad because they have no soul and gay because paradoxically they feel no sorrow. At the Last Judgement, which is reserved for the transformation of the *human* condition, they "melt out . . . like bright vapour." [26] This morality is reflected on the face of the Beloved, showing that she is now beyond life:

> And he saw young men and young girls
> Who danced on a level place
> And Bridget his bride among them,
> With a sad and a gay face.[27]

O'Driscoll is tempted with "the bread and wine" of fairy but is led away by his bride, thus recapitulating the denial of the sacramental breast which is the recurrent experience of the poet in *The Wind.*

> The bread and the wine had a doom
> For these were the host of the air.[28]

In his dream O'Driscoll sees his Beloved carried away by "The handsomest young man there," and awakes, in the earlier versions of the poems, to find his Beloved dead. In the later version he awakes only to hear the sound of Blake's piper. "The Host of the Air" is a dream poem making clear that the bride is only recovered in sleep and that she is the possession of the Eternal, and His alone. The piping of the fairies is that terrible sound issuing from the Golden Age or the Supernal Eden which we have studied: the song of that innocence of which man is incapable without the elaborate penitential process which is the subject of "The Blessed." As Cumhal's vision of the blessed souls is "like a drifting smoke," so O'Driscoll's dream of fairy vanishes "like a drifting smoke."

The formula of "The Stolen Bride" is the subject also of one of the last poems in *The Wind among the Reeds*. "Aedh Pleads with the Elemental Powers" was published in final form in the *Dome* in 1898. It first appeared in the *Bookman* in 1892, then in *The Second Book of the Rhymers' Club* in 1894. Revision of the poem took the form of a symbolic reinforcement of the psychological subject matter, as Yeats' knowledge of the occult background changed and grew more exact. The symbolic locality of the poem is what the *Hermetic Arcanum* calls the Philosopher's Garden.

The entrance of the Philosophers' Garden is kept by the Hesperean Dragon, which being put aside, a fountain of the clearest water proceeding from a seven-fold spring floweth forth. . . . Three kinds of most beautiful flowers are to be sought and may be found in this garden of the wise. . . . Thou shalt not sever such precious flowers from their roots until thou make the stone.[29]

The flower which Yeats conceives as growing in this paradise is the "Rose of Ideal Beauty . . . before it was cast into the world."[30] The drama is the Fall, as a result of which the Heavenly Logos descended into the world and commenced her relation to history. The last line of the quotation above expresses that impossible condition of human perfection required of man before Wisdom can once again be achieved. In the earliest version of the poem we see the Logos or Wisdom figure torn from her primordial place before the throne of God, where, looking on her, He created the world.

> The powers, not kind like you, came where
> God's garden blows,
> And stole the crimson Rose,

And hurled it from its place before His
    footstool white
Into the blinding night.[31]

In the 1899 version, the poem reads as follows:

AEDH PLEADS WITH THE ELEMENTAL POWERS

The Powers whose name and shape no living
    creature knows
Have pulled the Immortal Rose;
And though the Seven Lights bowed in their
    dance and wept,
The Polar Dragon slept,
His heavy rings uncoiled from glimmering
    deep to deep:
When will he wake from sleep?
Great Powers of falling wave and wind and
    windy fire,
With your harmonious choir
Encircle her I love and sing her into peace,
That my old care may cease;
Unfold your flaming wings and cover out of
    sight
The nets of day and night.
Dim Powers of drowsy thought, let her no
    longer be
Like the pale cup of the sea,
When winds have gathered and sun and moon
    burned dim
Above its cloudy rim;
But let a gentle silence wrought with music
    flow
Whither her footsteps go.[32]

The "Powers" of the first line are not the same as those of the seventh. A power without a name cannot be cabalistically controlled and that which removes the rose of "Ideal Beauty" from the garden belongs to the forces of what Yeats calls in his general way "objectivity." The rhetorical effect of this poem is intended to be the same as that of "Aedh Wishes His Beloved Were Dead," namely, the reassimilation of the Beloved to the garden of reverie from which she has been ravished into the world of life. The poet summons all the powers of harmony

7. Burne-Jones: "The Merciful Knight."

8. Burne-Jones: "The Baleful Head," showing the interposition of the "prior love"
between lover and beloved as in "Aedh Laments the Loss of Love."

which he can name in an effort to regain Wisdom as the prize of the perfected inwardness. But she has become angry and alien like a stormy sea, and the powers of song (lines eight and nine) will not serve to recover her.

The confusing verbal identity of the personages referred to in lines one and seven was carefully developed as Yeats worked and reworked the poem, and reflects the rule, which we have previously invoked, that obscurity occurs in Yeats where the problem of conflict would otherwise be most obvious. The "Powers" of the first line are those of God. The "Powers" of the seventh line, which refers specifically to the elemental Triplicities that Yeats so laboriously attempted to make his own, are those of the son to whom the garden of the alchemical quest belongs. Line one alludes to the Shemhamforash, the Tetragrammaton or mystic name of God, which cannot be spoken; as a result, the theft of the rose is the crime of the father himself, whom Yeats imagines to be the prepotent sexual force in the universe. The sexuality of the son, symbolized by the polar dragon, sleeps and is incompetent to recover its precious charge. We have seen repeatedly that Yeats in this period imagines himself as most powerful, closest to the Idea, when asleep or in trance and least effective in the world of objective conflict and objective sexual relation. The wresting of the sexual object into the world of history destroys the integrity of the tree of life, the primal image which is the special psychic possession of the poet, and leaves the powers of the son helpless. Yeats is here asserting both his intense desire that the sexual object be ideal and the equally powerful resistance of his mind to the process of sublimation.

One of the major problems which confront the lyric poet in the late nineteenth century is the withering away of techniques of personal idealization. Most of the major literary artists of the twentieth century, and most conspicuously Yeats, Lawrence, and Eliot, resisted in one way or another the secularization of the mind implied in the emergent nonrational psychology of which Freud's book on dreams (1899) was the landmark. As we have already observed, the function of Yeats' use of occult symbolism is to protect his self-image from the unmanageable real mechanisms of psychic events and to replace the real unconscious by a historical or pseudo-ontological entity which will express the power but not the cultural anonymity of the Freudian unconscious.

In "Aedh Pleads with the Elemental Powers," the expectation of ideality in the mind is betrayed and the Rose is dragged into the created world of the father, where she becomes terrible. The poet prays with force for the restoration of the lost realm of the spirit:

> Dim Powers of drowsy thought, let her no
>   longer be
> Like the pale cup of the sea,
> When winds have gathered and sun and moon
>   burned dim
> Above its cloudy rim.

The Beloved has two identities. As the Idea she is terrible because dead. She demands death of her lover as the sign of his readiness for consummation. She is the heavenly Wisdom, guarded by God the father, "Master of the still stars and the flaming door." In her second identity, as the descended Logos, she is even more terrible because she requires of her lover the abandonment of Ideality, which constitutes his whole realm of effectiveness, and because she is guarded by the father whose symbol is the created world against which Yeats as poet and son pitted every force in his power.

Chapter X

Spiritualise ton corps: sublime-toi!
                                    —Villiers de l'Isle-Adam, *Axel*

Stoop not down into the darkly splendid world wherein continually lieth a
faithless depth, and Hades wrapped in clouds, delighting in unintelligible
images, precipitous, winding, a black ever-rolling Abyss, ever espousing a
Body, unluminous, formless, void.—Regardie, *The Golden Dawn*

In the years of her age the most beautiful and the most flowery—the time
Love has his Mastery—Laura who was my life, has gone away leaving the
earth stripped and desolate. She has gone up into the heavens, living and
beautiful and naked, and from that place she is keeping her Lordship and
her rein upon me, and I keep crying out: Ohone, when will I see the day
breaking that will be my first day with herself in Paradise?—Synge, "He
Wishes He Might Die and Follow Laura"

The Calling of a Hound

THE phenomena to which Yeats avows credence in his essay on "Magic" are exactly those which form the data on the basis of which William James constructed his *Varieties of Religious Experience*. In England the rising field of nonrational psychology was represented by the scientifically legitimate Society for Psychical Research, founded in 1882. The chief document of that organization is Myers, Podmore, and Gurney's massive volume called *Phantasms of the Living*, in which, as in the case of James, the authors employ for scientific purposes the same data to which Yeats was being exposed at the feet of Madame Blavatsky.[1] The psychological and the transcendental "dream" were simultaneously developing concepts in the nineties. Yeats' work exhibits both the psychic necessities which called attention to these phenomena, and an artist's abhorrence of scientific conclusions about the mind, which in the twentieth century was to become typical.

In April, 1896, Havelock Ellis published in the *Savoy* an article by Cesare Lombroso called "A Mad Saint," which amply sums up in nineteenth-century psychological terms the predicament of the pseudo-sacramental sensibility which Yeats was soliciting.[2] There appeared in Lombroso's *clinique* a psychopathic woman whom he calls Maria G. She suffered from "hysterical" and "neuralgic" symptoms, and she claimed to be a saint, saw visions, and exhibited in every way the true mystic state of mind. The motive which led to the inclusion of this article in the *Savoy* is well indicated by Lombroso's conclusion.

Three or four centuries ago she would have attracted followers, founded monasteries, carried away crowds; she would have become an historical event. It is sad to reflect on the fate of so many men of genius, born before their time, or in lands incapable of understanding them, and dying sterilized, when they are not killed as rebels or heretics. Even among ourselves today, indeed, it is only after death that such men are admired and honored.

The germ of holiness, as well as that of genius, must be sought among the insane.[3]

The end which Lombroso contemplates for the insane genius is that which befell Michael Robartes in the "Rosa Alchemica." Yeats repeatedly equates the condition of the peasant when "taken" by the sidhe or the fairies (a psychotic syndrome) with the condition of the poet in the nineteenth century. His symbol of the "death" which precipitates the last judgement of the imagination implies a total dissociation of consciousness from the real, which in his or any time would be regarded as a symptom of madness. Lombroso's comment on the speech of Maria G. is of great interest.

The metre is nearly always the same . . . very sonorous, in rhymed quatrains of ten syllables; but the rhymes are often only assonances. . . . Sometimes while singing she falls into a condition of true ecstasy; the eyeballs are turned upwards, the eyelids become fixed, the arms extended, and she is able to support a much stronger electric current than that which gives her pain under normal conditions.

This persistent use of melody and rhythm certainly represents an atavistic return to primitive musical methods of expression which commonly accompanied emotional states among our ancestors. It is a kind of mental palaeontology . . . ; and it corresponds exactly to the vague uniform undifferentiated condition of her ideas.[4]

Lombroso's description of the "singing" of Maria G. suggests the kind of dramatic performance which Yeats and Florence Farr began to develop in 1892 when Yeats conceived the style of *The Wind among the Reeds*. Lombroso's interpretation of that style of speech would have satisfied William Sharp as a description of the Celtic poetic ambition. The "mental palaeontology" of Maria G. is the same thing as the search for the ethnic reality of the self which was the program of the Celticist. In nineteenth-century terms Yeats' speakers imitate the posture of the insane in order to recover "the germ of holiness." Seeking sanction in poetry for extreme states of mind, Yeats continually substituted ideality where the psychologist found mechanism.

One of the characteristics of Yeats' thought processes in later years is a habitual *dérèglement,* a technique of constructing symbols by reducing cultural to emotional phenomena and then identifying the emotional phenomenon with some impersonal historical image. In the early period he tended to bypass this process. The desired condition of the mind seemed to Yeats extreme, close to madness, and madness in its ideal construction is one of his most characteristic subjects. But the "dream" tended to disintegrate, to pass against his will from an ideal to a psychological status. This negative transformation became, therefore, one of the subjects of his early poetry. With respect to the human condition, Yeats would have concurred with Blake's Orc, who cries to the Shadowy Female:

> Take not human form, O Loveliest, take not terror
> Upon you.[5]

"Mongan Laments the Change That Has Come upon Him" and "The Song of the Wandering Aengus" are two carefully controlled examples of the Yeatsian *dérèglement,* the descent of the Idea into its motive. The context in which these poems can best be defined is the process of initiation, Yeats' characteristic technique of self-discovery.

Yeats wrote to Katharine Tynan shortly before the publication of "The Wanderings of Oisin" that it contained elements of meaning to which he alone had the key,[6] and afterward that " 'Oisin' needs an interpreter." [7] "Oisin," which was largely written before 1887 and which therefore preceded Yeats' intense exposure to the prophetic style of Blake, was most likely not constructed with any total symbolic order in mind and has not yet found an interpreter in the sense which Yeats' statement demands. But in 1896 the myth on which it was founded was given a lengthy symbolic reading by George Russell, who would have known better than anyone else the kind of meanings Yeats was likely to solicit between 1885 and 1889, when the poem was being written and revised.[8]

It [the story of Oisin] is purely occult. Oisin, Niam, her white steed, Tir-na-noge, the waters they pass over, are but names which define a little our forgotten being. Within Oisin, the magician, kindles the Ray, the hidden Beauty. . . . It is the Golden Bird of the Upanishads; the light that lighteth every man; it is that which the old Hermetists knew as the fair and the beautiful—for Niam means beauty; it is the Presence and when it is upon a man every other tie breaks; he goes alone with It, he is a dying regret, an ever increasing joy. And so with Oisin, whose weeping companions behold him no more.[9]

From Russell's point of view, Niam is the Wisdom figure who "calls" Oisin to the sacrificial commitment which in the later "Sailing to Byzantium" Yeats still seeks under the symbol of Russell's Upanishadic "Golden Bird." Russell continues at length his interpretive description of Oisin's journey, dealing now with symbols of "madness," the psychic resistance to the call of Wisdom.

As they pass over the waters, "they saw many wonderful things on their journey—islands and cities, lime-white mansions, bright greenans and lofty palaces." It is the mirror of heaven and earth, the astral light, in whose glass a myriad illusions arise and fleet before the mystic adventurers. Haunt of a false beauty—or rather veil hung dazzling before true beauty. . . . The transition from this to a subtler sphere is indicated. A hornless deer, chased by a white hound with red ears, and a maiden tossing a golden lure, vanishes forever before a phantom lover. The poet whose imagination has renewed for us the legend has caught the true significance of the hurrying forms.

> The immortal desire of immortals we saw in their
>   eyes and sighed.
> "Do not heed these forms!" cries Niam.[10]

There are centers in man corresponding to these appearances. They give vision and entrance into a red and dreadful world where unappeasable desire smites the soul—a dangerous clairvoyance.[11]

Then, in Russell's interpretation, the journeyer proceeds to battle with the self in order to conquer the "red and dreadful world" of the inwardness, the symbol of which is the primordial Fomorian.[12] "We too —would be mystics—are met on the threshold of diviner spheres by terrible forms embodying the sins of a living past." When these terrors are conquered, then the "power" in the form of the captive princess is released, and the mystic identity is achieved. "Tir-na-noge, the land of

Niam, is that region the soul lives in when its grosser energies and desires have been subdued, dominated, and brought under the control of light; where the ray of beauty kindles and illuminates every form which the imagination conceives and where every form tends to its archetype." [13]

The myth of Oisin from Russell's point of view is a representation of the process of initiation. The hound and deer symbolize that well-known emotional turbulence or madness that besets the aspirant at the beginning of the mystic undertaking. In alchemical terms, "the 'black beast,' the passional element of the lower nature, must emerge and be dealt with before anything further can be done." [14] Yeats' symbol of the beast of the inwardness is "the boar without bristles":

> Do you not hear me calling, white deer with no horns?
> I have been changed to a hound with one red ear;
> I have been in the Path of Stones and the Wood of
>   Thorns,
> For somebody hid hatred and hope and desire and
>   fear
> Under my feet that they follow you night and day.
> A man with a hazel wand came without sound;
> He changed me suddenly; I was looking another way;
> And now my calling is but the calling of a hound;
> And time and birth and change are hurrying by.
> I would that the boar without bristles had come from
>   the West
> And had rooted the sun and moon and stars out of the
>   sky
> And lay in the darkness, grunting, and turning to
>   his rest. [15]

Here Yeats deals directly with symbols which he first approached ten years earlier in "The Wanderings of Oisin." The title of the poem ("Mongan Laments the Change That Has Come upon Him and His Beloved") suggests that sadness which is part of the direct encounter with personal reality expressed in the other poem in *The Wind* attributed to the same speaker.

> I have drunk ale from the Country of the Young
> And weep because I know all things now.

In the poem at hand, the process of initiation has been arrested in the initial phase of emotional turbulence, of "unappeasable desire," which must be transcended in order to follow the Absolute.

When this poem first appeared, it was called "The Desire of Man and of Women." The "change," which is its subject, is the descent from the Dream into the sexual aspect of personal identity, the negative transformation. With infinite subtlety, Yeats records the meeting of Mongan with the Master of Love, Aengus:

> A man with a hazel wand came without sound:
> He changed me suddenly; I was looking another
> way.

The function of Yeats' mystic morality is to set personality above the complexities of extreme and conflicting emotions which violate the ideal simplicity of the self; but now, with an autonomy represented as unrelated to the will of the speaker, these feelings are awake and hunting like hounds.

> For somebody hid hatred and hope and desire and fear
> Under my feet that they follow you night and day.

The avenues of initiation have now become a source of suffering (a "Wood of Thorns"), and the willing acceptance of pain as a form of penance has vanished. The speaker becomes subject to change, as if through desire he were born for the first time into the world of "Time and Birth" from which the "dream" out of which he has just awakened protected him.

In the wand of hazel, one of the sacred trees of the Irish, the magical and the sexual symbols become equivalent; but we are justified, I think, in suspecting that the most important analogy is Wilde's sonnet "Helas," which has the same subject.

> To drift with every passion till my soul
> Is a stringed lute on which all winds can play,
> Is it for this that I have given away
> Mine ancient wisdom, and austere control?
> Methinks my life is a twice-written scroll
> Scrawled over on some boyish holiday
> With idle songs for pipe and virelay
> Which do but mar the secret of the whole.

> Surely there was a time I might have trod
> The sunlit heights and from life's dissonance
> Struck one clear chord to reach the ears of God:
> Is that time dead? lo! with a little rod
> I did but touch the honey of romance—
> And must I lose a soul's inheritance? [16]

The problem which both Wilde and Yeats are here approaching, namely, the difficulty of sustaining personal idealism, "the sunlit heights," in the face of the competing reality of the "red and dreadful world" of emotion, is fundamental to the literary environment of the late nineteenth century and is treated extensively both at the social and psychological levels. George Egerton's "Lost Masterpiece" describes the inspiration of a typical female prose writer in the ideal style destroyed by the sight of a fugitive from the East End, the psychical primitive in the form of the uncontrollable social phenomenon. Wilde puts the matter with force in *The Picture of Dorian Grey*: "I can sympathize with everything but suffering," and Yeats echoes the notion in his "Aedh Tells of the Rose in His Heart."

> All things uncomely and broken, all things worn out
>   and old,
> The cry of a child by the roadway, the creak of a
>   lumbering cart,
> The heavy steps of the ploughman, splashing the
>   wintry mold,
> Are wronging your image that blossoms a rose in
>   the deeps of my heart.[17]

This reversal of the Wordsworthian preference with respect to subject matter, both social and psychological, was the index of Yeats' real attitude toward the peasantry and indicates the affinity of aestheticism to the eighteenth-century tendency to construct the moral and the social hierarchy on the same vertical scale.

But "Aedh Tells of the Rose in His Heart" is an early poem compared with "Mongan Laments the Change," and the mark of the success of the latter is the absence of any solicitation of the protective maternal sensuality, the defensive subjectification of reality, which is the poet's normal resort in the face of symbols of his own violent inwardness. In "Michael Robartes Bids His Beloved Be at Peace," the poet hears the "Horses of Disaster" which "plunge in the heavy clay." [18] And in response to his own aroused virility, cries out:

> Beloved, let your eyes half close, and your heart beat
> Over my heart, and your hair fall over my breast,
> Drowning love's lonely hour in deep twilight of rest,
> And hiding their tossing manes and their tumultuous
>   feet.

In the poem assigned to Mongan, the black boar is directly invoked to precipitate the world of the son in the form of the "rough beast," the futile explosion of the denied aspect of personality.

> I would that the boar without bristles had come from
>   the West
> And had rooted the sun and moon and stars out of the
>   sky
> And lay in the darkness, grunting, and turning to
>   his rest.

The peculiar form of this cataclysm is the destruction of light. Not twilight but night comes upon the mind as a consequence of the negative transformation. This is the boar that destroyed Attis and Diarmuid, both lovers incompetent of the sublimity which had elected them.

One curious aspect of *The Wind among the Reeds* is the tension between the highly specific styles which it exhibits and the highly generalized subject matter which those styles serve. The cosmological purview is a form of psychological evasion which Yeats found very difficult to abandon. In "Mongan Laments the Change" the process of initiation, as Russell outlined it, is arrested at the most dangerous point, but the sense of personal exigency is diffused. Prophecy takes the place of anxiety.

If there is any doubt that Yeats' interpretation of the hound and deer corresponded to Russell's, one need only to turn to "The Shadowy Waters," where, as Forgael takes Dectora in his arms, this apparition troubles their sight.

> *Dectora.* (*Peering out over the waters*) O look!
> A red-eared hound follows a hornless deer.
> There! There! They have gone quickly, for already
> The cloudy waters and glimmering winds
> Have covered them.
> *Forgael.*   Where did they vanish away?
> *Dectora.*   Where the moon makes a cloudy light in the mists.
> *Forgael.*   (*Going to the steering oar*) The pale hound
>   and the deer wander forever
> Among the winds and waters; and when they pass
> The mountain of the gods, the unappeasable gods
> Cover their faces with their hair and weep.
> *Dectora.*   All dies among those streams.
> *Forgael.*   The fool has made
> These messengers to lure men to his peace,
> Where true-love wanders among the holy woods.[19]

Underlying Forgael's search for the love which is synonymous with
death is the vision of the sexual quest against which the gods rage in
vain. The key to Yeats' stylistic problem is the insistence with which
he dissociates strong emotion from consciousness. It is the fool of the
wood, or Aengus, who awakens the poet unaware of his own access to
feeling: "He changed me suddenly; I was looking another way." And
it is Aengus in the poet, and not the speaker of the poem, who pursues
the beloved.

> For somebody hid hatred and hope and desire and fear
> Under my feet that *they* follow you night and day.

Automatism of the emotions led to the dissociation within the self of
mortal and immortal elements, "the rending of the intellectual body,"
which Yeats symbolizes by the crucifixion and by the "Wood of
Thorns." In the case of "Mongan Laments," the only resolution is
cataclysm, the onset of night. This was Yeats' early and incomplete
fantasy of the solution of the problem of that dual self-conception
necessitated by the tradition of idealism.

But even within *The Wind among the Reeds* Yeats was capable, with
the aid of the imagery of the alchemical quest which we have seen in
"Breasal the Fisherman," to conceive of another conclusion.

The crucial poem in this respect is "The Song of the Wandering Aengus."

> I went out to the hazel wood,
> Because a fire was in my head,
> And cut and peeled a hazel wand,
> And hooked a berry to a thread;
> And when white moths were on the wing,
> And moth-like stars were flickering out,
> I dropped the berry in a stream
> And caught a little silver trout.
>
> When I had laid it on the floor
> I went to blow the fire a-flame,
> But something rustled on the floor,
> And someone called me by my name:
> It had become a glistening girl
> With apple blossoms in her hair
> Who called me by my name and ran
> And faded through the brightening air.
>
> Though I am old with wandering
> Through hollow lands and hilly lands,
> I will find out where she is gone,
> And kiss her lips and take her hands;
> And walk among long dappled grass,
> And pluck till time and times are done,
> The silver apples of the moon,
> The golden apples of the sun.[20]

Much work has been done on this poem, so that it only remains for us to indicate the main line of an appropriate interpretation rather than, as in other poems, to suggest a whole universe of sources.[21]

The central episode of the poem is the reduction of the fish or Wisdom symbol into its instinctual equivalent, the girl. This is the negative transformation which is the consequence of the onset of "madness." In the transitional region of Oisin's voyage from which the hound and deer are drawn, the voyager also encounters a fleeing female figure with an apple in her hand. The lover in Yeats' poem, who is Aengus by reason of his participation in the erotic quest, undertakes to solve the problem of love madness by fishing in that sea of the philosophers referred to in the comment on "Breasal the Fisherman."[22] The

Irish equivalent in Yeats' mind of the alchemical fish is the sacred
trout of Irish springs and wells which he found in the work of Samuel
Lover and anthologized in 1888.[23] The fisherman enters the wood in the
twilight before dawn:

> And when white moths were on the wing,
> And moth-like stars were flickering out.

Having caught the trout he undertakes to eat it, blowing up the fire of
life as does the old mother in the poem with which this is linked in *The
Wind among the Reeds.*[24] But as always in these poems, the oral
sacrament eludes the hunger of the mortal lover, the Wisdom figure
subsides into its denying identity and the endless quest is initiated.

The quest does not end; but in the last stanza the lover projects
rhetorically the desired consummation at the last judgement when the
hungry body will be united to the soul image and pluck the apples of
Wisdom. The origin of the gold and silver wood which bears upon the
same tree the apples of the male and female love, the objective and
subjective erotic mode, is the alchemical reading of Deuteronomy
33:13–16, Moses' blessing of Joseph, cited here in the form in which
Yeats knew it from Westcott's *Hermetic Arcanum.*

Joseph's Blessing spoken by the same prophet [Moses] will be sufficient to
the wise man. "Blessed of the Lord be his Land, for the apples of heaven,
for the dew, and for the Deep that liveth beneath: for the apples of fruit
both of sun and moon, for the tops of the ancient mountains, for the apples
of the everlasting earth." [25]

This is the earthly paradise of the philosopher's garden. The "earth" is
the alchemical first substance. Here the alchemical and the sexual quest
end simultaneously. It is significant for Yeats' early sense of totality
that this garden is a made thing of gold and silver. Fundamentally, it is
the sublime transfiguration of the dangerous wood of "The Seeker" and
that less ambiguous place of clarity won by penance in "The Blessed."
References to the apocalyptic forest abound in Yeats' poetry of this
period and later:

> The love of all under the light of the sun
> Is but brief longing, and deceiving hope,
> And bodily tenderness; but love is made

> Imperishable fire under the boughs
> Of chrysophrase and ruby and sardonyx.[26]

The description of the supernatural place as composite or "made" is normal in apocalyptic literature, but for Yeats it grows in his later poetry to represent a "sinking in," in the mystic sense, upon art as the ground of reality, as itself the superreality. If the natural thing is unreal, then the made thing or artifact must possess the desired reality which is the end of questing. Hence in "Sailing to Byzantium" the true instructors are the mosaics of the cathedral, and the eternity of which nature does not yield evidence is created by the fiat of the artist. The reversal of the order of nature and art was a commonplace of the *fin de siècle* which Yeats shared with Wilde as well as with Huysmans and Beardsley. Des Esseintes collects an elaborate array of exotic plants for the purpose of demonstrating that nature may be so far perverted that it can approach the perfection of art, and Wilde undertakes in *The Picture of Dorian Gray* and "The Portrait of Mr. W. H." to replace the fact by the image only to discover that art will not fill the place of lost modes of moral idealism. Yeats' technique of idealization was style, the immortality of the made thing, and it served him in a chancy way from moment to moment. The alchemist of the *Savoy* was the cosmetician. Beardsley's Barber can transform all women until he is faced with natural beauty itself. "The Ballad of a Barber" is a parody of Yeats' "Song of the Wandering Aengus."

> Her gold hair fell down to her feet
> And hung about her pretty eyes:
> She was as lyrical and sweet
> As one of Shubert's melodies.
>
> Three times the barber curled a lock,
> And thrice he straightened it again:
> And twice the irons scorched her frock,
> And twice he stumbled in her train.
>
> His fingers lost their cunning quite,
> His ivory combs obeyed no more;
> Something or other dimmed his sight,
> And moved mysteriously on the floor.[27]

In the end he kills her with a broken cologne bottle.

"The Song of the Wandering Aengus" concludes with the symbolic marriage of Luna and Sol on the tree of knowledge, the primordial apple tree. The sexual act is reassimilated to the Wisdom symbol, and body and soul are reconciled at the same time that man in the alchemical process is restored to the garden, which is the grace of God. From a rhetorical point of view, the problem of sublimation is solved.

As observed earlier, Russell assigns the symbols of these poems to the region of "dangerous clairvoyance" where madness threatens the mind. Yeats called "The Song of the Wandering Aengus" a mad song both before and after its publication in *The Wind among the Reeds*.[28] The formula of the second line ("because a fire was in my head") was first developed in "King Goll," upon whom madness and alienation come as "a whirling and a wandering fire." [29] "King Goll," "Fergus and the Druid," "The Man Who Dreamed of Fairyland," and many other poems of Yeats' earliest period document the descent of the mind into itself under the image of the aesthetic obsession. What is found is madness and alienation or, on the cosmological level, catacylsm. The resort to the self demanded by the aesthetic role destroys the mind, and death is a meaningless withdrawal from real relations. In "The Song of the Wandering Aengus" the successful repose of the made thing, the eternity of artifice, receives the energy of the mind, and the ever-living eternity of art provides the mode of transcendence of which the poet as instinctual man despairs.

Chapter XI

The Sacrifice

HAVING discussed the general tradition which defines Yeats' early notion of the woman and certain of the consequences of that notion, let us now return to the sacrificial concept of the second chapter, "The Muse of Ireland," in order to summarize and elaborate our conclusions about the nature of Yeats' early verse. We shall do this by way of an interpretation of "The Cap and Bells," which, after "The Lake Isle of Inisfree," is the most popular of the poems Yeats wrote before he was forty.

It will be well to have the poem before us.

THE CAP AND BELLS

The jester walked in the garden:
The garden had fallen still;
He bade his soul rise upward
And stand on her window-sill.

It rose in a straight blue garment,
When owls began to call:
It had grown wise-tongued by thinking
Of a quiet and light footfall;

But the young queen would not listen;
She rose in her pale night gown;
She drew in the heavy casement
And pushed the latches down.

He bade his heart go to her,
When the owls called out no more;

In a red and quivering garment
It sang to her through the door.

It had grown sweet-tongued by dreaming,
Of a flutter of flower-like hair;
But she took up her fan from the table
And waved it off on the air.

"I have cap and bells" he pondered,
"I will send them to her and die";
And when the morning whitened
He left them where she went by.

She laid them upon her bosom,
Under a cloud of her hair,
And her red lips sang them a love song:
Till stars grew out of the air.

She opened her door and her window,
And the heart and the soul came through,
To her right hand came the red one,
To her left hand came the blue.

They set up a noise like crickets,
A chattering wise and sweet,
And her hair was a folded flower
And the quiet of love in her feet.[1]

The narrative of this consummate and difficult poem is constructed upon a series of time indications distributed in the second, fourth, and sixth stanzas (ll. 6, 14, and 23). The address of the soul to the Beloved occurs in the still evening twilight of the garden ("When owls began to call"); the address of the body in the twilight before dawn ("When the owls called out no more"); the address of the aspect of the self symbolized by "cap and bells" in the apocalyptic morning whiteness when man dies and is reunited with the Beloved. Much of the elate completeness of the poem (Yeats describes his experience of it in a dream as "beautiful and coherent" conveying a sense of "illumination and exaltation") [2] derives from the simplicity and totality of the resolution of its symbolic elements. The soul whose meditation is the footfall of the Beloved and the body the affinities of which are to her hair are united in the completed symbol of the achieved woman:

> And her hair was a folded flower
> And the quiet of love in her feet.

The cap and bells, sign of the poet as jester, are not included in the ultimate unity of which the composed lady is the symbol. The soul is "wise-tongued" and the body "sweet-tongued." Beyond death their songs mingle, as they do not in life, like the voices of Homer's old men on the Skaian gates when they expressed their admiration of Helen.

> They set up a noise like crickets,
> A chattering wise and sweet.

The red and the blue cloths come from Morris' "Defence of Guinevere," where the mind is given the mysterious choice which haunts Yeats throughout his life; in that poem the mind chooses wrongly when it chooses heaven, a meaning which could not have failed to attract Yeats.[3] But the point of "The Cap and Bells" is the irrelevance of the choice. The poem is constructed with the utmost attention to aspects of simplicity, balance, and resolution. It is composed of nine stanzas of four lines. Each stanza, in contrast to the elaborate schemes which we have studied above, contains only one complete rhyme yoke. Stanzas two and three are devoted to the soul, stanzas four and five to the heart, stanzas six and seven to the "cap and bells," and stanzas eight and nine to the image of resolution. The symbolic order of stanzas four through seven is deliberately one of descending sublimity. The eighth stanza introduces the factor of balance both in the syntactic and the metaphysical image.

> She opened her door and her window,
> And the heart and the soul came through,
> To her right hand came the red one,
> To her left hand came the blue.

The final stanza resolves balance into unity in the symbol of the Lady.

The symbolic environment to which the poem refers is ostensibly chivalric. The tradition provides an analogue to Yeats' poem in Rossetti's "Staff and Scrip." There the pilgrim fights for the lady, as in Yeats the jester sings, and dies leaving behind the "staff and scrip" as the jester leaves the "cap and bells."

> Then stepped a damsel to her side,
> And spoke, and needs must weep:
> "For his sake, lady, if he died,
> He prayed of thee to keep
> This staff and scrip." [4]

The pilgrim warrior and his lady are united in heaven. Courtly motives dominated the Pre-Raphaelite sensibility in the form of a secularization of theological love of the dead woman. From the point of view of Yeats the courtly formula in which the Beloved is always the wife of someone else (Morris' Guinevere was certainly in his mind) corresponds to the cabalistic drama of Wisdom in relation to deity. Above all, the chivalric stereotype of the penitential trial by which the lover becomes worthy of the Lady would have attracted the young poet who spent his youth writing neo-Spenserian dramas such as "The Seeker." One can see in Symons' translations of Verlaine the influence, reflected in Yeats' poem, of the reawakening in France of interest in the *commedia dell' arte,* which led to such works as Dowson's *The Pierrot of the Minute.* Almost every poet of the nineties has one or two poems (like William Watson's "The Lute Player") involving the knight, the lady, and the minstrel or fool. Arthur O'Shaughnessy's *Lays of France* (1872) is but one of the many works which made the style of Yeats' "The Cap and Bells" inevitable.

> Fair ladies, give me leave to sing:
> God will I may die serving you.

But, as always, Yeats has left traces of the way in which he wishes the tradition of "The Cap and Bells" to be construed. In the revised edition of *The Celtic Twilight* he published a section called "The Queen and the Fool." [5] There we read:

I knew a man who was trying to bring before his mind's eye an image of Aengus, the old Irish god of love and poeetry and ecstasy, who changed four of his kisses into birds, and suddenly the image of a man with a cap and bells rushed before his mind's eye, and grew vivid and spoke and called itself "Aengus' messenger." And I knew another man, a truly great seer, who saw a white fool in a visionary garden, where there was a tree with peacock's feathers instead of leaves, and flowers that opened to show little human faces when the white fool had touched them with his cockscomb, and he saw at another time a white fool sitting by a pool, and smiling and watching images of beautiful women floating up from the pool.⁶

This passage, dated 1901, is apparently a transcription from Yeats' diary of visions sought for the purpose of constructing a Celtic ritual.⁷ The first man referred to in the quotation is Yeats himself, and the second George Pollexfen. "The Cap and Bells" is one of those poems, like "The Blessed," constructed in "the mind's eye" on the basis of the experience of Tatwa vision or scrying. Despite its apparent courtly tradition, Yeats is insisting that it has a visionary and, in fact, a folk origin.

I have heard one Hearne, a witch-doctor, who is on the border of Clare and Galway, say that in "every household" of Fairy "there is a queen and a fool," and that if you are "touched" by either you never recover. . . . He said of the fool that he was "maybe the wisest of all," and spoke of him as dressed like one of "the mummers that used to be going around the country." ⁸

Thus we find ourself in the Household of Fairy among the aristocracy of the other world. The wearer of the "cap and bells," though not Aengus himself, is a messenger of the god of love, suggesting that the cockscomb was, as in the poem, the key to the "pity" of the queen.

There are two current interpretations of "The Cap and Bells," both of which turn upon the meaning of the symbol which is the title of the poem. Ellmann puts it this way:

The jester, after first sending the queen the trappings of common romance, finally offers the cap and bells which are his alone, and she, obdurate before the familiar and grandiloquent gifts of heart and soul, yields when the jester sends what is most essential and individual in him. That Yeats recognized the meaning in the poem is suggested by the fact that in later lectures he would read "The Cloths of Heaven" as an example of "How not to win a lady," and "The Cap and Bells" as an example of how to win one.⁹

The error of Ellmann is in his disparagement of Yeats' symbols of body and soul, which are not merely "the trappings of common romance" but in fact the real elements of the nature of man and the terms on which the resolution of the poem is conceived. The interpretive mystery of

"The Cap and Bells" is the disappearance of its major symbol, the cockscomb, in the conclusion when body and soul are united beyond life in the symbol of the woman. In fact, the "cap and bells" are a unifying mode of the separate symbols of body and soul, rather than a third personal element "most essential and individual." The refusal of body and soul by the queen results from their dissociation, their presentation in terms of choice.

The cockscomb symbolizes a condition of being in which body and soul are not separate. It is catalytic but not substantive in precipitating the conclusion of the poem. Ellmann, as well as other critics, errs in not taking seriously Yeats' relation to what seem to them merely "the trappings of common romance." Following Yeats' suggestion that "The Cap and Bells" describes the way to win a lady, Morton Seiden presumes that the cap and bells are a genital symbol and that here in contrast to "The Cloths of Heaven" Yeats is offering the lady something that Freud would have recognized as pertaining to the real nature of love.[10] There is no doubt in my mind that not only the cockscomb with its patent sexual pun, but also the harp, were associated in Yeats' fantasy with the genitalia. But here, as in "King Goll," where the harp is torn, and in Yeats' poems and stories about decapitation, the act of giving the lady the organs of sex is accompanied by strong suggestions of the kind of penitential castration which can be observed in "The Hosting of the Sidhe." Sexuality is generally in Yeats a symbol for something else and is always overlaid by a very complex context of conditions.

If there were any doubt about the relevance of Yeats' later elaboration of the folk tradition of "The Queen and Fool" to the earlier poem which is our subject, we need only notice that in the earliest version of "The Cap and Bells" we are told that "The night smelled rich with June." In *The Celtic Twilight* we read:

"What month of the year is worst?" and I said, "The month of May, of May, of course." "It is not," he said; "but the month of June, for that's the month the Amadan [the fool] gives his stroke!"[11]

The identity of Yeats' fool is the key to the symbol of the "cap and bells." The unity of body and soul is not merely a genital fusion. The fool is the wise innocent whose wisdom is so much like emotion that it does not interrupt the primal continuum of body and soul. He is a shape changer and as such he represents that desired relation to the child-self and beyond to the tree of life which we have identified as poetic knowledge. The fool is the messenger of love.

What else can death be but the beginning of wisdom and power and beauty? and foolishness may be a kind of death. I cannot think it wonderful that many should see a fool with a shining vessel of some enchantment or wisdom or dream too powerful for mortal brains "in every household of them." It is natural too that there should be a queen to every household of them, and that one should hear very little of their kings, for women come more easily than men to that wisdom which ancient peoples, and all wild peoples even now, think the only wisdom. The self, which is the foundation of our knowledge, is broken in pieces by foolishness, and is forgotten in the sudden emotions of women, and therefore fools may get, and women do get of a certainty, glimpses of much that sanctity finds at the end of its painful journey.[12]

When the jester decides to give the queen his cap and bells, he also chooses death. The two choices are equally important.

> "I have cap and bells" he pondered,
> "I will send them to her and die."

Both the fool when he acknowledges his identity and the queenly woman are figures in the drama of Wisdom. In them the self insofar as it is related to the intellect and the real world is broken, and the alienating wound opened by the culture of consciousness healed.

The queen of the poem takes up the "cap and bells" as a mother would a child. There occurs that reunion with the breasts of the Wisdom figure which Yeats repeatedly fantasies as occurring only beyond death at the Last Judgement.

> She laid them upon her bosom,
> Under a cloud of her hair,
> And her red lips sang them a love song:
> Till stars grew out of the air.

We have seen the poet rooting the heavenly bodies out of the sky like a great boar or destroying them in some theosophic cataclysm of fire and water. In this poem they merely vanish, as at dawn the lesser light

disappears in the presence of a greater. Then the gates of the Supernal
Eden open, as do the doors and windows of the queen's chamber, and
body and soul are united in the presence of the Beloved. In the
consummation of the last two stanzas of "The Cap and Bells" the
symbol of the cockscomb disappears. Its relation to personal transformation is the same as that of poetry to culture. For Yeats in the early
period, eternity is the transformation of the self. The poem assists and
symbolizes that transformation but does not, as in the later period,
take the place of it. In the last lines of "The Cap and Bells," even body
and soul disappear, and the beloved exhibits that impossible tranquil-
lity, as after sexual consummation, which Blake called "desire grati-
fied."

> And her hair was a folded flower
> And the quiet of love in her feet.

The fool or jester is Yeats' image of the figure at the center. Therefore
he is dangerous. His identity does not negate those "trappings of
common romance," body and soul, but rather signifies a realm in the
self where they are no longer distinct. In this way "life" in any
common sense is broken and "unity" ensues.

As late as his American tour of 1919–20, Yeats read "The Cap and
Bells" and "Aedh Wishes for the Cloths of Heaven" in preference to
the large body of later love poetry which he might have presented.[13]
This was not merely because his audience preferred his early verse. It is
unlikely in postwar America that they did. It is rather because these
poems represented a part of Yeats' moral ambition which remained
central to his identity as a poet and because they preserved that
protective impersonality which he in large measure abandoned in his
later style.

As noted earlier, Yeats was reported by Hone to have commented on
these occasions that "The Cloths of Heaven" was an example of how
not to win a lady and the other poem of how to win one. "The Cap and
Bells," as we have seen, is a poem of consummation. But Yeats did read
both poems. "Aedh Wishes for the Cloths of Heaven" opens with the
same offering of the cloths signifying discrete aspects of personality

that we have examined in "The Cap and Bells." But, whereas the latter
is a poem of self-possession, the former expresses that incapacity to
own the real aspects of the self from which the jester as a Wisdom
figure is immune.

> AEDH WISHES FOR THE CLOTHS OF HEAVEN
> Had I the heavens' embroidered cloths,
> Enwrought with golden and silver light,
> The blue and the dim and the dark cloths
> Of night and light and the half light,
> I would spread the cloths under your feet:
> But I, being poor, have only my dreams;
> I have spread my dreams under your feet;
> Tread softly because you tread on my dreams.[14]

In the absence of the catalytic symbol of personal reality, the cockscomb, or the slower technique of penitential development under the
auspices of the master as in "The Blessed," the poet is abandoned to
the mid-region of indeterminate dream unable to compose either the
poem or the self. In contrast to the simple and complete rhyme scheme
of "The Cap and Bells," there are no rhymes in this poem. What seem
like rhyme yokes are redundancies.

What these two poems do have in common, however, is the factor of
sacrifice, which tends to render ambiguous the total consummation
which is the subject of "The Cap and Bells." As in the chivalric
relation of knight and mistress, so in the relation of poet and muse
there is a factor of service. Like the sidhe, the woman in her role as the
unifying Wisdom figure demands the sacrifice of the self. There is
always, in other words, a sense in which she is unreal. Yet the death
which she demands of her votarist is always actual. The type of the
predicament in "The Cap and Bells" is that of Nora Hopper's Aodh in
the Temple of Heroes.

"Give me thine hope, Aodh." "Give me thy faith, Aodh." "Give me thy
courage, Aodh." "Give me thy dreams, Aodh." So the voices called and
cried and to each Aodh answered and gave the desired gift. "Give me thy
heart, Aodh," cried another. "I am Maive, who knew much and loved
little." And with a sickening sense of pain Aodh felt slender cold fingers
scratching and tearing through his flesh and sinew till they grasped his
heart and tore the fluttering thing away. "Give me thy love, Aodh,"

another implored. "I am Aengus, master of love, and I have loved none." "Take it," Aodh said faintly.[15]

The capacity for sacrifice is in the early Yeats the measure of man's moral competence, and moral competence is not compatible with life. In the period after 1900 the jester signified for Yeats the gaiety which, desiring nothing, was in no way vulnerable to loss.

If we would find a company of our own way of thinking, we must go backward to turreted walls, to courts, to high rocky places, to little walled towns, to jesters like the jester of Charles the Fifth who made mirth out of his own death. . . . Certainly we could not delight in that so courtly thing, the poetry of light love, if it were sad; for only when we are gay over a thing, and can play with it, do we show ourselves its master, and have minds clear enough for strength.[16]

Nothing could be clearer than the contrast between this passage of 1907 and the jester of "The Cap and Bells." In the world of "The Cap and Bells" there is no component of mind. The poem of light love is troubled in its simplicity by sadness because it exists only in the mode of engagement. In the world of absolute affective commitment there is no possibility of gaiety, and the poet is inevitably the victim of his intentions. There is no mirth at the death of this fool. He has come to judgement.

Chapter XII

Whenas the garment of the glorified and sainted flesh shall be resumed, our person shall be more acceptable by being all complete.–Dante, *Paradiso*

For my own part I wish it to be clearly understood that I do not suppose that anything I shall say has the smallest tendency to prove that reality is not spiritual: I do not believe it possible to refute a single one of the many important propositions contained in the assertion that it is so. Reality may be spiritual for all I know; and I devoutly hope it is. But I take "Idealism" to be a wide term.—G. E. Moore, "The Refutation of Idealism"

The Last Judgement of
the Imagination

FEW of Yeats' symbols are not found in the Tarot. There the Fool wanders into infinity with his cap and bells; there is the Supernal Mother in the form of the High Priestess. The twentieth major trump of the Tarot is "The Last Judgement." "It is the card which registers the accomplishment of the great work of transformation in answer to the summons of the Supernal—which summons is heard and answered from within."[1] This is the consummation to which *The Wind among the Reeds* tends.

There is hardly a conceptual discipline in this century which does not seek to identify and heal some archaic division in the self having its origins in the history of culture. For the philosopher, Descartes is the villain; for the analytical psychologist, alienation occurred with the onset of culture itself. Eliot found Milton culpable, and Yeats in a later period drives the beginning of dissociation back to the early sixteenth century: "Had not Europe shared one mind and heart, until both mind and heart began to break into fragments a little before Shakespeare's birth." For the young Yeats the division was both personal and cosmic but not historical. As a young man he experienced and represented conflicting and interrelated impulses toward creation and extinction, identification and diffusion, art and experience, which obsessed his powerful nature under the great allegories of Time and Eternity. In the repertory of his early symbols "The Last Judgement" was the farthest reach of the imagination toward a resolution of these forces. In his study of Blake he wrote "When a man ascends wholly out of 'the wheel of birth' into 'the imagination that liveth forever' a last judgement is said to pass over him."

Men in general find it easier to acknowledge defect than to make comprehensible statements about the desired plenitude, and Yeats is no exception. To answer the call of the Supernals or the Host was to come to Judgement. But for Dante the *Paradiso* was part of the empirical ideal. It was irreducible. Yeats had no such tradition, and he was not a creative mystic. He had not the imagination of eternity. He could not really with hope desire to break the bonds of time; therefore, he undertook to disintegrate consciousness and to sink in upon the mind, where lost aspects of the self never ceased to have reality. But there too, as we have observed, actualization seemed to entail extinction. He could never resolve the competition of apparently mutually exclusive realities: the impersonal and the personal self, the sense of identity and the presence of the image, time and eternity, present and past, the conscious and the unconscious mind. He had never cried out in the blaze of the heaven of the sun: "Whoso lamenteth that we must die in the world to live up yonder, seeth not here the refreshment of the eternal shower." Therefore, as a young man he had no position except from moment to moment. The meaning of his symbols was a contingency of a reality which he had never experienced, and he was too ambitious in a true heuristic sense to rest in such a predicament.

One of the problems of discussing Yeats' poetry, and one of the fundamental difficulties in exacting useful moral statements of poetry in general, is the philosophic or dialectical meaninglessness of the categories which emerge. The student of Yeats' poetry in particular is abandoned in a terminological universe which has no philosophical stability. For such words as "The Absolute," "The Essence," "Eternity," "The Ideal," and even "The Subjectivity," and "The Self" Yeats provides and is conscious of providing no context or authority beyond the speaking voice, the identity of which is itself bound up with the inexpressible character of the preferred value. For all his elaborate prose utterance and endless explanations and confessions, Yeats never wrote a word of purely expository statement. The cost of affiliation with the Wisdom tradition is the reduction of the intelligible relations of statement. The complex context which we have provided for certain of Yeats' early lyrics augments their power, but not their intelligibility. What we have examined here are not the obscurities of the early lyrics but rather their authority, their right to power.

Yeats was born into the efflorescence of Neo-Hegelian Absolute Idealism in England and France. MacGregor Mathers' wife, who seems to have been the principal author of the rituals of the Golden Dawn, was the sister of Bergson. I am certain that Yeats as a young man was in a real sense more a Neo-Hegelian than a Neoplatonist, and I am certain also that he would have preferred not to understand the statement. Yeats is famous for saying in the year of his death that you can refute Hegel, but not the saint or the "Song of Sixpence," and that you can embody truth but not know it.[2] By this I take it he means that the only categories which have reality are moral, and that these have no existence or actuality beyond human mental states and human actions. *Above all, that which constitutes truth must be irrefutable, and it must be human.* The categories which Yeats uses to weld the terms of this paradox (the irrefutable *and* human statement) constitute the discursive unknown in his philosophic framework.

What are the possibilities?[3] The notion of "embodying truth," the incarnation, is late in its application to Yeats' thought and unrelated except by reversal to his early posture. The notion of transfiguration applies to the early period and suggests a vague disembodiment rather than the concrete sinking in upon real identity which is its sense in Christian symbology. The meaning of both terms is a contingency of the reality of Christian sacramental history. They are miracles, and Yeats, as he ultimately understood, could not truly claim them.

Yeats put the question in terms of the reality of human vision (the irrefutable statement). For the poet it is the central query in culture.

Are he and his blue-robed companions, and their like, "the Eternal realities" of which we are the reflection "in the vegetable glass of nature," or a momentary dream? To answer is to take sides in the only controversy in which it is greatly worth taking sides.

Yeats is here citing, as he was very fond of doing, Blake's "Vision of the Last Judgement." The Last Judgement involves the sorting of mankind and its eternalization according to its moral essence. But

Blake was uncertain about the relation of immortality to individuation, and both factors were essential aspects of human identity. If "Passion" was a State (Yeats' "Mood" or "Image") which visited man or in which man sojourned, what was its relation to individuality? If what is immortal and has no relations is inhuman, it must in the end join the other unusable abstractions of the discarded moral culture of the past. But then, what is the relation of man to the divine element which gives him his reality? How can mortal man become the vehicle of immortal utterance? Yeats was aware of this problem in relation to Bradley's idealism and bitterly repudiated Bradley's point of view along with the general impersonality of his own early attitudes in *A Vision:*

Professor Bradley believed also that he could stand by the death-bed of wife or mistress and not long for an immortality of body and soul. He found it difficult to reconcile personal immortality with his form of Absolute Idealism, and besides he hated the common heart: an arrogant, sapless man.[4]

Yeats needed a mid-ground between immanence, which for him was the destruction of the reality of the Idea, and transcendence, which was the destruction of the reality of man. Beyond conviction, the very nature of his mind demanded fusion, and yet he solicited (out of an instinctive terror of the demands of the absolute relation) the Neoplatonic mid-region where commitment to the Wisdom figure was incomplete, and he was there tormented. "Witches they are, and they come by on the wind, and they cry, 'Give a kiss, Fool, give a kiss.' "[5] We may call this terror instinctive with good reason because it was not an inevitable aspect of the tradition in which he worked.

The tradition in which Yeats located the reality of the images which he received was the tradition of knowledge, of which the presiding symbol is the Wisdom figure. With this tradition the concept of the Last Judgement is inextricably bound up:

> All would be known or shown
> If time were but gone.[6]

To put it as simply as possible and in literal terms, the Last Judgement means *death and cognitive success.* Both these relations are presented under terms reducible psychologically but altogether evasive from a philosophical point of view. They are created, like mystical ontology in general, by conceptual fiat. The dead are the irrefutable speakers. The authority of true utterance and the condition of true identity are not found in life. Implied in this statement is the historical criticism (the romantic convention) that they are not found *now* in life, and the metaphysical criticism (the idealist convention) that they are not found in *life*. Caught in this predicament, Yeats as a writer could only die or change, and as is well known he changed.

If Yeats had been either a cabalist or an alchemist, or a magician or an occultist, or a ceremonialist or a Catholic, or a nationalist, a decadent or a symbolist, *The Wind among the Reeds* would have been unified, and he could be more easily understood, because each of these historical postures is, within limits, self-defining. Certainly he never early or late sought empirical reality. Certainly he intended to be a realist in the sense that all mystics have a direct sensory relation to the empirical idea. But the ideal was unstable because neither the eternal reality (the impersonal self) nor the momentary dream (the actual self) was completely constructed. The factor of "indetermination" with respect to the real in Yeats' work had its origins in the nineties and is to the last the most general category applicable to Yeats' poetry as a whole. Ultimately, no authority which Yeats could command for the poet was capable of stabilizing the whole of reality from a conceptual point of view. The "imaginary culture" remained uncreated. For the tremendous energy and dignity which Yeats discovered in the gross human symbol, culture, as he conceived it, had no name.

The most comprehensive metaphor of Yeats' early imagination, then, is the Last Judgement, with its attendant mythology of the resurrection of the body.[7] This is the great Christian fantasy, resolving the conflict of man's infinite self-conception and finite condition which is the chief subject of tragedy. Tragedy requires acknowledgment of the external as real; it breaks the will. The mystical comedy of Christianity dissolves the real and releases the human self-conception from servitude to limits other than moral. The resurrection of the body heals the wound which opened when body and soul were distinguished, and man again becomes an undifferentiated moral continuum capable of total actualization. The Last Judgement in the Dantean sense is not the death but the completion of identity. Yeats' vision, and this is the important matter, lies wholly on the hither side of the ultimate cataclysm. The relation of time and eternity, or on the level of mystic art the relation of the poetic speaker and the ontologically real host of traditional images, is insoluble.

In "The Secret Rose," Yeats prays for death, "his hour of hours," which will precipitate transformation:

> Far off, most secret, and inviolate Rose,
> Enfold me in my hour of hours.[8]

The image is the primal white rose of Dante which in Yeats' imagination is inhabited by the Celtic and occult heroes of the absolute endeavor. Dante's image is dynamic. It includes both the female element of the rose, the last receptacle of the human identity, and also the presiding still point of infinite light, the seminal male element. Between the two elements, the fertilizing angels pass like golden bees. Yeats' vision is static, being composed of the female element only. The father, who in Dante greets the son's moral ambition by an answering real possibility, is the excluded and by defect the crucial element in Yeats' early fantasy. Those whom the Rose enfolds have achieved the desired centrality through madness, vision, questing, and death. They are the heroes of the Absolute.

> Thy great leaves enfold
> The ancient beards, the helms of ruby and gold
> Of the crowned Magi; and the king whose eyes
> Saw the pierced hands and rood of elder rise
> In Druid vapour and make the torches dim;
> Till vain frenzy awoke him and he died; and him
> Who met Fand walking among flaming dew
> By a grey shore where the wind never blew,
> And lost the world and Emer for a kiss;
> And him who drove the gods out of their liss,
> And till a hundred morns had flowered red
> Feasted, and wept the barrows of the dead;
> And the proud dreaming king who flung the crown
> And sorrow away, and calling bard and clown

> Dwelt among wine stained wanderers in deep woods;
> And him who sold tillage, and house and goods,
> And sought through lands and islands numberless years,
> Until he found, with laughter and with tears,
> A woman of so shining loveliness
> That men threshed corn at midnight by a tress
> A little stolen tress.

Hidden in the Rose, like Dante's redeemed souls, is Yeats' host of the reality-hungry sidhe. They are all male. The series opens with the occult titles of the adepts of the highest order in the Golden Dawn, the crowned Magi (ll. 2–3). Then follow Conchobar destroyed by a vision of the new world of the crucified Christ (ll. 3–6), Cuchullain who lost all that is real for the magical woman (ll. 6–9), Caolte who conquered the gods (ll. 9–12), Fergus who abandoned the kingdom of life for that of the imagination (ll. 13–15), and finally the mysterious folk figure, mostly Yeats' own invention, who seeks out and marries the woman whose hair is light. To these, images of his ideal self-conception, Yeats yearns to be gathered.

> I, too, await
> The hour of thy great wind of love and hate.
> When shall the stars be blown out of the sky
> Like sparks out of a smithy and die?
> Surely thine hour has come, thy great wind blows,
> Far off, most secret, and inviolate rose.

To be reunited to the Rose is Yeats' symbol of gnosis. It is the knowledge of origin, dreams of which are defeated until time is ended and the lost relation from which time alienates the mind is recovered. This is the world of the son. It is not the fantasy of sexuality in the genital sense, but in the diffused pregenital meaning which is always present but does not always dominate in coitus. Yeats longs to join the community of centrality where wisdom which is a state and not a possession will be his, the personal correlative of the metaphysical Absolute. This is the consummation of the relation of the hawk-headed youth and the white woman.

As we have seen, Yeats continually seeks through initiation and prophecy his own birth. Correlatively, his sense of unbornness is the symbolic aspect of his refusal to acknowledge a tradition and his continually frustrated attempt to construct one. The Irishman who undertook to write in the European tradition was, from a practical literary point of view, a man without origins. In his later period Yeats conceives man as having many identities; in the early period he has but one, and that is always to be sought in the dark world at the foot of the ladder of sublimation. From the point of view of the structures which we have elaborated, the turn of the century marks the birth of Yeats and the end of initiation. The hawk-headed youth dies, and with him total absorption in the impulse to "transcend form." Yeats ceases to be a mystic and becomes an artist, ceases to celebrate the impotence of the son and becomes a creative man, the father of many realities. But Yeats was born with the knowledge that reality is unitary. He experienced growth in a sense which he could never have intended. Maturity, as he so grandly achieved it, was a form of defeat, for the world of true divinity, the resurrection of the body, was "the Country of the Young."

One of the earliest memories recorded in Yeats' *Autobiographies* recalls his visits as a child to the sexton's daughter for writing lessons. "I found one poem in her School Reader that delighted me beyond all others, a fragment of some metrical translation from Aristophanes wherein the birds sing scorn upon mankind." [9] The passage, though Yeats does not locate it, is not difficult to recognize:

Weak mortals, chained to earth, creatures of clay as frail as the foliage of the woods, you unfortunate race, whose life is but darkness, as unreal as a shadow, the illusion of a dream, hearken to us, who are immortal beings, ethereal, ever-young and occupied with eternal thoughts.

The last lines of *The Wind among the Reeds* in the edition which is our subject echo the taunt of these birds, the everlasting voices. They are in the mouth of Mongan, Yeats' vehicle for the realization of the irreversibility of human time.

> I became a man, a hater of the wind,
> Knowing one, out of all things, alone, that his head
> Would not lie on the breast or his lips on the hair
> Of the woman that he loves, until he dies;
> Although the rushes and the fowl of the air
> Cry of his love with their pitiful cries.

The basis on which Yeats constructs his notion of the Absolute (which is the same as his notion of identity) is psychological, and therefore discursively meaningless. From this effort to dissolve the self (Yeats could conceive of the *solve* but not the *coagula*) the only possible development was the descent into tragedy. To change is to acknowledge the reality of time, and Yeats changed.

G. E. Moore records in his autobiography that his school masters, contemporaries of Yeats' father, attempted in vain to form his style according to the canons of the structural idealizing mode of prose of which Macaulay was the paradigm. But they could not. His stubbornness broke the momentary spell of idealism in England, and the world followed him, Yeats with the rest. But idealism, as G. J. Warnock remarks, being demonstrable only from within, can decay only from within. Such systems "are citadels, much shot at perhaps but never taken by storm, which are quietly discovered one day to be no longer inhabited." [10] In the end it was Yeats' incapacity to sustain a commitment to his own imaginative constructions which brought about the shift in his relation to them. The last poem which Yeats wrote before he died presents an image of this citadel besieged but still inhabited.

> Say that the men of the old black tower,
> Though they but feed as the goatherd feeds,
> Their money spent, their wine gone sour,
> Lack nothing that a soldier needs,
> That all are oath-bound men:
> Those banners come not in.

Abandoned but not dead, the soldiers of the inwardness await the revolution of history which will raise the siege. Yeats' concept of literary tradition as the totality of human culture here serves to interpret the isolation of the absolute ambition.

Yeats could not create, no single human imagination could, the conditions under which his early endeavor could longer be pursued. But his early effort served him as the memory of a lost dignity on which he constructed his whole later enterprise.

Poetry is the medium of the impersonal truth. It relies on traditions of *ordonnance*, metrical, generic, dictional, iconological, which must remain intact or poetry cannot continue to exist. However much the line or the total order of the poem may seem to be fragmented, closure, the capacity for the total conception, must remain possible or the poem will disappear as a man dies. Yeats understood, from beginning to end, that the only tradition of personal reality which could sustain the poetic role undiminished is the possession or memory of the unreal whole. The angel was necessary. Therefore the search into the process by which Yeats founded his poetic role is justified, for it must be undertaken in one form or another by any who would make or understand the poem. The origin of poetic authority is always, I venture to say, the Wisdom tradition, which is not religion or thought but the sense of the self in the highest mode imaginable. Therefore we may pray with the Hierophant at the close of the ceremony of the Golden Dawn:

May what we have partaken of this day sustain us in our search for the Quintessence; the Stone of the Philosophers; the True Wisdom and Perfect Happiness; and the Summum Bonum.

Appendix

Poem Titles

Notes and References

Index

An Appendix on "Wisdom"

B
EHIND Yeats' "white woman whom passion has worn" lies the tradition of the fallen Sophia, captive of the heresiarch Simon Magus. The *Ennoia,* a true archetype, is the gnostic Sophia or Wisdom, who is the first female principle emanating from the Highest God. This figure can be studied in Hans Jonas, *The Gnostic Religion* (Boston, 1958), and in Robert Grant (ed.), *Gnosticism: A Source Book of Heretical Writings from the Early Christian Period* (New York, 1961), in which translations of the early heresiological sources are printed. The Sophia is also identified with the Wisdom (*chochma*) of Proverbs 1–9 (see R. N. Whybray, *Wisdom in Proverbs* [London, 1965]) and with the second of the three Supernal *sephiroth* in the emanational system which Yeats found in the *Sefer Yetsirah,* translated in his period by Dr. Wynn Westcott and in S. L. MacGregor Mathers' *The Kabbalah Unveiled* (1887). The modern reader who wishes to pursue these matters should consult Gershom G. Scholem's *On the Kabbalah and Its Symbolism* and for the medieval and Renaissance Christian versions of the archetype Eugene F. Rice, Jr., *The Renaissance Idea of Wisdom* (Cambridge, 1958).

Although the archetype of the white woman was native to Yeats' mind, it was accessible to him in this period as part of the tradition in sources as diverse as Flaubert's *The Temptation of St. Anthony* in the translation of Lafcadio Hearn (1895) and Madame Blavatsky's hieratic compendiums, *Isis Unveiled* and *The Secret Doctrine*. In addition, Lionel Johnson's Neoplatonic readings of the fathers were clearly persuasive. Note, for example, Yeats' use of Augustine in the service of the archetype as an epigraph to *The Rose*. "Sero te amavi, Pulchritudo tam antiqua et tam nova! Sero te amavi." Yeats' habitual syncretism also bound into this tradition images from alchemy which he found in Westcott's *Hermetic Arcanum* (1893) and elsewhere. For the Philonic interpretation (based on Proverbs) of Wisdom as equivalent both to Logos and Mind, see Harry Austryn Wolfson's *Philo* (I, 255ff.) and Erwin R. Goodenough *By Light, Light the Mystic Gospel of Hellenistic Judaism* (Yale, 1935), *passim*.

The Wisdom figure, the creative power of God, became for the protomodern poet a sort of muse. The archetype assimilated the ethnically determined masks (discussed in Chapter II). She is not *a* symbol but functionally *the* symbol of the poet's resource in mind. Correlatively, the *magus* of whom the Samarian magician Simon is the prototype became the mask of the poet's self-identification. The ironies of much of the later Yeats can be felt in this passage from the "Clementine Homilies" (ii. 22–25) cited in Grant (*op. cit.*):

> Simon goes about in company with Helen and,
> even until now, as you see, stirs up the crowds.
> He says that he has brought down this Helen from
> the highest heavens to the world; she is
> Queen, since she is all-maternal Being
> and Wisdom. For her sake, he says, the
> Greeks and the barbarians fought, imagining
> an image of the truth. . . . But by allegorising
> certain matters of this sort, fictitiously
> combined with Greek myths, he deceives many,
> especially by his performance of many marvellous
> wonders, so that—if we did not know that he
> does these things by magic—we ourselves would
> also have been deceived.

Poem Titles

In the left-hand column below are the poem titles as they occur in 1899. In the right-hand column are the revised titles as found in *The Collected Poems* of 1949. The order is that of 1899.

1899	1949
The Hosting of the Sidhe	The Hosting of the Sidhe
The Everlasting Voices	The Everlasting Voices
The Moods	The Moods
Aedh Tells of the Rose in His Heart	The Lover Tells of the Rose in His Heart
The Host of the Air	The Host of the Air
Breasal the Fisherman	The Fish
A Cradle Song	The Unappeasable Host
Into the Twilight	Into the Twilight
The Song of the Wandering Aengus	The Song of the Wandering Aengus
The Song of the Old Mother	The Song of the Old Mother
The Fiddler of Dooney	The Fiddler of Dooney
The Heart of the Woman	The Heart of the Woman
Aedh Laments the Loss of Love	The Lover Mourns for the Loss of Love
Mongan Laments the Change That Has Come upon Him and His Beloved	He Mourns for the Change That Has Come upon Him and His Beloved, and Longs for the End of the World
Michael Robartes Bids His Beloved Be at Peace	He Bids His Beloved Be at Peace
Hanrahan Reproves the Curlew	He Reproves the Curlew
Michael Robartes Remembers Forgotten Beauty	He Remembers Forgotten Beauty

A Poet to His Beloved	A Poet to His Beloved
Aedh Gives His Beloved Certain Rhymes	He Gives His Beloved Certain Rhymes
To My Heart, Bidding It Have No Fear	To His Heart, Bidding It Have No Fear
The Cap and Bells	The Cap and Bells
The Valley of the Black Pig	The Valley of the Black Pig
Michael Robartes Asks Forgiveness because of His Many Moods	The Lover Asks Forgiveness because of His Many Moods
Aedh Tells of a Valley Full of Lovers	He Tells of a Valley Full of Lovers
Aedh Tells of Perfect Beauty	He Tells of Perfect Beauty
Aedh Hears the Cry of the Sedge	He Hears the Cry of the Sedge
Aedh Thinks of Those Who Have Spoken Evil of His Beloved	He Thinks of Those Who Have Spoken Evil of His Beloved
The Blessed	The Blessed
The Secret Rose	The Secret Rose
Hanrahan Laments because of His Wanderings	Maid Quiet
The Travail of Passion	The Travail of Passion
The Poet Pleads with His Friend for Old Friends	The Lover Pleads with His Friend for Old Friends
Hanrahan Speaks to the Lovers of His Songs in Coming Days	The Lover Speaks to the Hearers of His Songs in Coming Days
Aedh Pleads with the Elemental Powers	The Poet Pleads with the Elemental Powers
Aedh Wishes His Beloved Were Dead	He Wishes His Beloved Were Dead
Aedh Wishes for the Cloths of Heaven	He Wishes for the Cloths of Heaven
Mongan Thinks of His Past Greatness	He Thinks of His Past Greatness among the Constellations of Heaven

Notes and References

The following abbreviations and short titles are employed in the notes.

Autobiography   W. B. Yeats. *The Autobiography of W. B. Yeats.* New York: Doubleday Anchor, 1958.

Bibliography   Allan Wade. *A Bibliography of the Writings of W. B. Yeats.* London: Rupert Hart–Davis, 1958.

Celtic Twilight   W. B. Yeats. *The Celtic Twilight.* London: Lawrence and Bullen, 1893.

Ideas   W. B. Yeats. *Ideas of Good and Evil.* London: A. H. Bullen, 1903.

Letters   Allan Wade. *The Letters of W. B. Yeats.* London: Rupert Hart–Davis, 1945.

Mythologies   W. B. Yeats. *Mythologies.* New York: Macmillan, 1959.

SR   W. B. Yeats. *The Secret Rose.* London: Lawrence and Bullen, 1897.

TWATR   W. B. Yeats. *The Wind among the Reeds.* London: Elkin Matthews, 1899.

Variorum   Peter Allt and Russell K. Alspach (eds.). *The Variorum Edition of the Poems of W. B. Yeats.* New York: Macmillan, 1965.

Notes – Introduction

1. *Autobiography,* p. 102.
2. Frank Kermode, *The Romantic Image* (New York, 1964), pp. 9, 10. For an account of the white woman as Wisdom, see the Appendix on "Wisdom," below, p. 209.
3. *Hail and Farewell* (New York: Appleton, 1925), I, 241.
4. This claim by Moore had considerable impact and was widely noted. See, for example, Quiller-Couch's review in the *Speaker,* XX (June, 1899), 691.
5. XX, 499.
6. "W. B. Yeats' *The Wind among the Reeds,*" *Academy,* LVI (May, 1899), 501.
7. The *Mercure de France* (XXXI, 266ff.) reviewed *The Wind among the Reeds* together with Sharp's *The Dominion of Dream,* also published in 1899, as "deux oeuvres d'inspiration et de tendence identique." "Leurs ouvrages ont cette marque commune de leur race, une passion ardente et mélancholique pour d'innumerables rêves obscurs."
8. "A Group of Celtic Writers," *Fortnightly Review,* n.s. LXV (Jan. 1, 1899), 36ff.
9. *Ibid.,* p. 47.
10. "Mr. Yeats as a Lyric Poet," *Saturday Review,* XCI (May 6, 1899), 63ff.
11. *Ibid.,* p. 65.
12. *Ibid.*
13. *Ibid.*
14. *Ibid.,* p. 67.

Notes – Chapter I

1. "An Interview with Mr. W. B. Yeats," *Irish Theosophist,* II (November, 1893), 147.
2. "An Interview with W. B. Yeats," *Sketch, a Journal of Art and Actuality,* I (November, 1893), 83.
3. *Ibid.,* 84.
4. Dunlop, *op cit.,* p. 148.
5. *Variorum,* p. 800.
6. Of this literature Katharine Tynan, of course, provides the example closest to Yeats. The important thing to notice is that the native and Catholic literary culture was uncritical and ultimately nonliterary. The Protestant and English literary culture in which Yeats began his career was, on the contrary, highly critical and required the young Yeats to form a style in a sense that the young Miss Tynan and Catholic national Ireland did not then and does not to this day understand. Other examples are Jane Barlow, William Larminie, Emily Lawless, and Seumas MacManus.
7. *The Irish Literary Revival* (London: Ward and Donney, 1894), p. 25.

8. *Ibid.*, p. 29.

9. R. K. Alspach, "Some Sources of Yeats' *The Wanderings of Oisin*," *PMLA*, LVIII (1943), 849–66.

10. Sir Charles Gavan Duffy, who in the decade of the famine had founded the famous *Nation*, returned to Ireland in 1880 from Australia to become the representative of the continuity between '48 and the new national impulse. See *Autobiography*, p. 199.

11. *Op. cit.*, p. 134.

12. *Ibid.*

13. *Autobiography*, p. 331.

14. George Brandon Saul in his *Prologomena to the Study of Yeats' Poems* (Philadelphia: University of Pennsylvania Press, 1957), p. 36, suggests that the source of Yeats' title is Nora Hopper, *Ballads in Prose*, published in 1894. But Miss Hopper was a notorious plagiarist, and Yeats had, as we have seen, conceived his title at least a year earlier. Miss Hopper's cover was designed by one Walter West, as the symbolic weather vane in the lower left-hand corner suggests, and is adorned with shamrocks of the rising movement with which she is attempting to associate herself. Yeats did in fact later make use of material developed by Miss Hopper, including the format of her cover, but the title *The Wind among the Reeds* is his own.

15. That volume itself was initially conceived as *Under the Moon*. See *Letters*, p. 243.

16. *Autobiography*, p. 71.

17. John Unterecker, *A Reader's Guide to William Butler Yeats* (New York: Noonday Press, 1959), p. 93.

18. Of the remaining twenty-five poems, only two date from 1894 or before: the anomalous dream poem, "The Cap and Bells," which is probably the poem mentioned in the interview with Katharine Tynan which I have already cited, and the poem called in 1899 "Aedh Pleads with the Elemental Powers," which was first published in *The Second Book of the Rhymers* (1894) and was revised and reprinted in 1898 in a form that left little of the earlier poem intact. In the present state of Yeats' MSS a complete chronology of the composition of the early poems cannot be attempted. It can, however, be taken as a rule that before the first publication of any poem Yeats revised it in the light of the style which he practised at that time. Since the only accurate information about variants is contained in the Allt and Alspach *Variorum*, which deals only with published texts, I have confined my statements in general to published texts rather than attempt to profit from hints with respect to unpublished material which are scattered throughout the secondary literature.

19. *TWATR*, p. 1 (*Variorum*, p. 140). This is the first edition.

20. *Ibid.*, p. 3 (*Variorum*, p. 141).

21. *Ibid.*, p. 6 (*Variorum*, p. 143).

22. *Ibid.*, p. 15 (*Variorum*, p. 149).

23. *Autobiography*, pp. 191ff.

24. *TWATR*, p. 43 (*Variorum*, p. 165).

25. *Ibid.*, p. 54 (*Variorum*, p. 172).

26. *Ibid.,* p. 29 (*Variorum,* p. 157).

27. James Hall and Martin Steinman (eds.), *The Permanence of Yeats* (New York: Macmillan, 1950), p. 169.

28. *TWATR,* p. 21 (*Variorum,* p. 152).

29. *Ibid.,* p. 60 (*Variorum,* p. 176).

30. First published in 1895. See Chapter VII below.

31. *SR,* p. 20.

32. See below, Chapter VII.

33. The formulas, which constitute a specialization of romantic conventions, include at least thirty references to hair, six to eyes which are "dim" or "half-closed," twelve to pallor or whiteness, eighteen to "dream," and so forth. The function of the introduction of this diction is to simplify a heterogeneous body of poetic reference by pitting the accumulation of stable emotional symbols against the complexity of the tradition.

34. See Norman Jeffares, *W. B. Yeats: Man and Poet* (New Haven: Yale University Press, 1949), pp. 164ff.

35. J. Hastings, *Encyclopedia of Religion and Ethics,* s.v. "Gnosticism," VI, 236. This material is treated extensively in Chapter II, below, and in the Appendix.

36. Lafcadio Hearn (trans.), *The Temptation of Saint Anthony* (London: H. S. Nichols, 1895), p. 271.

37. Horace E. Scudder (ed.), *The Complete Poetical Works of Browning* (Boston: Houghton Mifflin, 1895), p. 2.

38. *SR,* p. 243.

39. *SR,* p. 241. Yeats is citing Burns' "Open the Door to Me O," where the moon is in fact "wan."

40. *SR,* p. 243.

41. Poems of this type are "Mongan Laments the Change," "The Valley Full of Lovers," "The Travail of Passion," "The Blessed," "The Secret Rose," and "Mongan Thinks of His Past Greatness."

42. *SR,* p. 250.

43. *TWATR,* p. 43 (*Variorum,* p. 165).

𝒩otes — Chapter II

1. T. Herbert Warren (ed.), *Poems of Tennyson* (London: Oxford University Press, 1946), p. 82.

2. *Autobiography,* p. 169.

3. C. M. Bowra, *The Heritage of Symbolism* (London: Macmillan, 1951), p. 3. Bowra of course knew Yeats during the latter's time at Oxford.

4. See, p. xxii above.

5. J. C. Smith and E. D. Selincourt (eds.), *The Poetical Works of Edmund Spenser* (Oxford: Oxford University Press, 1942), p. 598, l. 212.

6. *The Idiot* (London: William Leake, 1650), p. 6.

7. *Ibid.*, p. 10.

8. *Autobiography,* p. 169.

9. London: P. S. Ellis, 1887. "Some thirty years ago [1887] I read a prose allegory by Simeon Solomon, long out of print . . . and I remember or seem to remember a sentence, 'a hollow image of fulfilled desire' " (*Mythologies,* p. 329). What Solomon in fact wrote was, "The glory of her head was changed into the abiding place of serpents whose malice knew no lull; her beauty preyed upon itself; her face was whitened with pale fires, a hollow image of unappeased desire" (p. 13).

10. *Mythologies,* p. 37.

11. *Autobiography,* p. 209.

12. *Ibid.*, p. 19. In Yeats' life his mother represents the native tradition just as clearly as his father does the English and European. Throughout his early writings Yeats put consistent emphasis on the divine origins of the schizophrenic withdrawal so commonly observed among Irish peasants, a fact which is all the more important because after the family arrived in London in 1887 his mother suffered a breakdown and remained in a condition of passive withdrawal virtually until her death.

13. *Variorum,* p. 541.

14. The term was given currency by Rudolf Otto in his *The Idea of the Holy* (London: Oxford University Press, 1923), pp. 12ff. Otto's description of this phenomenon corresponds almost exactly to Yeats' experience in the nineties. It implies in the broadest sense the characteristics of "Awefulness," "Overpoweringness," and "Energy." The most typical statement of it in Yeats is the first poem of *TWATR,* "The Hosting of the Sidhe."

15. Yeats repeats the formula of the destruction of the harp more than once under various surrogates, of which the following from *The Countess Kathleen* is an example:

> *Kevin:*   Aye because her face
> The face of Countess Kathleen dwells with me
> The sadness of the world upon her brow
> The crying of these strings grew burdensome
> Therefore I tore them.

16. W. B. Yeats (ed.), *Fairy and Folk Tales of the Irish Peasantry* (London: Walter Scott, 1888), p. 81.

17. *Ibid.*, p. 146. Compare also W. B. Yeats (ed.), *Irish Fairy Tales* (London: T. Fisher Unwin), p. 230: "Her lovers waste away for she lives on their life. Most of the Gaelic poets down to recent times, have had a Leanhuan Shee for she gives inspiration to her slaves and is indeed the Gaelic Muse—this malignant fairy. Her lovers, the Gaelic poets, died young. She grew restless and carried them away to the other world for death does not destroy her power."

18. VIII (August, 1895), 138ff.

19. *Ibid.* The case of Nora Hopper emphasizes the fact that literary Celticism for the young English writer was one of the current literary manners in which the ideal style could be practised. According to a biography published in the *Bookman* in 1894, Nora Hopper had not, at the time of the publication of *The*

Ballads in Prose, been in Ireland. She was born in Exeter and spent nearly all her life in Kensington. Much later Yeats was to remark that Celticism had ruined her,

20. Ernest Dowson, *The Complete Lyrics* (Mount Vernon: Peter Pauper, n.d.), p. 8.

21. *Variorum,* p. 102.

22. *Ibid.,* p. 765.

ℜotes – Chapter III

1. *Collected Works* (London, 1787), II, 117.

2. *Bookman,* VIII (July, 1895), 100.

3. *Bibliography,* p. 35.

4. W. B. Yeats, "A Symbolic Artist and the Coming of Symbolic Art," *Dome,* n.s. I, 234. On the pages preceding Yeats' article three of Miss Gyles' drawings can be seen. So far as I am aware this is all that remains, beyond the Yeats covers, of the work of Althea Gyles.

5. This cover is reproduced with comment in Richard Ellmann, *The Identity of Yeats* (London: Macmillan, 1954), p. 65.

6. *Mythologies,* p. 296.

7. "A Symbolic Artist," p. 235.

8. This material is cited from Robert Bloomfield's *Nature's Music* in *The Remains of Robert Bloomfield* (London, 1824), I, 124–25.

9. *Ibid.*

10. *Ibid.,* p. 142.

11. *Ibid.,* p. 150.

12. Cited in Erika von Erhardt-Sieboldt, "Some Inventions of the Pre-Romantic Period and Their Influence upon Literature," *Englische Studien,* LXVI (1931), 347–63. Of spirit voices Madame H. P. Blavatsky remarks, "That of a pure spirit is like the tremulous murmur of Aeolian Harp" (*Isis Unveiled* [Covina: Theosophical University Press, 1950], I, 68).

13. James Macpherson, *The Poems of Ossian* (Philadelphia: Thomas Cowperthwaite, 1899), p. 360.

14. *Ibid.,* pp. 411–12.

15. Kingsford and Maitland, *The Perfect Way* (London: John M. Watkins, 1882), pp. 78ff. In his notes to *The Wind* Yeats makes the transition from the folk to the occult tradition in a prose passage which is somewhat more than usually specious. "These tales [that is, folk tales] are perhaps memories of true awakening out of the magical sleep, moulded by the imagination under the influence of a mystical doctrine which it understands too literally, into the shape of some well-known traditional tale." Apparently the occult tradition has a kind of historical prepotency, so that the folk transformation becomes a local expression of the more universal structure.

16. *Proclus: The Elements of Theology* (Oxford: Oxford University Press, 1933), pp. 313f.

17. Cornelius Agrippa von Nettesheim, *Three Books of Occult Philosophy,* ed. Whitehead (1898), bk. I, chap. vi, p. 44.

18. *Ideas,* p. 243.

19. *Mythologies,* pp. 352–53.

20. *TWATR,* p. 86 (*Variorum,* p. 806).

21. *Ibid.,* p. 51 (*Variorum,* p. 171).

22. *Ibid.,* p. 61 (*Variorum,* p. 177).

23. *Poems* (New York: Modern Library, n.d.), p. 161.

24. *Variorum,* p. 80, ll. 11, 12, 12a, 12b (variant).

25. *Ibid.,* p. 81, ll. 11, 24a–24j (variant).

26. Edward Dowden (ed.), *The Poetical Works of Percy Bysshe Shelley* (New York: Crowell, 1890), p. 384. See also *Ideas,* pp. 103–4.

27. Katharine Tynan, *Twenty-Five Years* (London: John Murray, 1913), p. 218.

28. *Shamrocks* (London: Macmillan, 1887), p. 143.

29. *Autobiograpy,* p. 131.

30. London: Trübner and Co.

31. *Ibid.,* p. 3.

32. "A Symbolical Drama in Paris," *Bookman,* VI (April, 1894), 14.

33. W. B. Yeats (ed.), *A Book of Irish Verse* (London: Methuen, 1894), p. xxi.

34. *Ideas,* p. 225.

35. This is part of the first sentence of a story called "Fergus O'Mara and the Demons," first published in P. W. Joyce, *Good and Pleasant Reading* (Dublin, 1886). The casualness of this source, which I cannot otherwise identify, suggests the obliquity of Yeats' scholarship, especially in view of the very general character of the conception.

36. See for example Lionel Johnson's in *Poems* (London: Elkin Mathews, 1895), p. 111.

37. "A Priestess of the Woods," *Irish Theosophist,* I (July, 1893), 99.

38. *Mythologies,* p. 315.

Notes – Chapter IV

1. Of this type the famous "Song of Amergin" will serve as an example.

2. This conception is a commonplace in the late nineteenth century. Pater had used it in his description of the "Mona Lisa." An example can be found in William Watson's "Beauty's Metempsychosis," in *The Poems of William Watson* (London: Macmillan, 1893), p. 155.

3. Of course Yeats was a very acute observer of the purely historical problems of literature, but insofar as the process of creation was a subject of poetry he represented himself in the early period as in search of the image, not the book. Being fundamentally a religious man he regarded literature, not as a value in itself but as a vehicle or agent of value.

4. London: Ward and Downey, 1892, p. 31.

5. On the other hand, John Butler Yeats writing to Dowden in December, 1869, attributes to Ellis expressions closely resembling those which W. B. Yeats employs twenty years later. "Excitement is the feature of an insufficiently emotional nature, the harsh discourse of the vibrating of but one or two cords. This is what Ellis also meant by 'violent and untiring emotion'" (Elizabeth D. and Hilda M. Dowden [eds.], *Letters of Edward Dowden and His Correspondents* [London: J. M. Dent, 1914], p. 48).

6. Edwin J. Ellis and W. B. Yeats, *The Works of William Blake* (London: Bernard Quaritch, 1893), II, 120. Hereafter referred to as *Blake*. The editors are building on the following passage from Blake's "A Vision of the Last Judgement," perhaps the work of Blake which Yeats found most compelling and cites most frequently. "Man Passes on, but States remain for Ever; he passes thro' them like a traveller who may as well suppose that the places he has passed thro' exist no more, as a Man may suppose that the States he has pass'd thro' Exist no more. Everything is Eternal" (Geoffrey Keynes [ed.], *The Complete Writings of William Blake* [New York: Random House, 1957], p. 606).

7. Yeats very occasionally suggests that the Moods are the sephirothic hierarchy. "Solitary men in moments of contemplation receive, as I think, the creative impulse from the lowest of the nine hierarchies, and so make and unmake mankind" (*Ideas*, p. 246). Hegel's notion of art as the sensuous embodiment of the Absolute Idea corresponds almost exactly with Yeats' concepts and may well lie behind Yeats by way of Ellis. Certainly Hegelianism and the Neo-Hegelian philosophers such as F. H. Bradley provide the only context in which Yeats' notions could be given an appropriate technical identity.

8. VIII, 105.

9. *Ibid.*

10. *Ibid.*

11. *Ibid.*

12. "The Common Sense of Theosophy," *Dublin University Review*, May, 1886, p. 43.

13. "The Poetry of Samuel Ferguson," *Dublin University Review*, November, 1886, p. 30.

14. *Ibid.*

15. W. B. Yeats, "Fiona MacLeod as Poet," *Bookman*, XI (December, 1896), 92.

16. "Irish National Literature," p. 167.

17. "Mr. Rhys' Welsh Ballads," *Bookman*, XIV (April, 1898), 14.

18. *A Book of Irish Verse* (London: Methuen, 1900), p. 250; first published in 1895. "Some verses in 'The Epicurean' were put into French by Theophile Gautier for the French translation and back into English by Mr. Robert Bridges. If any Irish reader who thinks Moore a great poet will compare his verses with the result, he will be less angry with the introduction to this book."

19. John Davidson, *A Full and True Account of . . . Earl Lavender* (London: Ward and Downley, 1895), p. iv.

20. *Mythologies*, p. 314.

21. *SR,* p. 23.

$\mathcal{N}$otes – Chapter V

1. *Bibliography,* p. 46.

2. *Letters,* p. 88.

3. *Pages from a Diary Written in Nineteen Hundred and Thirty* (Dublin: Cuala Press, 1944), pp. 18–19.

4. The rhyme scheme is *abacbaca.* The importance of this scheme lies, not only in the redundance of the *a* rhyme, but in the reversal of expectation in the *cb* rhyme cluster, frustrating any tendency of the poem to fall into two quatrains distinguished by the *b* and *c* rhyme variations.

5. *TWATR,* p. 3 (*Variorum,* p. 141).

6. Yeats in *Blake,* II, 13–14.

7. This point can be illustrated positively from the literature which Yeats regarded himself as rejecting. In the following lyric from Tennyson's "Maud" (V, iii) the speaker and the subject are fully identified by the narrative frame and the scope of symbolic suggestiveness thereby reduced:

> Silence, beautiful voice!
> Be still, for you only trouble the mind
> With a joy in which I cannot rejoice,
> A glory I shall not find.
> Still! I will hear you no more,
> For your sweetness hardly leaves me a choice
> But to move to the meadow and fall before
> Her feet on the meadow grass and adore,
> Not her, who is neither courtly nor kind,
> Not her, not her, but a voice.

The similarities between this and the Yeats poem are striking, but there is no evidence which would justify adducing it as a source.

8. Even so conventional a poem as "The Song of the Old Mother" (*TWATR,* p. 17 [*Variorum,* p. 150]) exhibits use of the distinction between young and old in the "occult" or folk sense of the difference between eternity and time.

9. *Celtic Twilight,* pp. 184f.

10. *TWATR,* p. 60 (*Variorum,* p. 176).

11. *Autobiography,* p. 47.

12. E. H. Coleridge (ed.), *The Works of Lord Byron* (London: John Murray, 1901), IV, 91.

13. This material can be most conveniently referred to in Virginia Moore, *The Unicorn* (New York: Macmillan, 1954), p. 134.

14. W. B. Yeats, "Is the Order of R. R. and A. C. to Remain a Magical Order?" (priv. ptd., 1901), p. 29.

15. Israel Regardie, *The Golden Dawn* (Chicago: Aries Press, 1937), I, 51; hereafter referred to as *Regardie.* This is the most reliable and extensive source for Golden Dawn material.

16. Regardie, I, 112. The four beast-headed figures arranged along the arms of the cross are of course the cherubic guards of the "heavenly fold."

17. Gershom Sholem, *Major Trends in Jewish Mysticism* (New York: Shocken, 1941), p. 37.

18. Regardie, II, 133.

19. W. W. Westcott, a London coroner and one of the founders of the Golden Dawn, translated the *Sepher Yetzirach* sometime in the eighties. It became one of the basic sources of Golden Dawn ritual. The only edition I have seen is the third of 1911. He translates *sephiroth* as "Voices" and "Divine Voices."

20. Regardie, I, 19.

21. Proverbs 8:22.

22. *Ibid.,* 29–31.

23. See above, p. 49.

24. I cannot locate the source of this phrase, which Yeats uses repeatedly, but the concept it implies comes ultimately from Dionysius Areopagiticus, who was known well enough within and without the subculture of occult discourse. (See, for example, *Blake,* I, 336, where the source is Lionel Johnson.) The notion of hierarchy does not accord with the image of the apocalyptic guardians, but Yeats was clearly seeking the large suggestion at this point. Their fire is the vigor which is the possession of God alone in the fallen world.

25. "Go to the guards of the heavenly fold. And bid them wander." The emphasis in reading should fall on *them.* The mechanism of intercession, which is fundamentally Catholic, may well suggest that the dominance of the female in *fin-de-siècle* occultism is determined by the Catholic influence. The same fruitless gesture of dismissal is found in "Hanrahan Reproves the Curlews" (*TWATR,* p. 26 [*Variorum,* p. 155]).

26. *TWATR,* 16 (*Variorum,* p. 149). Cf. *Blake,* I, 401. "Wandering is essentially mortal."

27. Regardie, II, 16. The banners reproduced in Fig. 5 are taken from the frontispiece of Vol. I.

28. *Ibid.,* II, 18. For another version of this ritual used in the Irish cult, see Virginia Moore, *op. cit.,* p. 79.

29. *TWATR,* p. 31 (*Variorum,* p. 158).

30. *Celtic Twilight,* p. 157.

31. Richard Ellmann in *Yeats: The Man and the Masks* (New York: Macmillan, 1948), pp. 142–43, cites from a MS book, presumably in the possession of Mrs. Yeats, eight drafts of a poem which he identifies as "To My Heart Bidding It Have No Fear." The latest version, dated November 19, 1894, reads as follows:

THE LOVER TO HIS HEART

Impetuous heart be still, be still,
 Your sorrowful love can never be told;
  Cover it up with a lonely tune;
He who could bend all things to His will
 Has covered the door of the infinite fold
  With the pale stars and the wandering moon.

The predicament in this poem is the same as in "The Everlasting Voices." Access to the Supernal Woman, symbolized by the "door to the infinite fold" is denied by the ministers of God, and the function of poetry ("Cover it up with a lonely tune") is simply to conceal hopeless desire. Between this poem and the later poem published in 1896 more than what Ellmann calls a "stylistic development" has occurred. The poet has in fact constructed a new work on the basis of a different relation to the process of initiation. He has commenced the ceremony ("the wisdom out of old days") which will eventually lead to the conquest of fear. The transformation of the poem on the basis of a new ritual source makes the poem no longer a complaint, but now a part of the process of psychic preparation which will lead to the conquest of the forbidden place. It should be noted that these drafts make it clear how hard it was for Yeats to confess that the concealed or occult element in his poetry was the sexual element. Four successive revisions of the same line yield the following sequence:

> The tale of tales may never be told
> The hidden things may not be told
> Your sorrowful thoughts may never be told
> Your sorrowful love may never be told.

32. W. B. Yeats, *The Cutting of an Agate* (New York: Macmillan, 1912), p. 124.

33. *TWATR*, p. 43 (*Variorum*, p. 165).

34. II, 16.

35. The London temple was dedicated to Isis-Urania, the mythological equivalent, according to Regardie, of Venus.

36. "The Marriage of Heaven and Hell," Plate 14. Obviously here man, not God, utters the ultimate command.

37. *Blake*, I, 298.

38. *Ibid.*, II, 36.

39. *TWATR*, p. 50 (*Variorum*, p. 169).

40. Yeats and Ellis comment on the cabalistic doctrine of the prior worlds in Vol. II, p. 63, in connection with the Edom of Blake's "The Marriage of Heaven and Hell" (Plate 3) with which they associate the world of nature. For the doctrine of sparks, see also Blavatsky, *op. cit.*, II, 421.

41. S. L. MacGregor Mathers, *The Kaballah Unveiled* (London: Kegan Paul, 1887), p. 301.

42. Chapter III above comments on a similar duality in the symbols of the creative and the destructive wind.

43. Cf. "Aedh Tells of the Perfect Beauty," *TWATR*, p. 42 (*Variorum*, p. 164).

> The poets labouring all their days
> To build a perfect beauty in rhyme
> Are overthrown by a woman's gaze
> And by the unlabouring brood of the skies.

In the last line the host is identified with those stars which, as we have seen, "The Secret Rose" describes as being destroyed when the poet is united with the Beloved. The woman is the mortal sexual object, enemy of sublimation.

44. See above, p. 139.

45. Regardie, III, 234.

46. *TWATR*, p. 35 (*Variorum*, p. 161). William Sharp, who also employs Order symbols in his poems, deals with the situation in his "Secret Gate" (*Poems and Dramas* [New York: Duffield, 1914], p. 289). In his review in 1899 of *TWATR* (*Fortnightly*, LXV, 36) he remarks, "Only the few may apprehend 'the flaming door.'"

47. *TWATR*, pp. 95–102 (*Variorum*, p. 808–811).

48. Regardie, II, 44. From the neophyte ritual.

49. *TWATR*, p. 52 (*Variorum*, p. 172). Ellmann's analysis of this poem occurs on pp. 69–70 of *The Identity of Yeats*.

50. It is a matter of considerable interest that "hyssop-heavy" remained in the text instead of the conventional "vinegar-heavy" until 1913. My reading presumes that "Our" of line 3 and the "We" of line 6 refer to the same entities, and that the last line is in apposition with the "you" of line 6.

51. II, 321.

52. *SR*, pp. 111f.

53. *Variorum*, p. 842.

54. *Irish Theosophist*, IV, 49.

55. *TWATR*, p. 5 (*Variorum*, p. 142).

56. *Ibid.*, p. 57 (*Variorum*, p. 174).

57. John 18:1.

58. Regardie, IV, 49.

59. *Op. cit.*, pp. 147–56. See also Regardie, II, 198–244.

60. *Ideas*, p. 308. These, needless to say, are the secrets of the father, who is dead and yet miraculously preserved, thus liberating the son from restraint and guilt simultaneously.

61. *Variorum*, p. 218.

Notes — Chapter VI

1. *Autobiography*, p. 68.

2. *Mythologies*, p. 300.

3. *TWATR*, pp. 73–74 (*Variorom*, p. 803).

4. Dublin, 1844, p. 40.

5. *SR*, pp. 144, 174, 185.

6. *Bibliography*, p. 72.

7. *Variorum*, p. 411.

8. See Ellmann, *Identity of Yeats*, p. 301.

9. The edition which I have used is *777 Revised; vel, Prolegomena Symbolica* . . . (London: Neptune Press, 1955), p. 42.

10. *Ibid.*

11. *Ibid.*

12. *TWATR*, p. 57 (*Variorum*, p. 174).

13. London: Theosophical Publishing Society, 1893–1902), V, 25. It is attributed to "L. O. et al." as editors. "L. O." is one of the Golden Dawn pseudonyms as yet undisclosed.

14. *The Works of Jacob Boehme* (London, 1764–81), III, 37.

15. Letter dated July, 1890, in *Letters*, pp. 153–54.

16. *Op. cit.*, I, xxxiv.

17. *Mythologies*, p. 311.

18. *Ibid.*

19. *Variorum*, p. 34, l. 178a (variant).

20. *Ibid.*, ll. 79–83a (variant).

21. *Ibid.*, ll. 79–87.

22. *Ibid.*, p. 794.

23. See "Cuchulain's Fight with the Sea," *Variorum*, p. 105.

24. Standish O'Grady, *History of Ireland* (London: Sampson, Low, Searle, Marston, etc., 1878–1880), II, 319.

25. *SR*, pp. 1ff.

26. *SR*, p. 9. This is, of course, a lethal example of the determination of the son's self-image by the father's image-making powers. This poem Yeats reprinted in *The Wind among the Reeds* without variants, except for the removal of indentation, as "Aedh Gives His Beloved Certain Rhymes."

27. Ellmann, *Identity of Yeats*, p. 305 (note to p. 52).

28. *The Collected Plays* (New York: Macmillan, 1953), p. 395.

29. The speaker in "Rosa Alchemica" is Yeats' most complete image of the inhabitant of an imaginary culture which requires a commitment of which he is incapable. The images by which he has surrounded himself have the same relation to the aesthete that the sidhe do to the peasant. "All those forms; that Madonna with her brooding purity, those delighted ghostly faces under the morning light, those bronze divinities with their passionless dignity, those wild shapes rushing from despair to despair, belonged to a divine world in which I had no part; and every experience, however profound, every perception, however exquisite, would bring me the bitter dream of a limitless energy I could never know. . . . I had heaped about me the gold born in the crucibles of others" (*Mythologies*, p. 269).

30. *Ibid.*, p. 271.

31. *Ibid.*, p. 275.

32. *Ideas*, p. 225.

33. *TWATR*, p. 27 (*Variorum*, p. 155).

34. *Savoy*, No. 2 (April, 1896), p. 188.

35. With respect to this image it is worth noting that the third sentence of Mathers' *Kabbala Unveiled* (p. 41) reads: "And the kings of ancient time were dead, and their crowns were found no more; and the earth was desolate." This is the description of the uncreated world.

36. *Mythologies*, p. 80.

37. *TWATR*, p. 37 (*Variorum*, p. 162).

38. *Ibid.*, p. 37, ll. 7–20.

39. They are, "Hanrahan Reproves the Curlew," "Hanrahan Laments because

of His Wanderings," "Hanrahan Speaks to the Lovers of His Songs in Coming Days."¹

40. New York: Duffield and Co., 1911, pp. 192–98.

41. *Ibid.*, p. 198.

42. *TWATR*, p. 26 (*Variorum*, p. 155).

43. I cite this later example because psychological references made by Yeats in occult terms are always more vivid than similar statements made in terms of Celtic mythology (*A Vision* [New York: Macmillan, 1959], p. 48).

44. *TWATR*, p. 90 (*Variorum*, p. 808).

45. *Variorum*, p. 299.

46. *SR*, p. 145.

47. *TWATR*, p. 51 (*Variorum*, p. 171).

48. See Yeats' note, *Variorum*, p. 171.

Notes – Chapter VII

1. *Mythologies*, p. 294.

2. Horace Scudder (ed.), *The Complete Poems of Browning* (Boston: Riverside, 1895), p. 1109.

3. *Autobiography*, p. 30.

4. *Ibid.*, p. 20.

5. *Wheels and Butterflies* (London: Macmillan, 1934), p. 102.

6. Walter Pater, *Marius the Epicurean* (New York: Boni and Liveright, n.d.), p. 102.

7. Pasadena: Theosophical University Press, 1952, p. 411.

8. *Ibid.*, p. 413.

9. The *Senate* existed between 1894 and 1897. Yeats' story appeared in Vol. III (1896), 406ff.

10. *Ibid.*, p. 408.

11. *Ibid.*

12. *Ibid.*, p. 411.

13. Joseph Hone, *W. B. Yeats* (New York: Macmillan, 1943), pp. 13, 20.

14. *TWATR*, p. 11.

15. P. 409.

16. *Variorum*, p. 177.

17. *TWATR*, p. 22 (*Variorum*, p. 153).

18. *Ibid.*, p. 61 (*Variorum*, p. 177).

19. Forty years later Yeats reworked the memory once more in "Mohini Chatterjee," *Variorum*, p. 495.

20. *On the Study of Celtic Literature* (New York: Macmillan, 1899), pp. 52, 53.

21. *Ibid.*, p. 54.

22. Lady Charlotte Guest, *The Mabinogion* (London: Dent, 1906), p. 263. Lady Guest's translation was first published in 1849.

23. *Ibid.*, p. 274.

24. Similarly, in "Fergus and the Druid" (*Variorum*, p. 102), the accession to fantasy results in the knowledge of the past of the self. The mark of the poet is his direct relation to the infantile self which, in the mind of the adult, cannot normally be recalled:

> I see my life go drifting like a river
> From change to change; I have been many things.

25. *Variorum*, p. 302.

26. *Ibid.*

27. *Ibid.*, p. 307.

28. Count Goblet d'Alviella, *The Migration of Symbols* (New York: University Book, 1956), p. 161. Originally published in English at Westminster in 1894. See *TWATR*, pp. 74–76.

𝒩otes – Chapter VIII

1. In "The Wisdom of the King" the child whose cradle is presided over by women with feathers instead of hair himself develops that characteristic.

2. *Plays*, p. 73.

3. *Ibid.*

4. In this sense, as an attempt to preserve the only human paradigm of personal reality and correlatively of poetic truth, Yeats' later tendency toward the political right can at least be understood.

5. *Autobiography*, p. 180.

6. *Ibid.*, p. 173 and *passim*.

7. *Ideas*, p. 245.

8. Horace Reynolds (ed.), *Letters to the New Island by W. B. Yeats* (Cambridge: Harvard University Press, 1934), p. 98.

9. *Ibid.*, p. 168.

10. *Ideas*, p. 299.

11. *Ibid.*, p. 304.

12. *Autobiography*, p. 177.

13. *Ibid.*, p. 249.

14. *Mythologies*, p. 294. This is the peculiarly Irish form of "criticism" which Yeats imagined that he was bringing to replace the rational didacticism of the English tradition. The Moods are the "mothers of nations," and they bring them to birth, as we have demonstrated, by destroying them in their temporal relations.

15. *Variorum*, p. 758.

𝒩otes – Chapter IX

1. "The Philosophy of Composition," *The Works of Edgar Allan Poe* (London: Shiells and Co., 1895), IV, 147.

2. London: William Heinemann, 1899, p. 90.

3. *Ibid.*

4. *Variorum*, p. 123.

5. *A Servant of the Queen* (Dublin: Golden Eagle Books, 1950), p. 141.

6. *TWATR*, p. 59 (*Variorum*, p. 175).

7. The notation of the rhyme scheme is as follows: *ababcadcefdef*. The first and third *a* rhymes are redundant, carrying the sound of "dead" far into the poem. The first five rhymes are normal for poems of this type in *The Wind*. But the separation of the *d* rhymes (thus avoiding the simple *defdef* conclusion) represents a subjectification of the rational aspects of poetic structure. The *d* rhyme introduces the second rhetorical section of the poem, following the emphasis of speech rather than of measure, and the spreading of the *c* rhyme yoke prevents the poem from falling into two parts.

8. *A Vision* (New York: Macmillan, 1956), pp. 23–24.

9. *TWATR*, p. 21 (*Variorum*, p. 152). Published in the *Dome*, May, 1898.

10. *Variorum*, p. 768.

11. *TWATR*, p. 40 (*Variorum*, p. 163).

12. Patty Gurd, *The Early Poetry of William Butler Yeats* (Lancaster, Pa.: New Era Printing Co., 1916), p. 24. Miss Gurd cites *The Fairy Queen*, bk. IV, can. 10, st. xxv. It should also be mentioned that the "wood" of "Aedh Tells of a Valley Full of Lovers" is no doubt the same as that in "The Blessed." A suggestion that Yeats intended it to mean "emotions made eternal by their own perfection" is contained in a quotation from an unpublished occult diary cited in Ellmann, *Identity of Yeats*, p. 83.

13. *Variorum*, p. 684.

14. *Ibid.*, p. 685.

15. *TWATR*, p. 10 (*Variorum*, p. 146). Ellmann, without citing his authority, dates the first drafts of this poem in 1893, which corresponds with its appearance in the first section of *The Wind among the Reeds* (*Yeats: Man and Masks*, p. 259).

16. P. 107.

17. "William Butler Yeats," *English Institute Essays* (New York: Columbia University Press, 1947), p. 87.

18. London, 1893, par. 46.

19. For a full discussion of the alchemical symbol of the fish, see C. G. Jung, *Aion* (New York: Pantheon Books, 1959), pp. 36–172.

20. It will be observed that Ellmann's early date (1893) for "Breasal the Fisherman" corresponds with the publication both of Westcott's *Hermetic Arcanum* and Waite's *The Hermetic Museum*.

21. Evelyn Underhill, *Mysticism* (New York: Meridian Books, 1955), p. 146.

22. *TWATR*, p. 29 (*Variorum*, p. 157).

23. *Variorum*, p. 482.

24. *Literature and the Occult Tradition* (New York: Dial, 1930), p. 94.

25. *TWATR*, p. 7 (*Variorum*, p. 143).

26. *Celtic Twilight*, p. 95. For the tradition which Yeats is following, see Robert Kirk, *The Secret Commonwealth of Elves, Fauns, and Fairies* (1691), which was edited by Andrew Lang (London: D. Nutt) in 1893: "So I say their

continual sadness is because of their pendulous state . . . as uncertain what will become of them at the last Revolution when they are locked up into one unchangeable condition."

27. *TWATR*, p. 8 (*Variorum*, p. 143).

28. *Ibid.*

29. Westcott, *op. cit.*, para. 54.

30. *Variorum*, p. 174 (Yeats' note).

31. *Ibid.*, ll. 1–4 (variant).

32. *TWATR*, p. 57 (*Variorum*, p. 174).

Notes – Chapter X

1. London: Society for Psychical Research, 1886.

2. I, No. 2 (April, 1896), 13ff.

3. *Ibid.*, p. 20.

4. *Ibid.*, p. 16.

5. Geoffrey Keynes (ed.), *The Complete Writings of William Blake* (New York: Random House, 1957), p. 499.

6. *Letters*, p. 88.

7. *Ibid.*, p. 111.

8. "The Legends of Ancient Eire," *Irish Theosophist*, III (March, 1892), 56ff.

9. *Ibid.*

10. Misquoted from "The Wanderings of Oisin," bk. III, l. 47.

11. Russell, *op. cit.*

12. As in Lombroso's psychological comment, the individual and the ethnic past are identical.

13. Russell, *op. cit.*

14. See above, p. 162.

15. *TWATR*, p. 22 (*Variorum*, p. 153).

16. *Poems* (New York: Random House, n.d.), p. vii. Compare *Autobiography*, p. 190.

17. *TWATR*, p. 5 (*Variorum*, p. 142).

18. *Ibid.*, p. 24 (*Variorum*, p. 154).

19. *Variorum*, p. 764.

20. *TWATR*, p. 15 (*Variorum*, p. 149).

21. See Saul, *op. cit.*, pp. 65–66.

22. See above, pp. 16off.

23. Yeats (ed.), *Fairy and Folk Tales*, pp. 30ff. and note p. 38.

24. Certain groups of poems seem to have been formed in *The Wind among the Reeds* by the collocation of certain symbols. "The Blessed" and "The Secret Rose" seem, for example, to be sequent because they are Rose poems. More obliquely, "The Song of the Wandering Aengus" and "The Song of the Old Mother" seem to be related by common reference to the seed of fire.

25. P. 23.

26. *Variorum,* p. 765.

27. "The Ballad of the Barber," *Savoy,* II, No. 3 (July, 1896), 91.

28. *Variorum,* p. 149 (title variants).

29. *Variorum,* p. 83, l. 28.

Notes – Chapter XI

1. *TWATR,* p. 32 (*Variorum,* p. 159).

2. *Ibid.,* p. 95 (*Variorum,* p. 808).

3. And one of these strange choosing cloths was
      blue,
   Wavy and long, and one cut short and red;
   No man could tell the better of the two.
   After a shivering half hour you said,
   "God help! heaven's colour, the blue": and
      he said: "hell."
   Perhaps you then would roll upon your bed.

For a similar observation with respect to the source of this aspect of "The Cap and Bells" see F. A. C. Wilson, *W. B. Yeats and the Tradition* (London: Victor Gollancz, 1958), pp. 251–52.

4. William M. Rossetti (ed.), *The Complete Poetical Works of Dante Gabriel Rossetti* (Boston: Roberts Brothers, 1894), p. 47.

5. *Mythologies,* pp. 112–16.

6. *Ibid.,* p. 115. This passage has been noticed by Miss Patty Gurd, *op. cit.*

7. See Virginia Moore, *op. cit.,* p. 72.

8. It is well to bear in mind that the sidhe are, in a significant sense, the peasant or folk memory of a native aristocracy.

9. *Identity of Yeats,* p. 251.

10. *Op. cit.,* pp. 76–84.

11. *Mythologies,* p. 113.

12. *Ibid.,* p. 115.

13. The evidence for this is Joseph Hone's statement in *W. B. Yeats* (New York: Macmillan, 1943), p. 159.

14. *TWATR,* p. 60 (*Variorum,* p. 176).

15. See above, Chapter II, Note 19.

16. *Cutting of an Agate,* p. 126.

Notes – Chapter XII

1. A. E. Waite, *The Pictorial Key to the Tarot* (New York: University Books, 1959), p. 148.

2. *Letters,* p. 922.

3. In 1903 Yeats published his *Ideas of Good and Evil.* On May 14 of that

year he writes: "I am no longer in sympathy with an essay like 'The Autumn of the Body,' not that I think that essay untrue. But I think that I mistook for a permanent phase of the world what was only a preparation. The close of the last century was full of a strange desire to get out of form, to get to some kind of disembodied beauty, and now it seems to me that contrary impulse has come. . . . The Greeks said that the Dionysiac influence preceded the Apollonic and that the Dionysiac was sad and desirous. But that the Apollonic was joyful and self-sufficient. Long ago I used to define to myself these two influences as the Transfiguration on the mountain and the Incarnation" (*Letters,* p. 402).

4. *Vision,* p. 219.

5. *Collected Plays,* p. 162.

6. *Variorum,* p. 510. "Crazy Jane on the Day of Judgement."

7. See *Blake,* I, 298.

8. *TWATR,* p. 48 (*Variorum,* p. 169).

9. P. 115.

10. *English Philosophy since 1900* (London: Oxford University Press, 1958), p. 11.

Index

Poetic Knowledge in the Early Yeats

was composed, printed, and bound by Kingsport Press, Inc., Kingsport, Tennessee. The types are Old Style Number 7 and Goudy Old Style, and the paper is Warren's Olde Style. Design is by Edward G. Foss.

9/69.
B + T
6.50